NEW YORK BREWERIES

2ND EDITION

0 11557 01229 3

NEW YORK
BREWERIES

2ND
EDITION

LEW BRYSON
Revised & Updated by DON CAZENTRE

STACKPOLE
BOOKS

Copyright ©2014 by Stackpole Books
First edition published 2003. Second edition 2014

Published by
STACKPOLE BOOKS
5067 Ritter Road
Mechanicsburg, PA 17055
www.stackpolebooks.com

The authors and the publisher encourage readers to visit the breweries and sample their beers and recommend that those who consume alcoholic bever-ages travel with a designated nondrinking driver.

Printed in the United States of America

10 9 8 7 6 5 4 3 2 1

Cover design by Tessa Sweigert
Labels and logos used with permission of the breweries

Library of Congress Cataloging-in-Publication Data

Bryson, Lew.
    New York breweries / Lew Bryson ; revised and updated by Don Cazentre.
    — 2nd edition.
        pages   cm. — (Breweries)
    ISBN 978-0-8117-1229-3
    1. Bars (Drinking establishments)—New York (State)—Guidebooks.
2. Microbreweries—New York (State)—Guidebooks.   3. Breweries—New York
(State)—Guidebooks.   I. Cazentre, Don.   II. Title.
TX950.57.N7B79   2014
647.95747—dc23
                                                            2013040188

Contents

Acknowledgments

When you tell people you're writing a book about beer, you often hear the response: "Wow, what a great job . . . do you need any help?" It was a great job, and I certainly did need help.

First credit goes to Lew Bryson, both for suggesting that I take over the updating and revising of the book he wrote in 2003, and for creating the template that I followed. Though there were a few times when I took his name in vain, all in all . . . thanks.

Thanks also to editor Kyle Weaver at Stackpole Books for his guidance and patience once I took the assignment.

Special appreciation goes to all the brewery owners, brewers, and staff who are the heart and soul of this book. They include many who have helped me understand the art, science, and passion of brewing ever since I began covering New York breweries in the 1990s, long before I started this book: Tim Herzog of Flying Bison Brewing Company; Chris Ericson of Lake Placid Pub & Brewery; Nick and Fred Matt of Matt Brewing Company (Saranac); Dan Mitchell at Ithaca Beer Co.; and everyone at Brewery Ommegang over the years, notably Don Feinberg and Wendy Littlefield, whose absence from Upstate New York is still keenly felt.

Then there's my hometown (Syracuse) beer crew that I couldn't get along without: Marc and Mary Rubenstein at Middle Ages Brewing Company, and David Katleski and Tim Butler at Empire Brewing Company. They're always there when I need them—and with a beer, too. And thanks to the folks who run my favorite local watering holes: Mike Yorton of The Blue Tusk; David Hoyne of Kitty Hoynes Irish Pub & Restaurant; and Ray Clark, whose Clark's Ale House was to make its return late in 2013.

All of the breweries featured in this book had folks who took valuable time to make me feel welcome. Each is worth noting, but here's a particular nod to the enthusiastic hospitality of John Carr at Adirondack Brewery and Pub in Lake George; Rick Davidson at Davidson Brothers Brewing Company in Glens Falls; John Urlaub at Rohrbach Brewing Company in Rochester; Steve Hindy at Brooklyn Brewery; Chuck Williamson at Butternuts Beer & Ale in Garrattsville; Jeff "Chief"

O'Neill at Peekskill Brewery; Alireza Saifi at Andean Brewing Company (Kuka) in Blauvelt; Hutch Kugeman at Crossroads Brewing Company; and Chris Cuzme at 508 Gastrobrewery in Manhattan.

I'm also grateful for the insights into the Hudson Valley, New York City, and Long Island offered by my *Ale Street News* reporting colleagues, Mark Marnell and Mary Izett. And to *Ale Street News* editor Tony Forder, who has been putting up with my blown deadlines longer than anyone.

Thanks to my sister, Julie Cazentre, who served as a frequent overnight host and occasional guide to the Albany/Hudson River region. Thanks also to my neighbor Jeff Stage for his gracious help in watching over the critters left at home during my travels. And thanks to my sister-in-law Bridget Hanson, whose timely gift of the *Oxford Companion to Beer* (edited by Brooklyn's Garret Oliver) made research a snap.

Speaking of books—a nod to the late Michael Jackson, whose *The New World Guide to Beer*, which I bought in London in 1991, was my first inspiration and guide to beer and beer-writing.

And a special shout-out to the genius who invented EZ Pass.

Most of the thanks goes to my wife, Maureen Fitzsimmons, who accompanied me on almost all the brewery visits, serving as navigator, assistant interviewer, extra taster, and most importantly, motivational guru when I needed it most.

—*Don Cazentre*

Introduction

New York is a big, beautiful state. I didn't know exactly how big, or how beautiful, until I started work on this book. It's a book about breweries, so I've seen lauter tuns and mash tuns, glycol-jacketed bright tanks and vintage oak barrels. I've seen more hoses and clamps, kegs and growlers than I can count.

I've also seen two Great Lakes and half a dozen Finger Lakes, Adirondack Mountains and Hudson River bluffs, the gritty Riverside district of Buffalo, and the sublime eastern forks of Long Island. I've stood in small town squares and under big city skyscrapers. I've driven the Northway, the Thruway, the Cross Bronx Expressway, the Southern Tier Expressway, and the Long Island Expressway. And no one who has ever tried to get around Rochester can forget the Inner Loop. I've taken the N train to Queens. I even survived a steep descent down the gravel-covered Bly Hollow Road in the Taconic Mountains.

And of course, there were always beers waiting for me at the next stop—pale ales and brown ales; Munich lagers and London porters; Belgian-style wits and French-influenced saisons; imperial stouts and "sessionable" IPAs; and beers infused with chamomile, inoculated with *Brettanomyces*, and injected with jalapeño peppers.

But as you page through this book, you'll see that it is mostly about the people I've met in the mountains, along the lakes, at the end of the highways, and in the outer boroughs. These are beer people—those who have chosen to make beer their business or their profession. They all began by having beer as their passion. Many of them are also wonderful storytellers, as you'll discover by reading these entries. They have a sense that they are part of a surging market, a business that is thriving in a time of economic uncertainty and one that is changing dramatically day by day (or sometimes, it seems, minute by minute).

The first edition of this book, written by Lew Bryson and published in 2003, had entries for fifty-four breweries, large and small. This edition has eighty-nine. Take into consideration the breweries in the first edition that have since closed, and you'll find fifty-two breweries that opened since 2003. And almost all of the breweries in the first edition that still exist have changed so dramatically that the entries for them needed to be completely rewritten. Some have new owners, and many have new brewers. Several changed location, and plenty doubled or tripled in size. Brewpubs morphed into production or packaging breweries, and production breweries added pubs and restaurants. In one case, a brewery from the first edition whose owner declared it would never be a brewpub is now primarily just that. Times change.

Many of the breweries that opened in the past year are small; they're called nanobreweries these days. Some of these operate commercially, brewing on systems that make only 1 or 2 barrels at a time—that's just 2 to 4 full kegs per batch. There are homebrewers with bigger systems. Meanwhile, several of the breweries are big and growing bigger. In 2013, in addition to the three breweries listed as "The Big Guys" in the first edition (Anheuser-Busch, Genesee, and Matt Brewing Company), there were a half-dozen breweries with 50-barrel or bigger brewhouses that either opened or were scheduled to open within a year. Outside the big three, there was only one that size in 2003.

That brings me to this word of caution: As I've noted, the brewing scene in New York, as elsewhere in the United States, is dynamic, constantly changing. Inevitably, there will be new breweries opening not long after this book goes to press. I've tried to list as many of these "in the pipeline" breweries as I can (the ones I'm aware of) in the

BREWERY LOCATIONS

introduction to each of the state's regions. There are also breweries, or brewing companies, that existed when I researched this book but didn't get full entries. I made the decision, for example, to not write a full entry on companies that don't make any of their own beer but instead exclusively contract with other breweries. Bottom line: A brewery is likely to get a full entry if it makes even a fraction of its own beer on its own premises. Contract-only breweries are mentioned in the introduction to each region.

However, you may also find that some of the newer, smaller nanobreweries didn't make it in either. In many of these cases, the brewery is operating in the owner's basement or garage, with no tasting room or tour opportunities. These breweries are not equipped to receive visitors with guidebooks in hand.

So in the end, New York will almost certainly have more than 100 breweries or brewing companies by the time you read this book. The National Brewers Association puts the total number of American breweries in 2013 at more than 2,400. New York, as one of the most populous states in the country, would seem to have room to add or grow breweries.

In the meantime, please use this guide to explore the ones we've listed. Drive the roads, take in the scenery, and get to know the "beer people." I think you'll agree New York is a big, beautiful state.

Western New York

It's the land of Niagara Falls, Buffalo Bills football, and the one-time glory of Eastman Kodak. It's where Lucille Ball was born, Ani DiFranco calls home, and Frank Lloyd Wright left an architectural legacy. It's the part of New York that can boast access to two Great Lakes, Erie and Ontario. It's New York's "West Coast," according to Flying Bison Brewing Company Manager Tim Herzog, a Rochester native who established his career in Buffalo.

In style, culture, and sensibility, however, it's really where New York meets the Midwest. The "City"—New York City—is a long way from here. Buffalo and Rochester are both grand old cities, and you can still see the landmarks left behind from their days as American industrial powerhouses. For old school beer drinkers, Buffalo means a blue-collar town with a tavern on every corner, and Rochester means Genesee.

You'll also find plenty of places serving Buffalo's great culinary contribution to the world—the chicken wing—and not just in Buffalo. (You'll want to be able to identify the stem from the flapper, and be able to move easily from atomic to nuclear.) And don't forget the beef on weck, a roast beef sandwich on a hard roll found in every tavern. In comparison, Rochester's food contribution just might be the "Garbage Plate." Let's just say there's a little bit of everything on it.

Outside the cities, the gently rolling landscape is home to grape vineyards (both grape juice and ice wine are major products here), apple and fruit orchards, and in the area toward Lake Ontario, the farm region known as the mucklands, where they grow things like potatoes and onions.

Western New York has its own mountains, too. The Alleghenies jut north from Pennsylvania into the state's southwest corner, providing plenty of outdoor opportunities like skiing and hunting. They can talk knowledgeably about hockey here, and if the accent of some of those hockey fans sometimes seems odd, remember there's a long, shared border with Canada.

I'll nominate the city of Niagara Falls as the most surprising location in New York State *not* to have a brewery, or more particularly a brewpub. (That's as of 2013, anyway.) As for the falls themselves, the hype is justified. You can sometimes hear the roar of the falls before you see them, and the sight, from either the United States or Canadian side, is unforgettable. They're also beautiful—perhaps even more so—in winter.

And yes, winter can be savage and long here, but people are used to it. When a blizzard hits, people come together to help each other clear sidewalks and pull cars out of roadside drifts. It's almost as if they enjoy it. Just remember to stock up on the beer when a winter storm is approaching.

Other brewing companies

Three Heads Brewing Co. (www.threeheadsbrewing.com/ThreeHeads Brewing/index.php) in Rochester is a major player with lots of tap handles around town, but is currently a contract-only brewer. Rogers Beer (www.rogersbeer.com) in East Rochester is a smaller contract brewer. Becker Brewing Company (www.beckerfarms.com) in Gasport has started making beers under contract. Hamburg Brewing Company (www.hamburgbrewing.com/brewery) opened south of Buffalo in 2013. In the pipeline, look soon for Big Ditch Brewing Company (www.big ditchbrewing.com), a production brewery under development in Buffalo, and new projects from the owners of Pearl Street Grill and Brewery.

Other beer sites

The Blue Monk (727 Elmwood Ave., Buffalo) is a Belgian-oriented gastropub; Cole's Restaurant (1104 Elmwood Ave., Buffalo) is noted for imports and craft brews; The Pizza Plant (5110 Main St., in the Buffalo suburb of Williamsville) has a top-rated craft beer selection; The Old Toad (277 Alexander St., Rochester) is a quintessential British pub with fine imports and crafts; and Tap and Mallet (381 Gregory St., Rochester) offers a top draft and bottled beer selection. Good beer stores include Premier Gourmet (3904 Maple Rd., in the Buffalo suburb of Amherst) and Beers of the World (2599 E. Henrietta Rd., Rochester).

Area Attractions

Niagara Falls is the reason most people visit western New York. Start with the Niagara USA Official Visitor Center (10 Rainbow Blvd., Niagara Falls, NY 14303; 716-282-8992; www.niagara-usa.com). The *Albright-Knox Art Gallery* (1285 Elmwood Ave., Buffalo, NY 14222; 716-882-8700; www.albrightknox.org) has a deep collection that's especially rich in postwar American and European examples. The *Buffalo and Erie County Naval & Military Park* (1 Naval Park Cove, Buffalo, NY 14202; 716-847-1773; www.buffalonavalpark.org) is located on the Lake Erie waterfront, near downtown Buffalo. The *Frank Lloyd Wright's Martin House Complex* (125 Jewett Parkway, Buffalo, NY 14214; 716-856-3858; www.darwinmartinhouse.org) is a fine example of the architect's Prairie style, and one of several Wright-related attractions in the Buffalo area. Graycliffe, an hour south of Buffalo, is another. The *Seneca Iroquois National Museum* (814 Broad St., Salamanca, NY 14779; 716-945-1760; www.senecamuseum.org/Default.aspx), located on the Allegheny Indian Reservation, is a small tribal museum with a longhouse, and is dedicated to the Six Nations of the Iroquois Confederacy. The *National Museum of Play* (1 Manhattan Square, Rochester, NY 14607; 585-263-2700; www.thestrong.org) is located inside Rochester's Strong Museum and dedicated to toys, dolls, games, and other items that celebrate play. The *George Eastman House* (900 East Ave., Rochester, NY 14607; 585-271-3361; www.eastmanhouse.org) is the world's oldest museum dedicated to photography and film. *The Lucy Ball Desi Arnaz Center for Comedy* (2 W. 3rd St., Jamestown, NY 14701; 716-484-0800; www.lucy-desi.com/center-for-comedy/) is a museum of all things Lucille Ball (the hometown girl) and Desi Arnaz.

Buffalo Brewpub

6861 Main St., Williamsville, NY 14221
(716) 632-0552 • www.buffalobrewpub.com

Here at a busy intersection in the Buffalo suburbs stands the oldest continuously operating brewpub in New York State. The intersection, at Main Street and Transit Road in Williamsville, has a lot to do with it. "It's a great location, a busy spot," said Keith Morgan, who has been with the place since day one and now serves as manager (including serving as brewing supervisor).

The house beers are made in a 10-barrel extract system, for which no one at Buffalo Brewpub sees any need to apologize. After all, the place has been in business since 1986, outlasting dozens of other breweries and brewpubs. It has plenty of beers on tap, including a large selection from New York's other craft brewers like Southern Tier Brewing Company, Ithaca Beer Co., Rohrbach Brewing Company, Brewery Ommegang, and Flying Bison Brewing Company. The house beers are tweaked on occasion, but essentially you're likely to find Amber Ale, Pale Ale, Weiss, and Lager. (The lager may sometimes be a pils, but you get the idea.)

The brewpub is also a comfortable place to meet friends, watch the Bills or Sabres, and enjoy the food. The menu is pub casual, as Morgan emphasizes. "We serve a pub-type menu and it's a great atmosphere," Morgan said. "I've seen other brewpubs try to do fine dining with a brewery attached, and that doesn't seem to work so well."

You can start with the free popcorn and roasted peanuts—just crack 'em open and drop the shells. You'll also find burgers, including one made from ground buffalo, and sandwiches, salads, wraps, pastas, and other casual fare. Don't overlook the Buffalo traditions: There's beef on weck, the classic Buffalo tavern sandwich of slow-roasted beef, in this case enhanced by seasoning in the house beer. And of course there are the Buffalo wings, which some local periodicals call the best in the city. And this is the city where they were invented.

The brewhouse is in a 30-foot by 10-foot space just off the dining room. The whole place is spacious, with a wide-open feel. Over the years, the

Beers brewed: Amber Ale, Pale Ale, Weiss, and Lager, with some occasional twists in the rotation.

The Pick: Buffalo Brewpub's Pale Ale is the most balanced of the bunch. It's not an over-the-top beer, in keeping with the general philosophy of the place.

pub has been brightened up a bit, but dark wood and flagstone floors still dominate. The brewpub was founded by Kevin Townsell, who had seen a similar operation on a visit to Welland, Ontario. The pub is now owned by his brother, John. Its opening marked the first return of any kind of brewing to the Buffalo area since the Iroquois and Simon Pure breweries closed in 1970. (Buffalo was also one of the largest producers of malt for the brewing industry, back before Prohibition.) Townsell also opened a similar brewpub in Rochester, but that has since closed.

Buffalo Brewpub has a legendary mug club—you know, where regulars join up and have their own glasses waiting for them inside a cupboard. There have been nearly ten thousand members since the place opened, with more than two thousand still active. The mug club also serves as a networking group; the pub publishes a listing of the members on its website, with info like email addresses and occupations. Members include everyone from doctors, lawyers, and engineers to dog trainers and even a bagpiper. The mug club seems to emphasize the vibe of the pub itself—when you're here, you're in good company.

With its long track record, Buffalo Brewpub sees no reason to change things up too much, certainly not to move toward an all-grain brewing system. "We don't really have the space," Morgan said. "Besides, it's been a long successful run the way it is now."

Buffalo Brewpub

Opened: 1986.
Type: Brewpub.
Owner: John Townsell.
Brewer: Keith Morgan.
System: 10-barrel Continental extract system.
Annual production: 130 barrels.
Distribution: On-premises only.
Hours: 11:30 a.m. to midnight Monday to Thursday; 11:30 a.m. to 1 a.m. Friday and Saturday; noon to midnight Sunday.
Parking: The brewpub has its own lot.

Community Beer Works

15 Lafayette Ave., Buffalo, NY 14213
(716) 759-HOPS • www.communitybeerworks.com

Once upon a time, Buffalo's west side was home to a thriving malt industry, with companies that took the grain stored in the city's massive elevators and turned it into the malt that is the basis of beer. Today, on the city's west side in a building formerly belonging to the George Meyer Malting Company, stands a tiny operation that turns malt into beer: Community Beer Works.

Community's three partners—Ethan A. Cox, Rudy Watkins, and Gregory Patterson-Tanski—began their nanobrewery in April 2012. "We were doing a lot of homebrewing . . . a lot of hauling our beer out of the basement," Cox said. "We thought, 'Why don't we just do this?' We realized that we could make this pay the bills." They started with a 1.5-barrel brewing system, with the hope of growing to a 7-barrel and perhaps eventually a 15-barrel system (they have the space) in a few years. "Our philosophy, as a bunch of homebrewers, is we like to do a wide range of things," Cox said. "We like everything. But then it has to be achievable. You know, reality."

The three partners came from different backgrounds—for example, Cox was a cognitive psychologist—but knew they wanted to do something new that would keep them in Buffalo. They set up the partnership with Cox as president, Patterson-Tanski as facility manager and head of community outreach, and Watkins as head brewer. But really, it's all hands on deck at most times.

Everything in the 3,300-square-foot brewhouse is custom-built. The building, originally used to store vehicles for the malting company, still has the look and feel of a garage. Inside, there's evidence of a lot of tinkering. "This kind of place is really all about DIY," Cox said.

That spirit is also embodied in the name of one of CBW's first beers: Frank. Yes, Frank is a beer, the brewery's flagship and the one with which they identify the most. Frank is also "a typical Buffalo character," Cox said. "Frank is that guy . . . Everybody's got that guy—the guy who can do your light plumbing, fix things, but who is also a

Beers brewed: The Whale (brown ale), The IPA, Frank (American pale ale), and De Maas (Belgian amber).

The Pick: Frankly, Frank is a pretty good pale ale, with an abundantly citrus-influenced aroma.

great guy to hang out with, drink a beer with. He's a blue-collar guy, but he can talk about *Moby Dick* too. That's a Buffalo thing. Everybody knows Frank."

Frank the beer is a 4.6 percent ABV pale ale with a pine and citrus aroma, courtesy of Zeus, Centennial, and Zythos hops. Other beers include a brown ale called Whale, a Belgian called De Maas, and an IPA called The IPA. Community Beer Works beers, all draft in 2012, are on tap at a number of better beer bars in Buffalo, including The Blue Monk and Cole's.

The brewery's philosophy is embodied in this statement on its website: "'Embeer Buffalo' is the slogan of Community Beer Works. Our motto. Our battle cry. Our goal is not only to succeed as a brewery, but to better the beer culture of Buffalo. Our city loves beer, and has the potential to be one of the premiere beer destinations in the country. Help make that happen. Embeer Buffalo."

At CBW, they take Buffalo seriously, including efforts to work with the community (hence the name). As one example, CBW sends its spent grain to the Massachusetts Avenue Project, an urban community garden that dabbles in aquaculture and raising chickens. "It's a Buffalo thing," Cox said. "It's all about Buffalo and the beer."

Community Beer Works

Opened: April 2012.

Owners: Ethan A. Cox, Rudy Watkins, and Gregory Patterson-Tanski.

Brewer: Rudy Watkins.

System: 1.5-barrel production nanobrewery.

Annual production: 400 barrels.

Distribution: Primarily on-site and at a nearby neighborhood farmers market.

Hours: 3 p.m. to 7 p.m. Thursday; 3 to 8 p.m. Friday; 11 a.m. to 7 p.m. Saturday

Parking: No off-street parking.

Ellicottville Brewing Company

28A Monroe St., Ellicottville, NY 14731
(716) 699-ALES
34 W. Main St., Fredonia, NY 14063 • (716) 679-7939
www.ellicottvillebrewing.com

Ellicottville, a small town at the northern tip of the Allegheny Mountains, used to count on winter as the busy season, when snow lured visitors to the Holiday Valley Ski Center and other nearby resorts. Those days are long in the past. The crowds come to Ellicottville year round now, and many of them find their way to the Ellicottville Brewing Company, a brewpub in the heart of the village, with a new production brewery right next door. "There is no slow season anymore," Ellicottville's Peter Kreinheder said. "It's a vacation town, if you like skiing, or hiking, or camping. A lot of people have second homes here. We're just an hour from Buffalo. And we get a lot of visitors from Ohio, Pennsylvania, [and] southern Ontario."

Family connections link Ellicottville Brewing to the ski center and to the Southern Tier Brewing Company (page 32), a little to the south near Jamestown. Kreinheder married into the family that runs the ski resort, as did Southern Tier owner Phin DeMink. Ellicottville Brewing came before Southern Tier (DeMink got his start working there). It opened in 1995 and was inspired, Kreinheder said, by a brewpub he spotted in Vail, Colorado, on a ski trip.

Ellicottville Brewing occupies a building that dates to the 1860s, with a black walnut bar that is more than one hundred years old and originated in Chicago. From the beginning, Kreinheder wanted a brewpub that would cater to the tourists and ski bums. "We're really a restaurant first," Kreinheder said. "The copper kettles [the brewery] bring everyone in the door. The food and the consistency keep them here." Sure it's pub food, but it's also more than that. You'll find steaks and

Beers brewed: Blueberry Wheat, EBC Pale Ale (Two Brothers), Buchan Nut Brown, EVL Amber, Toasted Lager, Black Jack Oatmeal Stout, Pantius Droppus, (Imperial IPA), and Mowmaster Ultra Pale. Small batch specials include a German Stein Beer, Raspberry Beret, Hopicity, Hop Bomb, Black Hops, and an oak-aged series.

The Pick: There's a lot to choose from, and I was really taken by both the CattCounty Cuvee oak-aged blonde and the Spruce Stein Beer. But the standard EBC Pale (Two Brothers) with its bold and citrusy Cascade aroma reminded me so strongly of the early West Coast pales that first turned me on to craft beer that I can't resist it.

burgers, comfort dishes like shepherd's pie and fish and chips, and everything from sesame tuna wontons to Belgian-style mussels and potato pierogies. So it has been at Ellicottville Brewing since it opened. "Our orientation is not to be ginormous," Kreinheder said. "It's a restaurant with a brewery, not a production brewery."

In 2012 Ellicottville began work on a 30-barrel production brewery, located next door to the EBC brewpub on Monroe Street. It opened in the summer of 2013. Is that a contradiction to Kreinheder's stated goal off a restaurant and brewery first? Not at all, he said. The production brewery, he hopes, eventually will chiefly support an export business, with some capacity devoted to the adjacent brewpub, and "boost" the town by providing jobs and more visitors.

The brewpub's 10-barrel system will change to almost exclusively producing Belgian-style beers for the brewpub, under the direction of head brewer Dan Minner, who prefers working "in front of people" in a brewpub setting. In 2012, the brewpub was making about 1,200 barrels a year on its in-house system (a fairly large layout that runs the length of the dining room). Another 5,000 or so barrels are packaged at Southern Tier. "We'll get to 8,000 barrels eventually," Kreinheder predicted.

In 2005, Ellicottville Brewing Company took over the former Barker Brewing Company in Fredonia, a state university college town on the Thruway south of Buffalo. That location still has a small (3.5-barrel) brewhouse, but it's rarely used these days. The place has a similar menu to the EBC brewpub and serves Ellicottville beers. Despite its proximity to SUNY Fredonia, Kreinheder doesn't think of his outpost there as a college bar. "It's more a crowd of faculty, administrators, and visitors to the school," he said. "Students go there when their parents are in town to visit."

EBC beers are eclectic and adventurous, and the brewpub makes twenty to twenty-five different styles per year, and standard, imperial, and oak-aged series. The bestseller is Blueberry Wheat, followed by EBC Pale Ale (known at the pub as Two Brothers Pale Ale). Or go for Pantious Droppus (think about that for a second), a big imperial pale ale; or Eagle Trail IPA, with its resiny bitterness; or Catt County Cuvee, a blonde Belgian. Ellicottville has also done specialty stein or stone beers in the German style. Its Spruce Stein Beer, at 5.8 percent ABV, has a citrusy taste from the spruce and offers a clean, woodsy aroma.

Despite the emphasis on the pub trade, packaged Ellicottville beers are available around western New York and beyond. Yet they've given up on one thing that made the brewery stand out a few years ago. Some of their beer used to be packaged in a "keggy," a self-contained, self-pressurized, self-tapped container that held about 1.5

cases. Kreinheder licensed them from a German manufacturer but gave them up because they were a pain to fill (and clean when customers returned them).

Kreinheder, running one of New York's older brewing operations, likes what he sees going on around the state, with brewery openings and expansion coming at a rapid clip. That includes his own climb from restaurant and brewpub to something bigger, but not quite "ginormous," as he puts it. "I think there is room for growth. All I hope is that the brewing community continues to cooperate like it always has," he said. "I've always been one to help out someone who's starting out. I hope that continues."

Like many business owners, Kreinheder is frequently asked to contribute to charitable events. Early on, he provided beer, when appropriate. Then he had another idea: He would offer a day in the brewhouse as an auction prize. "It's a mini brew school," he said. "They come in, learn the basics of malting and brewing, work with us, and they go home with a keg of beer. If we just gave them beer, that's what they'd have. Do you know what we've created at the end of a brew school day? An ambassador."

Ellicottville Brewing Company

Opened: 1995.

Type: Brewpub with adjoining production brewery.

Owner: Peter Kreinheder.

Brewer: Dan Minner.

System: 2-barrel Bohemian brewhouse.

Annual production: 1,200 barrels at the brewpub. The company had 5,000 barrels per year made under contract at Southern Tier, and expected to reach 8,000 with the opening of an adjoining production brewery.

Distribution: At the brewpub and around western New York; markets will expand as production brewery ramps up.

Hours: 11:30 a.m. to 10 p.m. Monday to Friday; 11:30 a.m. to 11 p.m. Saturday and Sunday. Taps open until 2 a.m.

Food: Full-service pub menu.

Parking: No off-street parking.

Fairport Brewing Company

Brewery: 1000 Turk Hill Rd., Suite 298, Fairport, NY 14450
Tasting room: 99 S. Main St., Fairport, NY 14450
(585) 678-6728 • www.fairportbrewing.com

Tim Garman likes to say "I can't see past 6 o'clock tonight." That's his way of saying he's not going to forecast the future for the nanobrewery he and partner Tom Bullinger opened in the Rochester suburb of Fairport in the fall of 2012. (The future had already changed by the middle of 2013, when Paul Guarracini replaced Bullinger as Garman's partner).

Fairport traces its actual founding date to 2010 and its origins to a homebrewing set-up in an upstairs flat that Garman and Bullinger called their "man cave," which "kept getting bigger and bigger, and we kept spending money on it, until we said 'How do we get some write-offs for doing this?'" Garman said.

The company started out with a half-barrel nanobrewhouse and tasting room located on the second floor of an old Crosswell Arms plant. (Crosswell is a maker of air guns and BB guns.) The brewery shares the complex with several other small businesses and manufacturers, including Flour City Pasta, whose not-to-miss pastas in various shapes and flavors are a hit at farmers markets and food co-ops across Upstate New York. The complex also overlooks the Erie Canal, which lends its heritage to a lot of Fairport's beer names.

In the summer of 2013, when Paul Guarracini came on board for most of the brewing, Fairport faced the nanobrewery dilemma of too much demand for too little beer. So Garman and Guarracini launched a Kickstarter drive to buy a 3-barrel brew system, which they planned to install in their original space. Meanwhile, armed with one of the state's new farm brewery licenses, which permit off-premises second locations, they opened a new tasting room at 99 Main St. in Fairport, a more visible location. They also moved the half-barrel system to the new tasting room, for pilot brewing and to be part of Fairport's ongoing project to team up with local homebrewers for demonstrations and brewing classes.

Garman's professional background is in the high-tech device industry, which shows in the

Beers brewed: Low Bridge Ale, Lift Bridge Lager, Raider's Red, Black Lager, and Trail Town Nut Brown Ale.

The Pick: How many small brewers can get away with a Black Lager that boasts strong coffee-toffee notes and a clean finish? Fairport does.

"board" listing the beers on tap at the tasting room: It's not a chalk-board, but rather a flat-screen TV powered by a laptop, and it lists the specifications of each beer. The beers, by the way—even low-alcohol, light-colored ones like the Low Bridge Ale (3.9 percent ABV)—are amazingly clean tasting, with no signs of any flaw that such beers often can't hide.

Like many small brewers, the guys at Fairport take advantage of their small batch sizes to do a lot of experimenting. They use several different yeasts and a lot of "trial and error," Garman said. "If it doesn't work out, it wasn't that big of an investment," Garman said. "But the community has been wonderfully supportive of us and the beers." That's why Fairport also hosts the local homebrewers for Community Brew Night. "We have the homebrewers in here and it's a lot of fun," Garman said.

With its two locations, Fairport is mostly supplying those who come to the brewery or tasting room, but the owners have hopes of selling to off-premises accounts, especially in the Fairport and east suburban Rochester area. Fairport likely will support the brewery in a big way. Garman points out that one of their beers, Raider's Red Ale, is named for the local high school mascot. "Fairport people support Fairport people," he said. "There's a saying, 'Once a Raider, always a Raider.' It's almost like a cult. So we have that support."

In addition to local trade, they draw in some of the folks who visit the beer trails, including the many who tour the Finger Lakes area south of Rochester. "The Finger Lakes is a destination for beer lovers," Garman said. "I don't see that getting any weaker. It's going to get stronger." But Fairport's growth is going to be cautious. "Our philosophy is: everything you see here is paid for," Garman said. "Our plan is managed growth, not going into debts that we can't handle." So how big will Fairport get? That's one of the questions to which Garman answers: "I can't see past 6 o'clock tonight."

Fairport Brewing Company

Opened: Fall 2012.
Owners: Tim Garman and Paul Guarracini.
Brewer: Paul Guarracini.
System: 3-barrel main brewhouse; 25-gallon pilot system.
Production: N/A.
Distribution: Mostly from the brewery and tasting room; draft only.
Hours: Check the website before you visit.
Parking: Yes.

Flying Bison Brewing Company

491 Ontario St., Buffalo NY 14207
(716) 873-1557
www.flyingbisonbrewing.com

There's much to admire about Tim Herzog and Buffalo's Flying Bison Brewing Company, and it all has to do with overcoming adversity. Herzog had a notion to open a brewery back in the 1990s. He and his friend, Red Mrozek, owner of a local homebrew shop, were inspired in part by a trip to Britain, where they sampled real, cask-conditioned ales. They were planning and raising money when Mrozek was killed in a motorcycle accident.

It took a few years, but Herzog and another partner finally got everything together and opened the brewery in 2000. On their first brew day, they experienced a problem with the fermentation temperature. Herzog, who had waited for this moment a long time, made the decision to dump it and start again. He figured it was better to have one more delay than to peddle bad beer. You've got to admire that.

Flying Bison has had its ups and downs since then. The major upside is that Herzog is one of the smartest people in the New York beer business. His Flying Bison beers (almost all of which have an aviation theme) started to take off in a notoriously difficult market. Buffalo is a hard-core Labatt Blue and Blue Light kind of place.

Herzog brewed, distributed, and marketed. But hard work has its limits and doesn't always pay the bills. That's where this story takes another dramatic turn. In 2010, Flying Bison briefly stopped brewing. Then a deal was struck: The Matt Brewing Company of Utica, makers of Saranac, bought the brewery, invested in new equipment, plotted marketing strategies, and perhaps most importantly, hired Tim Herzog as general manager. "Tim's the man," said company president Fred Matt. "It's his brewery to run, and of course, he knows Buffalo."

By 2013, Flying Bison was experiencing a 75 to 80 percent increase in year-over-year sales, centered in the immediate Buffalo metro area. There are still obstacles, the most important of which is finding a new location. Herzog opened the brewery

Beers brewed: Year-round: Aviator Red, Rusty Chain, Buffalo Lager, and IPA. Seasonals: Hell Diver, Oatmeal Pale, Buffalo Kolsch 716, Bisonfest, Blizzard Bock, and other limited releases.

The Pick: The malt-accented beers are the real stars here, and it's a toss-up between Aviator Red and the Rusty Chain. I'll go with the Chain, a Vienna lager bursting with toasted malt.

in the city's Riverside neighborhood, a gritty area north of downtown that has seen better days. But that doesn't stop loyal Flying Bison followers from stopping in, getting samples from the friendly tasting room staff, and spreading the gospel of Flying Bison by word of mouth. This is what attracted Fred Matt and his uncle, chairman Nick Matt, in the first place: loyalty. "Buffalo people are rabid," Fred said, while "Buffalo likes Buffalo" is how Nick put it. "There is a tremendous amount of Buffalo pride that we want to tap into," Nick said.

The beers will help. Herzog has always used one yeast and low fermentation temperatures to achieve clean taste in a series of beers that are bold and flavorful but not over the top. They are mostly recognizable English or European (German) beer styles, like pale ale, ESB, Kolsch, and Vienna lager. The core beers are Aviator Red (one of the earliest, named for Red Mrozek), Rusty Chain, IPA, and Buffalo Lager.

The story behind Rusty Chain is a good illustration of how Flying Bison works. It started with Herzog's idea to make a classic crisp and malty Vienna lager. Then the brewery was approached to make it as a benefit for a collaboration with three Buffalo civic groups: Green Options Buffalo, Buffalo Rising, and Buffalo Microparks. The goal was to raise money to support bicycle paths and parking in the city. So Vienna Lager became Rusty Chain and a seasonal became a signature, a year-round brew that shows Flying Bison's support of its city. It soon became the bestseller, so popular that Matt began producing it at the Utica plant. "There's a lot of versatility in the beer itself," Herzog said, "and there's also that link to bicycling culture and urban culture."

The Matts and Herzog envision a point when the bestselling Flying Bison beers are brewed in Utica, while the Buffalo brewhouse is used for both Flying Bison and Saranac specialties and limited release beers. But the focus will always be on the local brand. "We want to get it to where people in Buffalo know it as a Buffalo brand," Nick said.

Flying Bison Brewing Company

Opened: 2000; reopened after a brief hiatus in 2010.
Type: Production brewery.
Owner: Matt Brewing Company.
Brewer: Tim Herzog.
System: 20-barrel Criveller brewhouse.
Annual production: 3,400 barrels.
Distribution: Erie and Niagara counties. About 69 percent draft; 31 percent bottled.
Hours: Noon to 6 p.m. Thursday; noon to 7 p.m. Friday; 11 a.m. to 4 p.m. Saturday.
Parking: Yes.

Genesee Brewing Company

445 St. Paul Street, Rochester, NY 14605
(585) 263-9200 • www.geneseebeer.com/
Genesee Brew House: 25 Cataract St.,
Rochester, NY 14605 • (585) 263-9200
www.geneseebeer.com/brew-house

After nearly a century and a half in business, the Genesee Brewing Company in Rochester finally has a visitors center and tasting room. And it's pretty spectacular—as spectacular perhaps as the view of the famous High Falls of the Genesee River from the center's outdoor rooftop patio. This visitors center, called the Genesee Brew House, is part museum, part retail shop, part tasting room, part pilot brewery, and part restaurant and tavern. That's a lot of parts, but it seems fitting for Genesee, the oldest surviving brewery in the state. A one-time regional powerhouse, Genesee's products include Genesee Beer, Genny Light, and Genesee Cream Ale, once advertised on TV by such heavyweights as sportscaster Curt Gowdy.

Genesee itself is a component in a company with a lot of parts. Its immediate parent company is North American Breweries, which was purchased in late 2012 by the Florida Ice and Farm Co. of Costa Rica. FIFCo is better known as Cervecería Imperial, makers of the century-old Central American beer Imperial. North American Breweries, the FIFCo subsidiary, is also parent to the American craft brands Magic Hat, Pyramid, and MacTarnahan's (formerly Portland Brewing Co.).

Again, that's a lot of parts. The Genesee story includes a lot of history and, in the first decade or so of the twenty-first century, a lot of ownership upheaval. That's why North American Breweries CEO Rich Lozyniak sounded a little relieved when talking about the FIFCo takeover during an interview in early 2013. "These are folks who brew beer and build brands," said Lozyniak, who added that the new company is committed to keeping NAB headquartered in Rochester. "I don't think we could have ended up with a better owner."

Beers brewed: Genesee: Lager, Genny Light, 12 Horse Ale, and Genny Cream Ale. Dundee: Honey Brown Lager, Nut Brown, IPA, Porter, Stout, Pale Bock, Oktoberfest, Irish Red Lager, and other seasonals. Genesee Brew House: rotating specials and one-time only beers.

The Pick: It seems like there should be three, considering how this place works. I'll go with the slightly sweet and refreshing Genesee Cream Ale, the equally refreshing and malt-accented Dundee Pale Bock, and the rich and warming Oatmeal Stout.

There has been brewing on the site overlooking the High Falls since at least the 1850s, and the company that became Genesee was founded by the Wehle family in 1878. The Wehles kept it until 1999, when there was a buyout by a group of management employees. They reorganized the place as High Falls Brewing Co. and tried to keep the mainstream Genesee line going while also pumping up craft brands under the labels High Falls, JW Dundee, Koch's, Kipling, and Michael Shea's.

A bit of marketing nightmare, right? So, in 2009, a New York City financial investment company called KPS bought the operation, created a Rochester-based company called North American Breweries, added the above-mentioned craft lines to the portfolio, and even took over North American distribution of Labatt, the Canadian powerhouse. (And did I mention North American Breweries makes Seagram's alcohol beverages and other products under contract, too?) "KPS was great, putting a lot of money into it and building the brand," Lozyniak said. "But now we're part of a brewing company again."

The focus now is on returning to the legacy Genesee brands. The name was restored to the corporate moniker—not that most people had ever really called it High Falls—and the craft line has been consolidated and simplified as Dundee Ales & Lagers. The core market for these beers is New York, Pennsylvania, and Ohio. Production at the big Genesee brewery, with its 900-barrel brewhouse, peaked in the 1980s at 3.5 million barrels per year. By 2009, that had fallen to 1 million barrels, but rebounded to 2 million by 2013. Lozyniak thinks they may hit their stride again at 2.8 or even 3 million barrels within a few years.

History and legacy will always be a major part of Genesee. Ask most Upstaters of a certain age—let's say those born in the 1970s or earlier—and they are likely to tell you their first beer was a Genesee, most likely Genesee Cream Ale. (That beer actually dates only to 1960.) Unlike many of the famous breweries owned by German families elsewhere, Genesee always brewed both ales and lagers. Historic beers include Old Stratford Ale and Liebotschaner, once a generic name for a light pilsner (and since sold as a brand name to Red Lion in Pennsylvania). Today, there's Genesee Lager, Genny Light, Genesee 12 Horse (an ale), and Genny Cream (a hybrid brewed at lager temperature using ale yeast). Dundee, meanwhile, aims for the broad middle spectrum of the craft market, not too high in alcohol or extreme but still flavorful, very much like its sister Upstate former regional brewery, Saranac. "Dundee is an important brand focus," Lozyniak said, "but it's not a major contributor in the big picture. We see it as a strong regional craft brand."

The Genesee Brew House (the visitors center) will play a part in boosting all of the brands. "One of the nice things about the Genesee

Brew House," Lozyniak said, "is that it gives us a home to try new things, whether that's Dundee or even Genesee." The "big" Genesee Brew House is run by brewmaster John Fisher, who has been with the company for more than forty years. The 20-barrel pilot brewery at the Genesee Brew House is run by Dean Jones, a veteran of several Upstate craft breweries. He's like a kid in a candy store with this sparkling new Newlands brewing system. Referring to the "big" brewery, Jones said, "They call us the 'little brewery next store.'"

Jones works with the two Genesee house yeasts—one ale and one lager—but is not limited in what he can brew. His first beer was a Scotch Ale, followed by a Winter Warmer, an Oatmeal Stout, and a North German Pilsner. "We're going to do something different every time out," Jones said. "That's the point. Eventually, the best and most popular may transfer over to the big brewery." They've even talked about an "all malt" cream ale. "There's a bunch more fun yet to be explored," he said.

Exploring the fun is the business of the visitors center, with its tasting room for the pilot brews and lunch or dinner in the tavern, where the emphasis is on pub fare and some German specialties. After lunch, explore the museum-quality exhibits on Rochester's and Genesee's brewing history, which drew a quarter-million visitors in the first year. Like I said, history and legacy are a big part of Genesee's identity.

"Imperial is a century old," Lozyniak said, referring to the flagship of the company's Costa Rican owner. "Genesee is 135. Labatt [which the company distributes] is 160. Even our craft beers [Dundee] go back 25 years, and that's old in that segment. It's great to have all that heritage to fall back on."

Genesee Brewing Company

Opened: Genesee was founded in 1878.

Owner: North American Breweries, a subsidiary of Florida Ice and Farm Co. (Cervecería Imperial) of Costa Rica.

Brewer: John Fisher (Genesee), Steve Kaplan (Dundee lead brewer), and Dean Jones (pilot brewhouse).

System: 900-barrel (main brewery); 20-barrel (pilot brewhouse).

Annual production: 2 million barrels in 2013; capacity of 3 to 3.5 million barrels.

Distribution: Core market in New York, Pennsylvania, and Ohio.

Hours: Brew House: 11 a.m. to 9 p.m. Monday to Wednesday; 11 a.m. to 10 p.m. Thursday to Saturday; noon to 9 p.m. Sunday.

Food: Full menu at Genesee Brew House tavern.

Parking: Yes.

Gordon Biersch Brewery Restaurant

Walden Galleria, Galleria Drive,
Cheektowaga, NY 14225 • (716) 683-0050
www.gordonbiersch.com/locations

Gordon Biersch, the major national brewpub chain that started in California, decided to make its New York debut out west, in Buffalo. What was behind that choice? Probably real estate considerations. The brewpub opened in 2011 in a suburban mall owned by The Pyramid Cos., which also owns the Destiny USA Mall in Syracuse where Gordon Biersch installed its second New York location a year later (page 109).

But the Buffalo area does seem an inspired choice. Buffalo has a lot of residents with German, Czech, and Polish heritage, and it is a lager town, making Labatt Blue and Blue Light its top-consumed brands. And the mall in Buffalo, like the one in Syracuse, gets a fair share of Canadian visitors, eager for a taste of what Gordon Biersch has been selling since launching its first pub in Palo Alto in 1988: clean-tasting German- and Czech-style beers that adhere to the Reinheitsgebot, the German beer purity law (just malt, hops, and water, you know).

"Adhering to those standards and producing good quality beers with no off flavors is difficult," said Gordon Biersch's Buffalo brewmaster, Matt Redpath. "People sometimes don't realize how difficult that is." Gordon Biersch restricts its brewers in some other ways, too. All of them produce a series of core, year-round beers: a light lager called Golden Export, a traditional Bavarian Hefeweizen, a malty and mildly sweet Maerzen, a classic Czech Pilsner, and a roasted black Schwarzbier. There are standard seasonals, too: WinterBock, Maibock, SommerBrau (a Kolsch), and an Oktoberfest, which differs from the Maerzen (a real Oktoberfest in Germany), by being "a shade lighter with a bit more hoppiness to it," Redpath, a native of Portland, Oregon, said.

Every once in a while, Gordon Biersch cuts its brewers loose. Once or twice a year, Redpath gets to make a Brewer's Select beer, still of course adhering to those German standards. Among other things, he notes, "that means no dry hopping." (On the other hand, that keeps Gordon Biersch from

Beers brewed: Year-round: Golden Export, Hefeweizen, Schwartzbier, Czech Pilsner, and Maerzen. Seasonals: Maibock, SommerBrau (Kolsch), Oktoberfest, Winter-Bock, some Brewer's Select specials, and "gap" beers.

The Pick: Looking for a clean, balanced, delicately flavored pilsner without traveling to the Czech Republic? Look no further than Gordon Biersch's Czech Pilsner.

being a clone of every other brewpub out there.) For his first Brewer's Select in Buffalo, Redpath did a Weizenbock, a "nice, dark, heavy wheat beer," made with an ale yeast. Typically only Gordon Biersch's wheats are brewed with ale yeasts. Then he brewed a Rauch Schwarzbier, with 50 percent smoked malts. "With smoked beers, you either like it or you don't," Redpath said. "So I backed off a bit on the smoke."

Redpath also occasionally uses his 15-barrel brewing system to produce "gap" beers, which come out when one seasonal runs out before the next seasonal begins. One of these was an American-hopped bock. "I got to see how American hops react in a lager beer," he said.

Gordon Biersch bills itself as a brewery restaurant rather than a brewpub, so you know there's an emphasis on the food. The menu has its German influences, of course, but there are also Asian, southwest, Cajun, and other themes, including Californian. And check out those big "knife and fork" burgers. The place also sells growlers to go, both the twist-off tops and the German-style ceramic stopper varieties. The Buffalo location's rectangular layout allows plenty of vantage points for customers to look over the brewhouse.

In Buffalo, Gordon Biersch also participates in off-premises events, bringing its signature German-style beers on the road. Some of those take place at the Spring Garden in the Buffalo suburb of East Aurora, which celebrates German heritage with events like a Maifest in May and a Waldfest in July. "We actually had a wooden keg tapping and a brass band and all that," Redpath said.

Back at the pub, Redpath sometimes sees western New Yorkers stop by to celebrate their German culture. "It's cool to see some of the older folks who may have come from Germany," Redpath said. "They talk about our beer and how it reminds them of the beers they had back home."

Gordon Biersch Brewery Restaurant

Opened: 2011.

Owner: CraftWorks Restaurants & Breweries, Inc.

Brewer: Matt Redpath.

System: 15-barrel Specific Mechanical system.

Annual production: 1,500 barrels.

Distribution: Mostly on site, with growlers to go.

Hours: Restaurant: 11 a.m. to 10 p.m. Sunday; 11 a.m. to 11 p.m. Monday to Saturday. Bar: 10 p.m. to midnight Monday to Thursday; 10 p.m. to 1 a.m. Friday to Saturday.

Food: An eclectic, around-the-world menu.

Parking: Yes.

Pearl Street Grill & Brewery

76 Pearl St., Buffalo, NY 14202
(716) 856-2337 • www.pearlstreetgrill.com/home

Pan Am Grill & Brewery

391 Washington St, Buffalo, NY 14203
(716) 856-0062 • www.thehotellafayette.com/panam

Former brewmaster Phil Internicola shared this little oddity about Buffalo's Pearl Street Grill & Brewery: "Even though we sell 1,000 gallons of our own beer every week," he said of the downtown brewpub, "outside of the sports arenas and large venues like that, we are the number one outlet for Labatt products in the United States."

It just goes to show that Buffalo remains a hardcore Labatt Blue kind of town. Yet Pearl Street has thrived as a brewpub since 1997, and the owners have added a second brewpub a few blocks away, the Pan-American Brewery in the Lafayette Building. Their sights are also set on a third location along Buffalo's resurgent waterfront, in what is planned as a major entertainment district.

Pearl Street/Pan Am's ownership, led by managing partner Earl Ketry, has even dubbed this downtown area the "Brewery District." It's a part of downtown Buffalo that hearkens back to the turn of the twentieth century, when Buffalo was a bustling, important, and wealthy industrial city, and also home to a bustling, rough-and-tumble downtown and waterfront area.

Pan Am refers to one of the historic highlights of Buffalo history, the 1901 Pan American Exposition, a sort of world's fair marred by the assassination of President McKinley during his visit. Buffalonians prefer to remember the second part of that incident: Theodore Roosevelt, McKinley's vice president, came to the city a few days later to take the oath of office as president. Why go

Beers brewed at Pearl Street: Lake Effect Pale Ale, Lighthouse Premium Blond, Saber's Edge Double IPA, Street Brawler Stout, Trainwreck German Amber, Wild Ox Wheat, seasonals, and limited releases.

Beers brewed at Pan Am: Year-round: City of Light (pale German lager), Rough Rider (English-style brown porter), Roosevelt Red (Irish red ale), and The Terminator (American pale ale). Seasonals: Nickel Town Brown, Th' Wee Beastie, and Dusseldorf Altbier.

The Pick: Pearl Street's Sabre's Edge may not get the Sabres to the Stanley Cup, but it is a highly addictive, citrusy sweet American India pale ale. You definitely want at least a hat trick's worth of these.

into all this in a beer book? Because that history—that era—seems alive and well in Buffalo, and its influences show up at both the Pearl Street and Pan Am brewpubs. Because they are just blocks apart, with the same owners and brew team, I've combined them into one entry. Internicola left the company in late 2013. The new head brewer is Noah McIntee.

The Pearl Street Grill & Brewery opened in 1997 at the corner of busy Pearl Street and Seneca Street, where all roads leading to downtown Buffalo seem to meet. The brewhouse, visible from the street and the main dining room, is the same 15-barrel Specific Mechanical system installed in 1997. Pearl Street has two distinct identities. The first is that it's a popular sports bar, jammed to the rafters on a night when the Buffalo Sabres are home at the nearby First Niagara Center. (An older arena, nicknamed "The Aud," used to be directly across the street.) "That move didn't make any difference—the hockey fans will come here no matter what," Internicola said. That's where the Labatt drinkers fit in.

Pearl Street's second identity is that it's a brewpub. The place seems to have a little steampunk feel to it, another echo of the turn of the twentieth century and the fascination with the mechanical devices of the Victorian period. Your eyes are drawn to the old-fashioned ceiling fans powered by one long leather belt that snakes around the place. That apparatus dates back more than a century, when the building housed a sewing machine factory.

The beer at the Pearl Street is steeped in the classic European traditions: German, English, and Belgian, plus the American styles that descended from them. The bestseller at Pearl Street is the Train Wreck Amber, a malty and nutty German-influenced lager. "That's our signature and outsells any other two combined," Internicola said. It's followed in popularity by Lighthouse Premium Blond, which also serves as the base for the popular blueberry ale called Blue Eyed Blond. Pearl Street's flavored beers are not shy. The Blue Eyed Blond has an explosive blueberry aroma; the raspberry and chocolate beers offer similar powerful flavor notes. Only the Don Cherry What softens the flavor, allowing the wheat character to shine through.

The food at Pearl Street is classic pub fare, from pizzas and burgers to salads and sandwiches. There's also a nearby spot, under the same ownership, called Brawler's Deli.

The Pan Am Grill & Brewery satellite opened in 2012 with its own brewhouse. At 15 barrels, the brewhouse is the same size as Pearl Street's, but the number and size of fermenters and other tanks makes its output smaller. "We had the one at Pan Am made for us," Internicola said. "We wanted to have as close as possible the same equipment in both locations, so we could have the interchangeability of personnel, process, and so on."

Pan Am is associated with the hotel in the grand LaFayette Building, and is outfitted in a lush, early 1900s décor. The food is a little more upscale than at Pearl Street; there's confit of duck at Pan Am that you won't find in the other pub, for instance. The beers are different, too. The popular beers here include City of Light Lager and Roosevelt Red, a take on Irish red ale.

At both Pearl Street and Pan Am, the brewers strive to balance the competing nature of Buffalo's beer scene. "Buffalo people are traditional," he said. "There are still people who are new to craft beers. So we provide both lighter styles and bolder beers that allow [people] to graduate up the scale."

Pearl Street Grill & Brewery/Pan Am Grill & Brewery

Opened: Pearl Street opened in 1997; Pan Am opened in 2012.
Type: Brewpubs.
Owners: Partnership led by Earl Ketry.
Brewer: Noah McIntee.
System: Each pub has a 15-barrel Specific Mechanical brewhouse. There is more fermentation and tank space at Pearl Street.
Annual production: 2,100 barrels at Pearl Street; 500 barrels at Pan Am.
Distribution: Primarily on-premises only.
Hours: Check the websites.
Food: Pearl Street is pub fare; Pan Am is more upscale.
Parking: On-street parking or nearby lots and garages.

Roc Brewing Co.

56 South Union St., Rochester, NY 14607
(585) 794-9798 • www.rocbrewingco.com

It says a lot about Roc Brewing Co. that its flagship beer is a Dark Mild. That's a statement about Roc and about its customers. Let's face it: Mild ale has long been a hard sell in the United States, and it's not exactly a barn burner in its native England these days, either. But Jon Mervine and Chris Spinelli seem perfectly capable of joining the craft beer bandwagon, and of going off in their own direction while doing it.

The customers at their hybrid nanobrewery and tap room in downtown Rochester seem to enjoy being challenged. "The demographic here is everything from twenty-two-year-old college kids to grandparents," said Mervine, the brewer. "It's great. They're beer enthusiasts. There's no boundaries to that." Late Saturday afternoon at Roc is when many customers come in for tasting flights of whatever Mervine has on tap, anything from a Golden Pale Ale to a wet-hopped IPA to a Belgian Blonde. Or maybe the Union 56—the "house" pale ale that changes with every batch—or What the Fuggles IPA, which turns bold American IPA on its head with the earthy British hop variety.

During my first visit, one customer, nosing his beer, actually looked up and asked: "So this was a warmer fermentation, right?" You don't find that in every bar, not even in every brewery or brewpub, but it fits with Roc's outlook. Mervine and Spinelli don't offer their customers a set of extreme or over-the-top beers, but they don't offer only safe alternatives either. Mervine views the Dark Mild, for example, as "an educational thing." This beer is relatively light, at 4 percent, but with big, bold flavor. "Someone might say 'I want a lighter beer,'" he said. "So I say: Lighter alcohol? Lighter body? It can mean a lot of different things."

Roc Brewing opened in 2011 alongside the Inner Loop in the heart of urban Rochester. It's just "an 8-iron shot away," Mervine notes, from one of Rochester's other beer destinations, The Old Toad, an authentically British-style pub. Roc seems different from many craft beer joints. The tasting and

Beers brewed: An ever-changing lineup includes Golden Pale Ale, Cullinan's Revival (Irish red), Dark Mild, Amber Ale, and a host of seasonals, one-offs, and series.

The Pick: Want a session beer with attitude? The Dark Mild is big and bold, fruity and earthy, but easily drinkable at just 4 percent ABV.

taproom feels more like a bar, and you can order pints. Mervine brews beer all week—with a 1-barrel system, he needs to brew frequently to keep up with demand. They do plan to scale up the size of the brewhouses, perhaps to 3 barrels and later to 7. In the meantime, some of their more popular beers are brewed under contract at Rohrbach Brewing Company, the granddaddy of Rochester craft brewers.

Mervine and Spinelli met while studying economics at the Rochester Institute of Technology. Spinelli's mother, Patty, suggested they start homebrewing. A couple of years later they opened Roc, with Patty as a partner. The location is a former VFW hall they share with an architectural firm. The architects replaced the front wall with a floor-to-ceiling glass window for a sleek, modern, urban look.

The state license requires something in the way of food, so Roc serves a soft pretzel. But never fear: Just as Roc has lured those seeking interesting beers, it's also managed to be a magnet for Rochester's food trucks. On any given night, you might find a truck specializing in burgers or other meaty sandwiches, or one featuring Peruvian cuisine, or one called Le Petite Poutine, which serves variations on the Canadian bar food classic of fries, cheese curds, and gravy. "People go out, get food, and come back in," Spinelli said. "It's a nice little collaboration."

Mervine also believes in collaboration with his beers. Take the smoked porter called Nano Roc made along with Community Beer Works, a similar-sized outfit in Buffalo. Mervine has also worked with a Rochester coffee roaster called Joe Bean on a series of coffee-infused beers, including a coffee Belgian stout called Kyoto Protocol. You won't see that in every brewery.

Roc Brewing Co.

Opened: 2011.

Type: Hybrid nanobrewery with a licensed bar selling beer; other beer made under contract.

Owners: Patty Spinelli, Chris Spinelli, and Jon Mervine.

Brewer: Jon Mervine.

System: 1-barrel brewhouse at the bar (with plans to scale up to a 3-barrel).

Annual production: 150 barrels at the pub; about 800 barrels under contract.

Distribution: Primarily on-premises; limited off-premises accounts in the Rochester area.

Hours: Limited: 5 p.m. to 9 p.m. Wednesday; 5 p.m. to 11 p.m. Thursday; 3 p.m. to 11 p.m. Saturday.

Food: Look for the food trucks parked outside.

Parking: It's in a city neighborhood.

Rohrbach Brewing Company

97 Railroad St., Rochester, NY 14609
(585) 546-8020
Rohrbach Brewpub: 3859 Buffalo Rd.,
  Rochester 14624
(585) 594-9800 • www.rohrbachs.com

Anyone who has ever driven in Rochester is familiar with the Inner Loop, a sunken highway that circles the city center. So it's fitting that Rohrbach Brewing Company—the city's longest surviving craft brewery— has made something of a loop of its own. Call it the Brotherhood of the Traveling Brewhouses.

Rohrbach started as a brewpub back in 1992 with a 7-barrel brewhouse on Gregory Street in the city's South Wedge neighborhood (just south of downtown). Then, in 1995, owner John Urlaub branched out with a second pub in the western suburbs (the Gates–Chili area), and installed a 20-barrel brewhouse. In 2001, he closed the Gregory Street brewhouse (a loss that beer lovers in Rochester still lament) when its lease expired. The brewhouse loop was closed, in a way, in 2008 when Rohrbach launched a production brewery back in the city, on Railroad Street in the Market District east of downtown. Then brewhouses started revolving. Urlaub moved the 20-barrel system from the suburban brewpub to the production brewery. He sent the 7-barrel brewhouse from the first pub, which had been in storage, out to the brewpub on Buffalo Road in the Gates-Chili area.

Urlaub calls himself a "city guy," so he's excited to once again have a presence in the heart of Rochester. "The Finger Lakes is great with all its breweries in a rural setting," Urlaub said, alluding to the burgeoning brew scene in the area just south of Rochester. "But I've always thought of brewing traditionally as an urban operation. That's the history of brewing—breweries in the cities."

Rohrbach's production brewery is just down the street from the Rochester Public Market, a

Beers brewed: Year-round: Scotch Ale, Highland Lager, Railroad Street IPA, Sam Patch Porter, Patty's Irish-Style Cream Ale, Red Wing Red Ale, and Pilsner. Seasonals: Vanilla Porter, Blueberry Ale, Oktoberfest, Kim's Kristmas Ale, Winter Warmer, Black IPA, and many more, plus one-offs. (Six are typically available at the brewery and fourteen are on at the pub.)

The Pick: I believe John Urlaub when he speaks so eloquently about balance, and that's why I go with the Railroad Street IPA, which builds its hop accents on a firm base of malt. At the pub, I enjoyed the Black IPA for the same reason—nice hop bitterness atop a toffee-like dark malt base.

year-round farmers and producers market with a large following. "The market is a jewel in the city of Rochester," Urlaub said. "And it's a good fit for us, for what we do. We make beers, and the farmers and the chefs and producers have their products. It's a bit of a foodie thing that we can be part of."

People shopping at the market do indeed take the short walk down to the brewery, especially on Saturdays. What they see when they walk in looks an awful lot like a brewpub. There's a tasting room bar, and a warm and inviting seating area, finished with lots of wood and equipped with four long tables and stools that give it the appearance of a European beer hall. (It also has one of the nicest, cleanest rest rooms I've seen in a brewery.) It's all part of a renovation in 2012.

It looks like it's a place ready to serve food, but as of 2013 that hasn't happened. "A lot of people ask about food when they come in, but all we're serving here is beer samples," said Mitch LaGoy, head brewer. There are usually a half dozen on the taps, some made on the premises, and some made at the brewpub.

The well-appointed tasting room is adjacent to a bustling and expanding production brewhouse. Rohrbach makes about a half-dozen year-round beers and another half-dozen or so seasonals, and serves as a contract brewer. (Clients include Roc Brewing Co. in Rochester.) The striking thing about Rohrbach's production facility, at least in 2013, is the amount of energy devoted to prefilled growlers. It's unusual for many brewers, but a major part of Rohrbach's business, especially since one of its biggest customers for the growlers is the Rochester-based Wegmans supermarket chain. Rohrbach is looking into adding a bottling line and possibly phasing out the growlers.

LaGoy said Urlaub leans toward beers that are malt-accented, while Urlaub's take on it is that he believes in balance. "I don't believe in going too far over the top in either direction," Urlaub said. "Just like a good chef balances the spices he uses, I think good brewers balance the malt and the hops." Nevertheless, the brewery's flagship bestseller is a malt-accented Scotch Ale, made with 1 percent roasted barley. It has a sweet but not cloying taste. The second bestseller is Highland Lager, a beer modeled after the lagers from Sam Adams or Brooklyn.

LaGoy, meanwhile, has tinkered with a beer that used to be called Stock Ale but is now known as Railroad Street IPA. It's hopped with Willamette, then dry hopped with Centennial and Cascade. "It's an East Coast IPA," LaGoy said. There's also a beer called Patty's Irish Style Cream Ale. "It's risky doing something called cream ale in Rochester," LaGoy said, acknowledging the preeminence of the famed Genesee Cream Ale made by the big brewer in town. "This is different—it's more like a Wexford's [Irish ale]." Another well-known Rohrbach product is Red Wing Red Ale, brewed for the Triple-A Rochester Red Wings baseball team and their downtown ballpark, Frontier Field.

Despite his belief in the urban tradition of brewing, Urlaub said he finds himself spending more of his time at the brewpub on Buffalo Street. "I like the restaurant business," he said, admitting that's ironic "because all I ever wanted was to be a brewer." The pub has the usual array of pub food, plus a full page of German specialties like schnitzel and a sausage plate. There are usually fourteen house beers on tap. The 7-barrel brewhouse is located in the rear of a backroom that once housed the bigger 20-barrel system. Much of that room is a new dining area, and with a patio open in nice weather, the pub can seat up to 190 people.

It seems that Rohrbach has been on the Rochester beer scene forever. But Genesee Brewing Co., which dates to the mid-nineteenth century, is clearly far older, and there was another brewpub in the area—the long-since closed Rochester Brew Pub—when Urlaub founded his business. Even though breweries existed then, Urlaub more or less fondly recalls having to hunt down a brewery license application back in 1991. Times have changed.

Urlaub enjoys the camaraderie of today's Rochester beer community, noting that all the brewers in town, large or small, production or contract, get along. "Rochester has a great beer scene," he said. "We have the breweries, some great beer bars, [and] Wegmans. We have a strong home-brewer community, and all the brewers support each other. Genesee has been supportive of everyone. I'm proud of Rochester."

Rohrbach Brewing Company

Opened: Rohrbach Pub & Brewery, 1995; Rohrbach Brewing Co., 2008.

Owners: John and Patty Urlaub.

Brewers: Mitch LaGoy (brewery) and Eric Bishop (brewpub).

System: 20-barrle Criveller (brewery); 7-barrel (brewpub).

Annual production: Aiming for 5,500 barrels in 2013, of which 4,500 will be at the brewery.

Distribution: Primarily in the greater Rochester area; growlers sold at Wegmans supermarkets.

Hours: Brewery/tasting room: 10 a.m. to 5 p.m. Monday to Wednesday (beer sales only); 1 a.m. to 5 p.m. Thursday and Friday (beer sales and sampling); 9 a.m. to 3 p.m. Saturday (tours and tastings). Brewpub: 11 a.m. to 11 p.m. Monday to Thursday; 11 a.m. to midnight Friday; 11:30 a.m. to midnight Saturday; noon to 9 p.m. Sunday.

Food: Full pub menu at the brewpub; no food at the brewery tasting room.

Parking: The brewpub has its own lot.

Southern Tier Brewing Company

2072 Stoneman Circle, Lakewood,
New York 14750 • (716) 763-5479
www.stbcbeer.com

Imagine standing in front of the mild-mannered Bruce Banner and watching him explode into the Incredible Hulk. That's what it has been like to watch the Southern Tier Brewing in Jamestown for much of the past decade. It grows right before your eyes—bulking up, bursting out of its space, ready to take on the world—but with a set of 660-barrel fermenters and a 12,000-bottle-per-hour packaging line instead of bulging muscles and a green complexion.

It's hard to believe that Southern Tier Brewing Company was not in the first edition of this book, published in 2003. It didn't exist. It's hard to believe, because less than ten years later Southern Tier has built one of the strongest reputations for quality in the state, and in 2012 was counted among the fifty largest breweries in the country. It was actually thirty-seventh among craft breweries and forty-eighth among all breweries, according to the Brewers Association. In size, that puts Southern Tier between Long Island's Bluepoint Brewing and California's Lost Coast Brewing (and this was before its most recent expansion, which is going to jack up its numbers). All the while, almost every beer fan I've ever met agrees with me when I say this: I've never had a Southern Tier beer I didn't like a lot. It is, to use a word found in the name of one of Southern Tier's beers, *unearthly*.

So where did it all come from? Credit Phin DeMink, who started out as a brewer at the Ellicottville Brewing Company brewpub about an hour away in the Allegheny Mountains. DeMink left his mark in Ellicottville, producing its highly successful pale ale, then headed west to Chicago's Goose Island production brewery. He later returned Upstate, and built a then-modest-sized brewery in an existing building in an industrial park in Lakewood, just outside Jamestown, near Chautauqua Lake.

Eventually, the brewery moved across the road into a larger purpose-built building and added an

Beers brewed: Core beers are IPA, Porter, Phin & Matt's Extraordinary Ale (an American pale), 2XIPA, 2XStout, 422 (a pale wheat session ale), and Live (a bottle-conditioned), plus seasonal imperials, the Blackwater Series (imperial stouts and porters), and other specials.

The Pick: Impossible. Okay, I'll try. Imperial Pumking is an 8.6 percent ABV fall seasonal with a full but not overpowering pumpkin flavor, a spicy complexity, and a teasing sweetness.

on-site pub and beer garden. In 2012, it launched a massive expansion. Already operating a 50-barrel brewhouse, it added a 110-barrel system. That's an addition to the 50-barrel set-up, not a replacement. The brew crew is now working seven days a week. "We are never not changing," said brewery spokesman, graphic designer, and marketing guy Nate Arnone, in something of an understatement. The day I was there, the brewery took a delivery for two 660-barrel fermenters. It looked like a couple of space shuttles were being delivered.

This is New York's southwesternmost brewery. Jamestown is a former industrial city, a furniture manufacturing center that, like many other Upstate cities, has seen better days. It may be best known as the hometown of Lucille Ball. The name Southern Tier refers to the hilly, sometimes mountainous region that hugs the Pennsylvania border from Binghamton west to Jamestown and Chautauqua. At first glance, it seems out of the way. But if you take the New York State Thruway south from Buffalo on your way to Erie, Pennsylvania, or Cleveland, Ohio, for example, it's less than an hour's drive from the exit. That's why Southern Tier considers some of its core territory to be Buffalo, Cleveland, and Pittsburgh. That's a top-notch beer-drinking region, but would be shortchanging the market. Southern Tier is now in about thirty states and several foreign countries. It's the beer that put it on all those maps.

DeMink and cofounder Skip Yahn began with a couple of brews: a Mild Ale (alas, since dropped), a Pilsner, and an IPA. Today it still makes seven core beers: IPA, Porter, Phin & Matt's Extraordinary Ale (an American pale), 2XIPA, 2XStout, 422 (a pale wheat session ale), and the newest Live, a bottle-conditioned beer. To that, add seven seasonals, a complement of big stouts and porters called the Blackwater Series, a couple of year-round imperials, four seasonal imperials, and a couple of limited edition beers.

Where to begin with all this? To get an idea, take the two year-round imperials. One is called UnEarthly, a 9.5 percent imperial IPA the brewery calls "an uninhibited infusion of hops." It's piney, citrusy, and resinous, but with a lot of malt backbone, too. The other year-round imperial is Iniquity (9 percent), a beer so dark and opaque that no amount of light could ever penetrate it. It has the pine and citrus qualities of UnEarthly, but with the addition of dark-roasted malts to give it flavors of toffee and cocoa. I could also go on about the Blackwater Series, which has evolved over time. One of the newest in the series is Plum Noir, an imperial porter brewed with Italian plums. But don't think everything they do is big and heavy. Many people I know consider the seasonal Hop Sun their go-to summer quencher.

Southern Tier seems to be everywhere these days, but it's worth checking out their on-site pub and tasting room, The Empty Pint. It's a nicely appointed room, made of stone and dark wood, with an outdoor seating area for nice weather. The beer selection is great, of course, though the menu is limited, offering just a pulled pork sandwich and some snacks. But it's worth the drive. Stop, sip a beer, and watch the brewery grow around you.

Southern Tier Brewing Company

Opened: 2003.

Type: Production brewery with on-site pub.

Owners: Phin and Sara DeMink.

Brewers: Dustin Hazer (head brewer) and Joe Reynolds (R&D director).

System: Two brewhouses: a 50-barrel system (a tandem of a 20-barrel kettle and a 30-barrel kettle), plus a 110-barrel Steinecker brewhouse.

Annual production: 70,000 to 75,000 barrels.

Distribution: 12- and 22-ounce bottles and kegs, with sales in about thirty states and parts of Australia, Denmark, Japan, Philippines, Singapore, Ontario, British Columbia, and the United Kingdom.

Hours: The pub is open 4 p.m. to 10 p.m. Thursday and Friday; noon to 10 p.m. Saturday; and noon to 6 p.m. Sunday. Tours are offered every Saturday at 1 p.m., 2:30 p.m., and 4 p.m.

Food: Limited menu at the on-site pub.

Parking: The brewing company has its own lot.

Woodcock Brothers Brewing Company

638 Lake St., Wilson, New York 14172
(716) 333-4000 • www.woodcockbrothersbrewery.com

Fishing, fruit orchards, wineries—and now a brewery. This is Wilson, a lakeside community about twenty-five miles east of Niagara Falls, where the Woodcock brothers, Mark and Tim, and their wives, Andrea and Debbie, have brought craft beer brewing to the state's northwest corner.

While pondering why a tourist-driven town like Niagara Falls (the New York side) *doesn't* have a brewpub, let's consider that the much smaller and less well-known Wilson does. "This is a small town," Andrea Woodcock said. "There's only one other full-service, year-round restaurant in town." Still, Wilson is a three-season-per-year fishing destination, home to apple and other fruit orchards, and located right in the middle of the state's Niagara Wine Trail.

To hear Andrea tell it, the reason they're in Wilson, aside from the fact that Tim and Debbie live there, is the one-hundred-year-old former cold storage building they found that seemed perfect for a brewery. Mark and Tim had talked for years about doing a brewery project, and it came together after they discovered the place on Lake Street (despite the address, the brewery is actually about a mile from the water). None of the family had commercial brewing or restaurant experience before. So, naturally, they decided on a brewpub. "We've had some learning curves," Woodcock said. "But we saw the potential and decided to go big with this."

The brewpub they built has a wide-open feel, and the brewhouse, which is in the basement, is visible through a glass wall behind the bar. Mark and Tim tinkered around the beers for five years before the place opened, using a "hodge-podge" 30-gallon system. They opened the brewpub with a 10-barrel Criveller brewhouse and started in November 2012 with three house brews. They had boosted that to seven by the summer of 2013. They also usually have one guest tap serving light beer and sometimes BlackBird Cider, made just outside of Rochester.

The house beers made by the Woodcock brothers fall into a range of brewpub-comfort ales:

Beers brewed: Amber, American Pale Ale, India Pale Ale, Porter, Cold Storage Ale, and Summer Ale.

The Pick: Malty and bitter—that's what a Porter made by an American brewpub ought to be.

a pale, an IPA, an amber, a porter, and a summer ale. The strongest is the Porter, at 5.8 percent ABV, with a combined roasted malt flavor and noticeable bitterness courtesy of Warrior and Willamette hops. The IPA is hopped with Nugget and Fuggles. These beers are available at the pub and to off-premises accounts while Cold Storage Ale, a 4.5 percent lightly hopped and malt-accented beer, is served only at the pub.

So do they serve beer novices or beer geeks? "Yes and yes," is Woodcock's answer. "We get people who come in and say, 'I don't really like beer,'" she said. "And I answer, 'Well, welcome to our brewery.' But then we get people like this one couple who say they are visiting every brewery in the country. They told us we were number 581. So we get all types."

Woodcock Brothers food is built largely around its wood-fired pizza oven and includes Greek, stuffed pepper, margherita, roasted vegetable, and a white version. It's western New York, so there's also wings and beef on weck (roast beef on a hard roll); and it's near Canada, so there's poutine, the fries, cheese curds, and gravy combo that is a classic beer-drinkers' comfort food.

The Niagara Wine Trail, noted especially for the quality ice wines produced by its members, runs in and around Wilson, and Woodcock Brothers in an associate member of the trail. "It's great being on the trail," Woodcock said. "That and the great fishing in the harbor bring us a lot of visitors."

Woodcock Brothers Brewing Company

Opened: 2012.

Type: Brewpub.

Owners: Mark and Andrea Woodcock, and Tim and Debbie Woodcock.

Brewer: Tim Woodcock.

System: 10-barrel Criveller brewhouse.

Production: N/A.

Distribution: Mostly on-premises; some off-site accounts.

Hours: noon to 10 p.m. Monday to Thursday; noon to 11 p.m. Friday to Saturday; noon to 8 p.m. Sunday.

Food: Full-service restaurant specializing in wood-fired pizzas.

Parking: Yes.

Beer Traveling

First things first: "Beer traveling" is not about driving drunk from brewpub to brewpub. Beer outings are similar to the wine trips celebrated in glossy travel and food magazines: They're pleasant combinations of carefree travel and the semi-mystical enjoyment of a potion in its birthplace. To be sure, the vineyards of France may be more hypnotically beautiful than, say, the streets of Troy, but you won't get any special-make hot dogs with famous Zippy sauce in the Rhone Valley, either. Life's a series of trade-offs.

Beer traveling is sometimes the only way to taste limited-release brews or brewpub beers. Beer is usually fresher at bars and distributors near the source. And the beer you'll get at the brewery itself is sublimely fresh, beer like you'll never have it anywhere else—the supreme quaff. You'll also get a chance to see the brewing operations and maybe talk to the brewer.

One of the things a beer enthusiast has to deal with is the perception that beer drinkers are second-class citizens compared with wine and single-malt scotch connoisseurs (although admittedly, that is changing as craft beer takes hold). Announcing plans for a vacation in the Napa Valley or a couple weeks on Scotland's Whisky Trail might arouse envious glances. A vacation built around brewery tours, on the other hand, might generate only mild confusion or pity. Microbreweries sell T-shirts and baseball caps, and beer geeks wear them. I've never seen a Beringer "Wine Rules!" T-shirt or a Chandon gimme cap. Beer-related souvenirs are plastic "beverage wrenches" and decorated pint glasses. Wine paraphernalia tends to be of a higher order: corkscrews, foil cutters, and tasting glasses. How do you, as a beer enthusiast, deal with this problem of perception? Simple: Revel in it.

When you're planning a beer outing, you need to think about your approach. If you want to visit just one brewery, or perhaps tour the closely packed brewpubs and bars in Syracuse, you can first settle in at a nearby hotel. Get your walking shoes ready, and you'll be set to work your way through the brewery offerings. If you plan to visit several breweries in different towns, it is essential that you travel with a non-drinking driver.

You should know that the beer at brewpubs and microbreweries is sometimes stronger than mainstream beer. Often brewers will tell you the alcohol content of their beers. Pay attention to it. Keep in mind that most mainstream beers are between 4.5 and 5.0 percent ABV, and judge your limits accordingly. Of course, you might want to do your figuring before you start sampling. About that sampling: You'll want to stay as clear-headed as possible, both during the day so you can enjoy the beer, and the morning after so you can enjoy life. The best thing to do is drink water. Every pro I know swears by it. If you drink a pint of water for every two pints of beer you drink (one to one is even better), you'll enjoy the beer more during the day. Drinking that much water slows down your beer consumption, which is a good thing. Drinking that much water also helps keep away the *katzenjammers*, as the Germans call the evil spirits that cause hangovers. There is, however, no substitute for the simple strategy of drinking moderate amounts of beer in the first place.

Beer traveling is about enjoying beer and discovering the places where it is at its best. You could make a simple whirlwind tour of breweries, but you'll want to find other things to do, too. Beer is only part of life, after all. You'll probably enjoy trips to breweries more when you mix in other attractions.

The Finger Lakes

The Iroquois legend holds that the Finger Lakes were formed when the Great Spirit blessed the land with his outstretched hand. Geologists say the long, narrow, deep lakes came about with the retreat of glaciers. Drive through the rolling Finger Lakes countryside and you may be inclined to believe both versions.

Try this little exercise when you're touring the area: You can generally tell when you're approaching one of the lakes by a sudden disappearance of land on the horizon. When you're high on a ridge, you may see that before the water. Try it in the middle of Seneca County and you'll spot the disappearing horizon both to the east and west.

At the southern end of the lakes, you'll find an abundance of scenic gorges and waterfalls, including the state's highest, Taughannock Falls (higher than Niagara, but not nearly as wide). Six of the lakes—Canandaigua, Keuka, Seneca, Cayuga, Owasco, and Skaneateles—form the core. Smaller lakes are on either end.

The region is perhaps most famous today for the one-hundred-plus wineries that dot the shorelines. The principal grape is Riesling, but other aromatic whites and even some reds are starting to win acclaim. The lakes, most of which are so deep they do not freeze, provide a warming buffer for the vineyards that climb up from the shore. Besides the wineries, you'll find a growing food culture, from several highly regarded farm-to-table restaurants, to the new Finger Lakes Cheese Trail, to a bounty of locally grown fruits, vegetables, and even meat products. Also look for the plentiful Amish farm markets.

You'll also discover that the Finger Lakes is a region of charming, old-fashioned small towns. Take Seneca Falls, for example, where the Women's Rights movement began in the 1800s, and which later became known as the most-likely inspiration for Bedford Falls in the movie *It's a Wonderful Life*. It still has a mid-century feel, part mid-nineteenth and part mid-twentieth. Shop the main streets of places like Watkins Glen, Corning, Penn Yan, and Hammondsport for a throwback to the way life used to be in simpler times. (Although the modern Waterloo Premium Outlets mall is one of the region's big attractions, too.) Discover historic sites related to Mark Twain, William H. Seward, and Harriet Tubman. And then there's Ithaca, home to the Ivy League Cornell University and Ithaca College. It's often found on the list of the best small cities in America.

The Finger Lakes is also home to the most dynamic brewing region in the state. As this book went to press, there were more breweries opening (or in the pipeline) here than in any other region. All in all, this is an area to explore. Get out and take a cruise. You never know what'll be over the next hill—a pristine lake left by the Great Spirit's hand, or perhaps New York's newest craft brewery.

Other breweries and beer companies

The Finger Lakes includes several tasting rooms—many adjoining wineries—that have their beer made under contract. These include Miles Craft Ales (www.mileswinecellars.com/beer), Starkey's Lookout/G.C. Starkey Beer Company (www.starkeyslookout.com), and War Horse Brewing Company (www.3brotherswinery.com/war-horse.html). The Seneca Lodge in Watkins Glen (www.senecalodge.com/Brewery/) has a small brewhouse that operates seasonally. Other breweries expected to open in 2013 or the near future include Crafty Ales and Lagers (www.drinkcraftyales.com) in Phelps, Abandon Brewing Co. (www.abandonbrewing.com) in Penn Yan, Brewery of Broken Dreams in Hammondsport, The Site Cyber Bar & Grill (www.thesitecyber barandgrill.com) in Corning, Climbing Bines Craft Ale in Penn Yan, Heavily Brewing Company (www.heavilybrewingcompany.com) in Montour Falls, and 3 Herons Brewing Co. in Trumansburg.

Other beer sites

MacGregor's Grill & Taproom (759 S. Main St., Canandaigua); Ithaca Ale House (111 N. Aurora St.); Tinker's Guild (78 Franklin St., Auburn); The Chapter House (400 Stewart Ave., Ithaca); and Village Tavern (30 Mechanic St., Hammondsport). Also check out the Finger Lakes Beverage Center store (605 W. State St., Ithaca) and The New York Wine & Culinary Center in Canandaigua (see page 41).

Area Attractions

There are more than one hundred *Finger Lakes wineries* in the region (www.fingerlakeswinecountry.com). For more information, see the New

York's wine regions section (page 232). Many **gorges and waterfalls** are located throughout the region. Ithaca boasts more than 150 waterfalls within 10 miles of downtown. Major regional attractions include the Letchworth Gorge in Letchworth State Park (716-493-3600), with 17 miles of steep-sided gorge, punctuated by 3 spectacular waterfalls; Taughannock Falls State Park (607-387-6739), with the highest falls in the state at 215 feet high; and Watkins Glen State Park (607-535-4511) with its mile-and-a-half hike through a wonderland of stream-carved rock, waterfalls, pools and potholes, tunnels, and stairways.

The New York Wine & Culinary Center (800 S. Main St., Canandaigua, NY 14424; 585-394-7070; www.nywcc.com) is dedicated to the food, wine, and beer of the state, with an on-site restaurant and demonstration kitchens. *Corning Museum of Glass* (1 Museum Way, Corning, NY 14830; 607-937-5371; www.cmog.org) offers an exploration of every facet of the art and industry of glass. The *Watkins Glen International Raceway* (2790 County Route 16, Watkins Glen, NY 14891; 607-535-2486; www.theglen.com) hosts a NASCAR Winston Cup race and a number of Sports Car Club of America events. *Cornell Plantations* (124 Comstock Knoll Dr., Ithaca, NY 14850; 607-255-2400; www.cornell plantations.org), has a botanical garden, arboretum and natural area adjacent to Cornell University. The *Montezuma National Wildlife Refuge* (3395 Route 20 East, Seneca Falls, NY 13148; 315-568-5987; www.fws.gov/refuge/montezuma) is a major flyway for migratory birds, with bald eagles and blue herons among the feathered visitors.

The Finger Lakes also has many historical sites. The *Women's Rights National Historical Park* (136 Fall St., Seneca Falls, NY 13148; 315-568-0024; www.nps.gov/wori/) consists of the visitors center, including the Women's Rights Hall of Fame, and historical properties related to the First Women's Rights Convention held here in 1848. *Mark Twain's Sites* (1 Park Place, Elmira, NY 14901; 607-735-1941; www.marktwaincountry.com/mark-twain/) include the study, now located at Elmira College, where the author wrote major portions of *Tom Sawyer* and *Huckleberry Finn*. His grave is in the city's Woodlawn Cemetery. The *Seward House Historic Museum* (33 South St., Auburn, NY 13021; 315-252-1283; www.sewardhouse.org) is the well-preserved home of Abraham Lincoln's secretary of state and the man behind the purchase of Alaska. *The Harriet Tubman Home* (180 South St., Auburn, NY 13021; 315-252-2081; www.harriethouse.org) is where the Underground Railroad leader lived after the Civil War.

Bacchus Brewing Company

15 Ellis Drive, Dryden, NY 13053
(607) 844-8474 • www.bacchusbrewing.com

Bacchus may primarily be known as the ancient Roman god of wine, but surely he would have enjoyed a good beer now and then, right?

The story at Bacchus Brewing Company in Dryden is that owner Dave McCune somehow got through college without drinking beer. He didn't like it—at least, not the mass-produced beers he was exposed to. Over time, McCune developed a passion for craft beer. Later, he encountered the homebrews made by Christina Poulos, a geologist and researcher then working at the SUNY campus in Binghamton. The meeting was a stroke of good fortune. McCune had recently started a physical therapy office and an adjacent fitness center in a building just outside the village of Dryden, a small community on the road between Cortland and Ithaca. The trouble was, the nearby community college opened a fitness center at the same time. Dryden isn't really big enough to support two fitness centers, especially when one is owned and operated by a state-supported college. So McCune was looking for something else to do with his space.

Enter Poulos and her beers. A lot of brewers can go on and on (and on) about the technical aspects of their beer, even discussing the esoteric details of their water treatment. When Poulos, the founding and former head brewer at Bacchus Brewing, talked about those things, you got the sense she really knew what she was talking about. Though Poulos moved on in 2013, leaving the brewery in the hands of Richie Shallcross, she put her stamp on Bacchus and its beers. During her time in Dryden, she was also the only female head brewer at any of the breweries in this book. She was used to that. "When I give talks in geology, I look out and there's not a lot of women," she said. "There's not a lot in brewing, either, but that's changing."

Bacchus opened for business in March 2012 with a Blonde Ale, an Irish Red, and an IPA. A Pale Ale, the first seasonal, debuted later in 2012. Shallcross, who came to Bacchus after a few years brewing at nearby Ithaca Beer Co. and now handles the 7-barrel brewhouse, introduced Flora's

Beers brewed: Year-round: Blonde Ale, Irish Red Ale, Bacchus IPA, and Pale Ale. Seasonals: Flora's Fate, Harvest Ale, and more to come.

The Pick: The Blonde Ale, at 6.3 percent ABV, has nice citrus aromas and a dry finish, courtesy of Perle and Liberty hops. It's a first-rate thirst quencher.

Fate, a session pale ale, and has been working on a Double IPA, a Harvest Ale, and other beers. Flora's Fate is named for the Roman goddess of flowers (and possibly drinking). Shallcross hopped it with Chinook, Ahtanum, and Falconer's Flight, giving it a floral aroma.

Dryden is a small town surrounded by farmland, just off the eastern edge of the Finger Lakes wine region. There are colleges and universities no matter in which direction you look—Cornell University and Ithaca College in nearby Ithaca, Cortland State University to the west, and Tompkins-Cortland Community College, just outside of town. That gives Bacchus a built-in source of customers. Bacchus is also included in Finger Lakes Beer Trail, which prints a brochure guide to the area's breweries and touts them actively on social media.

And like many Upstate New York breweries, Bacchus plans to use local ingredients whenever possible. "There's just a lot in the Finger Lakes, a lot of things that grow here, that we can use in the beers," Shallcross said.

Bacchus Brewing Company

Opened: 2012.

Type: Production brewery.

Owner: Dave McCune.

Brewer: Richie Shallcross.

System: 7-barrel DME brewhouse.

Annual production: About 400 barrels.

Distribution: Mostly in the Ithaca–Dryden–Cortland area, with a lot of sales through the tasting room.

Hours: 3 p.m. to 6 p.m. Wednesday to Friday; noon to 6 p.m. Saturday.

Parking: The brewery has its own lot.

Bandwagon Brew Pub

114 N. Cayuga St, Ithaca, NY 14850
(607) 319-0699
www.bandwagonbeer.com

Before we get to serious beer business, here's a little nugget about Bandwagon Brew Pub, courtesy of head brewer Lars Mudrak: The brewpub in downtown Ithaca employs a 2-barrel brewing system cobbled together from old dairy tanks and other equipment, some of which came from Cornell University's agriculture school. "I can't swear this is true, but we were told that the boil kettle we use now was used in the production of the very first chicken McNuggets, up at Cornell," Mudrak said. It's certainly possible. The late Cornell professor Bob Baker is widely credited as the inventor of the chicken nugget

But don't let that anecdote fool you. Bandwagon is all about gourmet food and craft beer, with some lofty ambitions. These include, eventually, a production brewery, hop yard, and malting operation (under way). The pub opened in December 2008, when the recent explosion in the number of Finger Lakes area brewing companies was just starting. The first brewhouse was a 10-gallon Sabco system, and it quickly grew into the slightly larger, homemade brewery.

The brewpub is near the Ithaca Commons, a downtown district of eclectic eateries, bars, and shops. Bandwagon is below ground level and cozy inside, with a bar area separating a dining area and a lounge area. The pub attracts a knowledgeable beer-and-food crowd early in the evening, and then later turns into "more of a nightclub-type scene," Mudrak said. "It's more like a college bar later, with a younger crowd."

There are always five or six house brews on tap and another fifteen or so guest lines, mostly centered on quality craft beers from New York state, with a few national and international examples. Bandwagon has about fifty beers in its repertoire and counting. The core house beers include

Beers brewed: Year-round: Hidden Rabbit Hefeweizen, Pedro's Pale Ale, Ezra Red Ale, Pirate Eye I.P.A., The Honey Brunette, Tartan 80/ Scottish Ale, High Step Weizenbock, and Sully's Irish Stout. Seasonals: Humulus Hefeweizen, Strawberry Cream, Watermelon Wheat, Loc-ale, Pop's Session Ale, Raspberry Jalapeno, Pumpkin Ale, Frosty's Winter Ale, Scotch Ale, and Peanut Butter Chocolate Stout.

The Pick: One of my visits to Bandwagon came on a blazingly hot day (for Upstate New York), so I tried the seasonal Watermelon Wheat. It's not at all sweet, but has a taste so real you want to spit the seeds out.

the bestseller Pirate Eye IPA, in which all the hops are added late in the boil to provide floral and citrus aromas without lots of bitterness. Other beers usually found on tap are the malty Ezra Red Ale (named for university founder Ezra Cornell); Hidden Rabbit Hefeweizen (made with coriander and chamomile flowers); and High Step Weizenbock, at 9.3 percent ABV a true-to-German-style strong wheat beer. The Weizenbock won the medal as best craft beer in New York state at the 2012 TAP New York festival. Another brew usually available is Peanut Butter Chocolate Stout, exactly what it sounds like and pretty popular. The rest of the range runs the gamut from Humulus Hefeweize, with a classic German wheat base but hopped like an IPA, to Watermelon Wheat.

Bandwagon's owners—there are five partners—are in the process of putting together a production brewery, to be located in the village of Interlaken, north of Ithaca between Seneca and Cayuga lakes. Initially conceived as a potential 30-barrel brewery, it'll likely end up at 7- or 15-barrels, Mudrak said. There are plans to grow hops nearby. Meanwhile, some of the Bandwagon owners have also started a malting operation in the nearby town of Dryden. It was just getting under way in 2013. That malt found its way into a beer called Loc-ale, which is comprised of 90 percent locally grown barley, plus local honey. But local sourcing isn't just for the beer. Bandwagon's food also includes elements of the bounty of the Finger Lakes region, from meats to cheeses to produce. There are house-made condiments and a menu especially rich with chipotle and curry.

Bandwagon is now one of more than a half-dozen breweries or brewpubs in the immediate Ithaca area, which also abounds with wineries and vineyards. "It's getting close to the point where you really can do the breweries in a tour, just like the wineries," Mudrak said.

Bandwagon Brew Pub

Opened: 2008.

Type: Brewpub.

Owners: A partnership that includes Alex Johnson, Michael Johnson, and John Hughes.

Brewer: Lars Mudrak.

System: 2-barrel, homemade brewhouse.

Annual production: 250 barrels.

Distribution: Mostly at the pub, with a handful of Ithaca-area draft accounts. Limited 750-milliliter bottles available at the pub and at a few off-premises location in town.

Hours: 5 p.m. to 1 a.m. Monday to Thursday; noon to 1 a.m. Friday to Sunday.

Food: Upscale pub menu.

Parking: No off-street parking, but there are municipal lots in the area.

Birdland Brewing Company

1015 Kendall St., Horseheads, NY 14845
(607) 796-2337 • www.birdlandbrewingco.com

Like a lot of people in the brewing business these days, Dennis Edwards started as a homebrewer. "First in the kitchen, then the garage, and now this," Edwards said of his 1-barrel nanobrewery and tasting room in the village of Horseheads, just outside Elmira in the state's Southern Tier. He's a partner in the brewery with his wife, Susan, and their friend Mike Hess.

Unlike many others perhaps, Edwards had the name of his brewery established long before he went commercial. The Edwards live in a development where the streets are all named after birds. "I was already calling my homebrew Birdland Brewing and naming the beers after birds," Edwards said, "so we kept that when we opened."

The commercial Birdland Brewing Company opened in November 2012 on Black Friday. Edwards serves as the brewer and works his 1-barrel system about four days a week. He and his partners hope one day to expand—perhaps to a 7-barrel system—but are taking it slowly. "We're not going to rush this," Edwards said. "When it's time to expand, we'll know." That means brewing on a small system for now. "The tour takes thirty seconds," Edwards notes, as he shows off his rig in a building that once housed a car wash. The first thing you notice are the "Cajun cookers," made by the Bayou Classic Co. Edwards, a mechanical engineer, converted them to gas to use for mashing and boiling.

Birdland Brewing is the third microbrewery to open in the town of Horseheads, though it's the first in the village that bears the same name. The other local breweries are Horseheads Brewing Co., and Upstate Brewing Company. That probably gives Horseheads the highest number of breweries, per capita, of any town in New York. "When we sent in the applications, no one batted an eye," said Hess, who previosly served twenty years as a state trooper.

The Birdland crew knows the area's drinkers are mostly Bud, Miller, and Coors fans, and they

Beers brewed: Year-round: Mountie Brees, Kewlerskald, Red Wing, and Blue Jay. Seasonals: Sap Sucker, Blue Bird, Falcon (stout), and more. They also serve Flabingo, a "malternative."

The Pick: When the "light" beer, in this case Mountie Brees, packs that much flavor, it's tempting to give it the shout-out. But we'll go with the seasonal Blue Bird, a chocolate blueberry porter whose layers of flavor tickle the taste buds.

tailor their beers to acclimate those trying to move up to craft beer. But even their lightest "starter" beer, a pale ale called Mountie Brees, has character. It's got a caramel-malt flavor and a nice hop finish.

"But wait," you're saying. "Aren't all the beers named for birds?" Not all of them. Mountie Brees is an early homebrew recipe that Edwards named because he used Canadian pale malt (hence the Mountie part) and brewed it with a friend from a nearby town called Breesport. There's an even better story attached to the amber ale he calls Kewlerskald. That's not a bird either. During a homebrew session, the cooler holding the hot liquor sprung a leak, splashing Edwards on the leg. "I got scalded by water from a cooler," he said. "That's where that comes from." It's one of his oldest recipes.

It should be noted that Edwards has since taken an online class through Chicago's Siebel Institute, so that might minimize some of those homebrew disasters. His experimentation with new brews includes the seasonal Sap Sucker, made with fresh local maple syrup, and a "no malt, no hops" alcohol beverage called Flabingo. It's tart and refreshing, and at 10 percent ABV could be cut with soda.

Most of Birdland's brews are sold at the shop, in both 64-ounce and 32-ounce growlers and in ⅙- and ¼-kegs. They also have a few accounts at local bars and restaurants. Like the other breweries in the Southern Tier and Finger Lakes region, Birdland hopes to benefit from the sheer number of breweries and wineries that lure visitors. They are listed on the maps and web listing for the Finger Lakes Beer Trail, and as at other Finger Lakes breweries, more people are coming just for beer. "We had a couple of guys from Tonawanda [near Buffalo] stop in on a tour of breweries," Hess said. "They said we were their last stop, and they were happy to see us."

Birdland Brewing Company

Opened: November 2012.

Type: Production brewery.

Owners: Dennis and Susan Edwards, and Mike Hess.

Brewer: Dennis Edwards.

System: 1-barrel, custom-built.

Annual production: Up to 200 barrels.

Distribution: Kegs and growlers from the brewery; a growing list of off-premises draft accounts.

Hours: noon to 6 p.m. Wednesday to Thursday; noon to 7 p.m. Friday; 11 a.m. to 5 p.m. Saturday; noon to 4 p.m. Sunday.

Parking: A shared lot out front.

CB Craft Brewers

300 Village Square Blvd., Honeoye Falls, NY 14472
(585) 624-4386 • www.cbsbrewing.com

Sampling beers in the CB Craft Brewers tasting room in Honeoye Falls is like taking a tour of Upstate New York while standing in one place. Want to sample beer from War Horse Brewing Co. near Geneva, or Miles Craft Brewers on Seneca Lake, or Three Heads Brewing Co. in Rochester? You'll find those and many more at CB's—including beers brewed under the CB's label.

It's all part of the fairly unusual business model pioneered by Mike Alcorn, who started the company, originally under the name Custom Brewcrafters, in 1997. His brewery is all about making beer, whether for itself or for someone else. It has been such a success that CB's, as most people in western New York call it, far outgrew its original location and moved into what locals refer to as "the big red barn" on the outskirts of town. "It's been a fun ride," said Alcorn, who runs the business with his wife, Luanne.

In fact, Alcorn said his brewery now has four unique parts, each of which represents about a quarter of his business. One quarter is the beer the company makes under Alcorn's own CB's label for distribution off-site. Another quarter comes from the retail sales at his brewery and tasting room, which includes merchandise like T-shirts and hats, as well as growler fills and packages of all the beers made on-premises. A third quarter is "custom" beer, and the final quarter is "contract" beer.

So now you want to know the difference between custom and contract, don't you? In a nutshell, custom beers are those made for bars, restaurants, or other venues that simply want a beer—really just a tap handle—they can call their own. Typically, CB's devises the recipes and makes the beer. The custom beer owners put it on at their bars and that's that. Contract brewers, on the other hand, are companies that have recipes and

Beers brewed: CB's branded beers include Caged Alpha Monkey, Canandaigua Lake Pale Ale, EPA (English Pale Ale), Double Dark Cream Porter, and many seasonals and one-off beers.

The Pick: Why buck popular opinion? The Caged Alpha Monkey bursts with pineapple, grapefruit, pine, and citrus aroma. It's like walking through a citrus fruit forest.

marketing strategies that go beyond a single venue. These companies don't have their own brewing equipment and often don't have a tasting room of their own, either. In the Rochester area, a company called Three Heads Brewing is one of these. It has beer made at CB's on tap across the region.

There are other brewers with their own equipment and tasting rooms who contract with places like CB's to make a portion of their beer. Typically, these brewers make use of CB's or a similar facility to make their most-popular beers, freeing up capacity in their own brewhouses. Alcorn sums up the difference between his custom business and his contract business: "Our custom accounts are not selling beer on the open market," he said. "The contract guys are selling their beer up against mine."

It's the contract work that has been booming of late, Alcorn said. CB's does all this in a 10-barrel brewhouse. Head brewer J.P. Liberatore and his colleagues will do double or triple batches for some orders. They always "hold back" some of the beer they make for other accounts, which is why you'll find twenty-five or more beers on tap in the tasting room, under various names. Overall, CB's makes about sixty different beers that can be found in more than forty locations, Alcorn said.

Alcorn's business grew bigger and faster than he expected, which is why after eight years he left the original location closer to the heart of Honeoye Falls and built the new place. It now includes a pub, called The Pint and Goblet, where you can order a full pint and get some food. The brewery tasting room is just twenty minutes or so (with no traffic) from downtown Rochester. "We wanted a place where people could come, be comfortable, and have an enjoyable experience," Alcorn said.

As successful as the custom and contracting work have been, it's clear Alcorn relishes the response CB's has been getting to its proprietary brews. The first two beers were a Golden Ale and English Pale Ale, which Alcorn said were brewed to keep a revenue stream going between other jobs. The bestsellers among those beers are Caged Alpha Monkey, the flagship CB's brand, and Canandaigua Lake Pale Ale. Caged Alpha Monkey, a 6.5 percent ABV IPA, came about because the IPAs that the brewery made for other accounts often ended up being those brands' bestsellers. "We've even had to change some of the custom IPA recipes because side-by-side, people were always coming back to the Monkey," Alcorn said. "Now they [CB's own beers] are a bigger part of the brewery than we first thought," he said. "It's all been pretty breathtaking, really."

CB Craft Brewers

Opened: 1997.

Type: Production brewery, with on-site pub and tasting room.

Owners: Mike and Luanne Alorn.

Brewer: J.P. Liberatore.

System: 10-barrel Criveller.

Annual production: 6,000 barrels.

Distribution: At the tasting room and locations throughout the Rochester and Finger Lakes area.

Hours: Noon to 8 p.m. Monday to Wednesday; noon to 9 p.m. Thursday and Friday; 10 a.m. to 9 p.m. Saturday; noon to 6 p.m. Sunday.

Food: Pub menu served on-site.

Parking: Yes.

Finger Lakes Beer Company

8462 State Route 54, Hammondsport, NY 14840
(607) 569-3311 • www.fingerlakesbeercompany.com

You can't say Mark Goodwin has relaxed much since he retired from Verizon a few years back. First, he cofounded Keuka Brewing Co., just north of Hammondsport. After a couple of years, he left there (amicably) and cofounded a second brewery, Finger Lakes Beer Company, closer to Hammondsport. He knows the brewery business: "My philosophy of brewing is it's 80 percent cleaning and 20 percent brewing," he said. "You can't mind getting your hands wet." Some retirement.

Finger Lakes Beer started in 2010, and Goodwin was the primary brewer for the first two years. His partner, Wayne Peworchik, retired in the fall of 2012, and the two now work together more often. They started with a bit of luck. They bought a 7-barrel brewhouse from the defunct Walla Walla Brewing Co. in Washington state in 2009, before the explosion in breweries nationwide caused the price of equipment, both new and used, to soar.

Goodwin and Peworchik were both avid home-brewers. Peworchik had previously worked for years in the sheet metal business. "It's nice having him around because when you need something, he can knock things together pretty quick," Goodwin said.

Finger Lakes Beer shares a circumstance common to other breweries in the region: It's a heavily touristed area, especially in the summer and fall, when visitors flock to the more than one hundred wineries, fine restaurants, and spectacular views of the lakes and waterfalls. That's one reason Goodwin and Peworchik "tossed around" the idea of a brewpub, but ultimately decided they liked the production and retail business. They operate a spacious brewery for visitors, with a tasting room and separate gift shop area.

Being in wine country also means hosting the tourists who come by bus and limo, especially in summer and fall. "The wineries are good to us," Goodwin said. "They send a lot of people our way." But Goodwin, like other brewers in the Finger

Beers produced: Year-round: Aviator Wheat, Newton's Pale Ale, 11/11 IPA, Copperline, Ring of Fire, Hammonds-Porter, and M&W Root Beer. Seasonals: Mr. Melon and Indian Summer, and a spiced winter WHITE-OUT Wassail.

The Pick: Newton's Pale Ale has a good back story. A local newspaper reporter interviewed Goodwin, then called him Mark Newton in her story. Showing a sense of humor, Goodwin named this beer for the non-existent Mr. Newton. The beer is a good session ale, with a dry finish and noteworthy hop aroma, courtesy of Columbus and some locally sourced Willamette.

Lakes, has noticed more visitors coming specifically to check out the breweries. That's helped by the sheer numbers—this book counts about twenty in the region. All of those are reasons Goodwin and Peworchik decided to start with a 7-barrel system they could grow into. "When you're trying to service retail accounts and the buses and limos start coming, you can get behind pretty quick," Goodwin said. Finger Lakes Beer has more than a dozen retail accounts in the Keuka Lake region and a little beyond. In mid-2012 they started up a modest bottling operation for 22-ounce beers. The brewery makes use of abundant Keuka Lake water, and Goodwin and Peworchik have brewed with local hops when possible. Goodwin said he's intrigued by talk of barley growing and malting in New York state. "We would love to get to the point where we use nothing but New York state ingredients," he said. "We try to use American-made stuff. . . . It may cost a little more, but I think people see 'Made in America' and they're willing to pay a little more."

Finger Lakes makes a wide variety of beers, including Aviator Wheat; Newton's Pale Ale; 11/11 IPA; Copperline, a coppery red ale; Ring of Fire, a Scotch ale with smoked malt; and Hammonds-Porter, with Madagascar vanilla beans added. Seasonals include Mr. Melon, a summertime watermelon wheat; Indian Summer, a pumpkin and spice beer for fall served in a sugar-and-spice rimmed glass; and a spiced winter WHITEOUT Wassail, aged in Jack Daniels whiskey barrels.

Reflecting on his experience in the modern brewery business, Goodwin was quick to cite the fellowship and friendliness shared by his fellow brewers. "Other industries are cutthroat," he said. "The camaraderie in the brewing industry amazes me, it really does. I had a guy call me and ask if I had some wheat malt. Not a problem. If I was 50 pounds short in a mash, I could turn to someone who'd help me out. That's the way this business is."

Finger Lakes Beer Company

Opened: 2010.

Type: Production brewery.

Owners and Brewers: Wayne Peworchik and Mark Goodwin.

System: 7-barrel Ripley system.

Annual production: 400 barrels.

Distribution: Brewery tasting room and retail accounts around the Finger Lakes region; bottling started in 2012.

Hours: noon to 6 p.m. Monday, Wednesday, and Thursday; noon to 8 p.m. Friday; noon to 6 p.m. Saturday; noon to 5 p.m. Sunday.

Parking: Yes.

Hopshire Farm & Brewery

1771 Dryden Road (Route 13), Dryden, NY 13053
(607) 279-1243 • www.hopshire.com

People get into the craft beer business for many reasons, most notably because of a passion for making beer. Randy Lacey's passion is this: To preserve brewing and beermaking traditions. "It's about the heritage," he said. That's why the purpose-built brewery on a 35-acre farm located a few miles east of Ithaca was designed to look like a classic nineteenth-century Upstate New York hop barn. Lacey studied the dimensions and built an exact copy.

This is not just a historic replica: Lacey is growing hops on 4 acres adjacent to the brewery and will, by 2014, grow enough to justify using the cupola attached to the brewery to dry his freshly harvested Cascade, Willamette, Perle, and Centennial hops. And he's not just a hop grower. The 7-barrel brewhouse is also at the center of Lacey's plan. He applied for and received one of the state's first farm brewery licenses, which offers tax incentives and other benefits for brewers who use local ingredients.

Lacey is a realist: He knew when he opened in 2013 that there weren't enough suppliers yet to satisfy his demand. So he decided to make two of his early beers exclusively with New York ingredients. (The rest are made with conventional sourcing.) "If I spread the New York ingredients across all the beers, what's the point?" he said, pointing to his malty ESB. "If I put New York pale malt in this, it would get lost."

The two New York heritage beers he made in 2013 shared something else. Since the amount of malt and hops produced in the state was still fairly limited, he revved these up with other ingredients. Beehave, for example, adds locally produced basswood honey to the New York-grown malt and hops. The Blossom, a cherry wheat, uses New York-grown wheat and cherry extract obtained from a western New York orchard. Neither beer is

Beers brewed: Beehave (honey blonde), Blossom (cherry wheat), Daddy-O (English pale ale), Zingabeer (Belgian wheat with ginger), Shire Ale (Scottish), Nearvarna (IPA), Hop Onyx (black IPA), and other releases.

The Pick: At the time I researched this book, I was becoming accustomed to the many grapefruit-heavy IPAs made with Mosaic or Falconer's Flight hops, but rarely encountered one so dark as Hop Onyx. At the same time, that Daddy-O did taste a lot like Bombardier . . .

excessively hoppy, but that's okay with the man who named his brewery Hopshire. "In these beers, what [we] don't have in malt and hops we make up for with the other ingredients," Lacey said. "We'll leave the more standard levels [of hops and malt] to the other beers."

Lacey bought a 7-barrel brewhouse formerly used by the Horseheads Brewing Co. farther west in the Southern Tier region. (Horseheads graduated to a 15-barrel system.) It's a bit cobbled together. There's a kettle and mash tun made by Pub Systems, a mash tun converted from an old dairy tank, and other fermenters and tanks gathered from here and there. Another piece of equipment is essential to Lacey's mission: His "hop rocket" attachment on his serving tanks adds an extra hop infusion and provides filtering through a fresh hop bouquet as the beers are drawn off. The beers are then served in a tasting room with decorative bits like carved dark wood trim found in an old house, and the bar that once stood in a downtown Ithaca restaurant.

Though Hopshire is not directly on the nearby wine trails, it's close enough. "We want the tasting room experience to mimic what you find in the wineries," Lacey said. "It's an inviting atmosphere, and we're here to talk about the beer, the hops, the history, and so on."

Aside from his all-New York brews, Lacey has offerings that are generally adaptations of European and American classics, from a Scotch Ale to a Black IPA. The board behind the tasting counter groups the seven beers available at any time according to three categories: Mellow, Middling, and Mighty. "That's basically according to both ABV [alcohol level] and hops," he said. So the two low-hopped New York beers are Mellow, while the early best-selling IPA called Nearvarna (named for a nearby town) is Mighty. In the middle are beers like the Daddy-O ESB, which bears a strong resemblance to the English Wells Bombardier. He intends the slightly sweet Scottish ale, called Shire Ale, to be the flagship. It's made with a Scottish ale yeast and flaked oats, and fits in the "Middling" category at 6.3 percent ABV. But he's willing to see where the market leads. Early on, the Nearvarna was flying out of the tasting room.

Lacey, whose fulltime job is director of facilities engineering at nearby Cornell University, has his eye on the future while upholding the past—and keeping it realistic. He has, for example, thought about growing his own grain, but will probably stop short of malting it. "Between growing the hops, making the beer, and doing the tasting room, that's probably enough," he said. "There's enough heritage in those things."

Hopshire Farm & Brewery

Opened: 2013.

Type: Production brewery and farm.

Owners: Randy Lacey and Diane Gerhart.

Brewer: Randy Lacey.

System: 7-barrel, with some Pub Systems equipment.

Annual production: 300 barrels.

Distribution: Mostly directly from the tasting room.

Hours: Tasting room: 4 p.m. to 8 p.m. Wednesday to Friday; 11 a.m. to 6 p.m. Saturday; 1 p.m. to 6 p.m. Sunday.

Parking: Yes.

Horseheads Brewing Co.

250 Old Ithaca Rd., Horseheads, NY 14845
(607) 739-8468 • www.horseheadsbrewing.com

Ed and Brenda Samchisen hit the ground running when they opened Horseheads Brewing Co. in 2007, and they haven't stopped since. Horseheads traded in its original 7-barrel system for a 15-barrel brewhouse after just a few years, and Ed, the brewer, has his heart set on replacing that with a 30-barrel system in late 2013 or early 2014.

It's not just about size. Horseheads won the title of Best Brewery in New York State at the annual TAP New York Craft Beer and Food Festival in 2010, just three years after opening. Individual beers, notably their pumpkin ale and their specialty Hot-Jala Heim chili beer, have won numerous medals. All this in a brewery located on the outskirts of an evocatively named little village in the state's Southern Tier region.

Visit the tasting room, and you'll find Brenda Samchisen loves to tell stories. One is about how Horseheads got its name. During the Revolutionary War, George Washington sent an American general named John Sullivan to Upstate New York to "clear" away Indians who sided with the British. The Sullivan Expedition of 1779 eventually reached the area now known as Horseheads. "There are two stories," she said. "One is that the troops ran out of food and had to kill the horses and eat them. The other is that the horses were spent, and they killed them to put them out of their misery. Either way, they killed a lot of horses and left them here. The Indians came back later and saw the horse skulls bleaching in the sun. They put signs up marking this as the valley of the Horses' Heads." The story also leads to the names Horseheads Brewing Co. gives some of its beers, like Pale Expedition Ale, Sullivan's Stout, and Iroquois Wheat.

Brenda has another story, this one about the beer that caused so much buzz around Upstate New York when she and Ed began touring beer festivals. Lines formed so people could try their Hot-Jala Heim. It began, Brenda said, a few months after the brewery opened, when she and Ed

Beers brewed: Year-round: Iroquois Wheat, Chemung Canal Towpath Ale, Brickyard Red Ale, Horseheads IPA, Newtown Brown Ale, Pale Expedition Ale, and Hot-Jala Heim. Seasonals: Horseheads Orion, Chocolate Porter, Black Horse Ale, Maple Amber Ale, and others.

The Pick: It's tempting to say a beer like the Hot-Jala Heim is great for a small taste, but do you really want a whole pint or more? After several tastes over several years, I'd say yes, in certain circumstances. So I'll go with it.

attended the Great American Beer Festival in Colorado. "At the GABF, I saw a chili beer," she said. "I thought, 'What's next—garlic beer?' But I got in line and tried it, and I immediately said, 'Oh my God, we've got to make this.'" She convinced Ed to try it and they agreed: Horseheads needed a chili beer. They experimented with every kind of chili pepper they could find: serrano, Anaheim, jalapeño, chipotle, poblano, and more. They ended up settling on jalapeño and Anaheim.

"People kept trying to talk us out of it, and all our relatives said no, you can't do this," Brenda said. "I thought, we'll make a 5-gallon batch, and if it's no good, we'll dump it." That didn't happen, because the beer is more than a gimmick. "It's a perfect winter beer for Super Bowl parties," Brenda said. "It's warming. It's a junk food beer." Hot-Jala Heim made it onto Horseheads' regular rotation and remains popular whenever Ed and Brenda pour it at festivals. "I'm just glad we didn't listen to our relatives," Brenda said.

According to Ed, he had to do some persuading himself before Brenda agreed to open the brewery. Ed, a mechanical engineer by trade, started out as a homebrewer. His first batch was an extract brew. "I guess it's my engineering background—I thought extract was boring," he said. "Then I did a whole grain batch, with a mash and everything, and I was hooked. It took me two years to talk Brenda into opening a brewery." Now they make an interesting array of year-round beers and seasonals. Their Chocolate Porter won two medals at TAP New York in 2012, and their Pumpkin Ale—which Brenda calls a "cash cow"—beat such notables as Southern Tier and Weyerbacher in a pumpkin beer contest. Brenda encourages Ed's love of tinkering to come up with new beers . . . but nothing too crazy. Almost everything they do falls between 6 and 8 percent ABV.

One day, Brenda had a request. She told Ed: "I want it dark, I want it Belgian, I want it to have lots of hops, I want it to have everything." He came up with Horseheads Nebula (now called Orion). It's a winter seasonal in a style probably unimagined before: Belgian-style Dark IPA. "In this beer you can taste everything but the water," Brenda said. "You taste the grain, you taste the hops, you taste the yeast."

If you press Ed, he'll admit he's still a little surprised he can get away with these beers in the Southern Tier area. "This is definitely a Bud and Labatt Blue type of place," he said. But the brewery does get a lot of tourists from the nearby Finger Lakes wine region, and his off-premises accounts are as far away as Syracuse and Rochester. He's even ventured into a deal with a New York City distributor.

Horseheads, it seems, has definitely turned some heads. Mark Goodwin, cofounder of Finger Lakes Beer Company (page 51) in

Hammondsport, specifically mentions Horseheads when he cites breweries he wants to emulate. "Ed and Brenda have just done a tremendous job," said Goodwin, who opened Finger Lakes in 2010. "They've got it right."

"I guess we have built a reputation for ourselves," Ed said. "We don't want to get too big, but we'd like to supply New York state."

Horseheads Brewing Co.

Opened: 2007.

Type: Production brewery.

Owners: Ed and Brenda Samchisen.

Brewer: Ed Samchisen.

System: 15-barrel brewhouse.

Annual production: About 1,200 barrels.

Distribution: Throughout the Finger Lakes and some into New York City; draft and bottles.

Hours: Noon to 6 p.m. Tuesday to Thursday; noon to 8 p.m. Friday and Saturday; noon to 5 p.m. Sunday.

Parking: The brewery has its own lot.

Ithaca Beer Co.

122 Ithaca Beer Drive (off Route 13), Ithaca, NY 14850
(607) 273-0766 • www.ithacabeer.com

Ithaca sometimes seems to have it all. It has Cornell University, the prestigious Ivy League college. It's in a stunning location amid the hills and valleys at the southern end of Cayuga Lake, hence the slogan "Ithaca is Gorges." It's constantly listed in magazines and on websites as one of the best small cities in America, praised for its diversity, livability, progressiveness, and mentality, to name a few. And to top it off, there are almost a half-dozen breweries or brewpubs in the immediate area and another twenty or so in the surrounding Finger Lakes (plus about one hundred wineries).

Just when it seemed Ithaca couldn't get any better, Dan Mitchell embarked on a major renovation and expansion of his Ithaca Beer Co. Founded in 1997, it's the oldest and largest brewery in the area. It now has a 50-barrel production brewhouse, a 5-barrel pilot system, and a showpiece tasting and taproom, complete with a wood-fired oven for pizzas and an outdoor beer garden for the summer. "What we've done, really, is change the relationship we have with our customers when they come to the brewery," Mitchell said.

While we're talking about super-sustainable Ithaca, note that Mitchell now has the land to grow hops and other ingredients for his kitchen and brewery. Although this means Ithaca can tap into New York's new Farm Brewery Law, which gives tax credits to beer makers who use locally sourced ingredients, that wasn't Mitchell's motivation. "It's just a personal thing," he said, "a direction I really wanted to go in."

It all took just a little longer than Mitchell had anticipated. His original plan, back in the mid-1990s, was to open a brewpub somewhere near the Cayuga Lake shoreline. Over time, that plan changed to a production brewery on the edge of town. The space wasn't much to look at—a small

Beers brewed: Year-round: Pale Ale, Nut Brown Ale, Apricot White, Cascazilla (Red IPA), and Flower Power IPA. Seasonals: Ground Break, Gorges Smoked Porter, Cold Front, Country Pumpkin, and Partly Sunny. Excelsior! series: White Gold, Excelsior, Le Blue, and AlpHalHa.

The Pick: Summers are gorgeous in the Finger Lakes, and winters can be too, even though they're sometimes a bit harsh. That's why I look forward each year to the Gorges Smoked Porter, a deep, rich, and satisfying brew (7.5 percent) with just the right amount of smoke to provide some warmth.

building with a small tasting room and a very crowded brewery out back. The success of Ithaca's beers only added to the congestion.

Ithaca Beer launched its first brews, taking advantage of the "Finger Lakes" identity in its labeling. The Pale Ale, Nut Brown Ale, and Apricot Wheat were soon joined by Flower Power IPA and Cascazilla, a hoppy Red IPA. Then there were seasonals like Ground Break, a spring saison, and Gorges Smoked Porter for the fall and winter. Ithaca also became the first brewery in the state to make a commercial beer using exclusively New York state hops, helping to launch a small but growing local hop resurgence. Over time, Ithaca added its own line of sodas and continued its line of special anniversary beers, launching a series of big beers in 750-milliliter bottles, called Excelsior! after the New York state motto. The Excelsior! beers include such creative brews as Brute, a sour golden ale; Le Bleu, a sour blueberry ale; Old Habit, a rye ale; and AlpHalpHa, a "double honey bitter" made with local honey.

The new 50-barrel brewhouse will crank out a lot of Ithaca's best-sellers, like the leading brand Flower Power, and will help fill spaces in the brewery's seven-state market. "We're not really looking to expand territory as much as we're meeting the demand in our current market," Mitchell said. The brewery made about 12,000 barrels a year in the old system, and Mitchell said he hopes for 20,000 in the first full year (2013) of the new one. Eventually, he'll add storage tanks and fermenters, in the hope of bringing the annual capacity to 40,000 barrels.

That all sounds pretty big, and Ithaca has positioned itself on the larger side of New York's craft brewing scene. But Mitchell doesn't want to focus too much on that. "Size doesn't really matter to us," he said, "as long as we're making beers that are good [in] quality and creativity." And with the 5-barrel pilot system, the brewing team can experiment. "We're having a lot of fun with the pilot brewery," Mitchell said. "That's where the R&D part comes in—the new beers and the creative side."

Ithaca Beer Co.

Opened: 1997.

Owner: Dan Mitchell.

Brewers: Mike Bank, Andrew Schwartz, and Bill Ballweber.

System: 50-barrel primary brewhouse; 5-barrel pilot system.

Annual production: 20,000 barrels in 2013.

Distribution: Available in bottles and draft in seven states.

Hours: noon to 9 p.m. Wednesday through Sunday.

Food: On-site pub and restaurant, featuring wood-fired pizza and more.

Parking: Yes.

Keuka Brewing Co.

8572 Briglin Rd., Hammondsport, NY 14840
(607) 868-4648 • www.keukabrewingcompany.com

Let me get this out of the way first: All of the Finger Lakes are spectacularly beautiful. While I was driving around the region for this book, I got a chance to see all of them from just about every angle. I hereby declare Keuka Lake to be the most spectacular, with steep hillsides overlooking nearly its entire shoreline. It's also noted for being shaped like a "Y" instead of a finger, unlike the other lakes. And a hint on its pronunciation can be found on T-shirts sold in the area: They read "QKA." To pronounce it like the locals, say "cue-ka." (Nearby Cayuga Lake is generally pronounced "cue-ga." Try telling the difference after a few beers.)

That brings us to Keuka Brewing Co., founded in 2008 on a steep hillside overlooking the bottom prong of the lake, a few miles north of the village of Hammondsport, near famed Finger Lakes wineries like Dr. Konstantin Frank and Heron Hill. Run by Richard and Linda Musso (after original partner Mark Goodwin left to form Finger Lakes Beer Company in Hammondsport), the brewery, like most others in the region, has been growing. But they're taking it slow and easy.

The tasting room has doubled in size and the brewery building has had a few rooms added. In mid-2012, Keuka traded in its original 1-barrel nanosystem for a 3.5-barrel system. That may still seem small, but Keuka has a way of seeming bigger than it is. That's because it has two of its more popular beers brewed and bottled at CB's in Honeoye Falls (page 48). That still leaves Mark Musso, Richard and Linda's son and Keuka's brewer, plenty to do. The brewery has a rotation of almost a half-dozen year-round beers and regular seasonals, plus a selection of big one-offs under its Old Urbana series. Most are available on draft and in bottles.

Beers brewed: Afterburner Habanero Ale, White Cap Wheat, Hoppy Laker IPA, KBC Pale Ale (contracted out), Briglin Road Red (contracted out), Bluff Point Brown, Local Mocha Coffee Stout, Pumpkin Cream Ale, and the Old Urbana series (these change each year).

The Pick: This is a toss-up between two contrasting styles: The Local Mocha Stout is balanced, smooth, and not overpowered by the coffee, a great beer for a cold day. The Hoppy Laker IPA, despite its 7 percent ABV and plentiful hops, is balanced with the addition of bitterness-cutting lemon zest. As Mark Musso said, it's a "sessionable, take-it-out-on-your-boat IPA." With a lake as beautiful as Keuka, that's got to be the choice.

Musso likes experimentation. On my visit, I started by sampling a beer called Afterburner Habanero Ale. It's based on a 3.3 percent ABV light ale, to which Musso adds habanero peppers he buys from local Amish farmers. (The peppers are fresh in season; some are dehydrated for winter use.) There's also a beer called Local Mocha Stout, made with semisweet and bittersweet chocolate and coffee from Keuka Roasters in the nearby village of Penn Yan.

It has taken a few years to settle on the beers in the rotation, but Mark Musso thinks they've arrived. That prompted the start of the high-alcohol, boldly flavored beers in the Old Urbana line, named after a steamship that once plied Keuka Lake's waters. "We've found our groove now, the beers we want to keep," Musso said. "We use the series to try new things." Beers in the Old Urbana series debut each April—Musso spends the relatively slow winter season tinkering with them. The first was a barleywine; the second was a Russian Imperial Stout. On my visit, Musso was in mid-tinker on a planned Belgian Tripel. He brewed three versions, each with a different yeast, but appeared to be settling on a Chimay-like yeast. Musso once worked at the nearby Heron Hill winery, so it's not surprising to hear him use some wine-aficionado descriptors for his beers. He described the Russian Imperial Stout, for example, as having "dark currant and dark fruit" aromas.

Keuka has a handful of accounts in the Finger Lakes area and has sold its bottled beers as far away as Rochester and Syracuse. The tasting room gets much of its traffic courtesy of the nearby wine trails and the tourists they bring. Like other brewers in the Finger Lakes, Keuka has seen a change in that pattern in recent years. "Originally, people happened to be out on the wine tour, saw the beer sign, stopped in, and liked what we had," Musso said. "Now they go tell their friends. Now people have heard about the beer and a lot of them come up just for the breweries."

Looking ahead, the slow and steady growth at Keuka may be starting to ramp up. Mark Musso looks forward to the day when he has the space to brew all of his beers instead of having some contracted out. The Musso family has also been in talks with the new owners of one of the old and defunct wineries in the area about the possibility of relocating there. The benefit of that? Keuka's current setup uses ambient temperatures in its fermentation room to chill the beers, with help from a window air conditioning unit. The old winery has caves where wine used to be stored—and where Musso could try to do some lagers. "It's fun to be here and look down the road and imagine all the beers we could do," Musso said.

Keuka Brewing Co.

Opened: 2008.

Type: Production brewery.

Owners: Richard and Linda Musso.

Brewer: Mark Musso.

System: 3.5-barrel brewhouse.

Annual production: About 300 barrels on-site; more through contract brewing.

Distribution: Mostly on-premises; some distribution off-site, including New York City.

Hours: Hours vary seasonally; check the website.

Parking: Yes.

Market Street Brewing Co. & Restaurant

63 W. Market St., Corning, NY 14830
(607) 936-2337 • www.936-beer.com

It's called the Gaffer District, and it's just about the most hopping little business district in any small Upstate town. Market Street is the primary artery running through the Gaffer District in Corning, and that's where you'll find Market Street Brewing Co. & Restaurant, a brewpub established in 1997. The Gaffer District looks Victorian, but it's really a rebuilt restoration of a Victorian downtown. Blame Hurricane Agnes in 1972. The hurricane brought a flood, and the government-aided rebuilding project brought the Gaffer District. "If you were sitting here having a beer in 1972, you'd have had to be a fish," said Pelham McClellan, who runs Market Street with his wife, Theresa. (She's listed as the owner; Pelham is one of the brewers, along with Shane Stahl.)

Even though Corning Inc. is not the major manufacturer of cookware and other glass products that it once was, the nearby Corning Museum of Glass is still a major attraction. Between the museum and the nearby Finger Lakes wine region, the area lures half a million visitors a year. But when it comes to the question of what draws people to the brewpub, McClellan has seen some changes since the place opened, including a lot more knowledgeable beer drinkers than there used to be. "I compare it to the wineries," he said. "People used to go to the wineries and say 'Give me a Chablis or give me a Burgundy.' Same way people said, 'Give me a beer.' Now they know what they want and what they like, and they ask for it."

Market Street obliges with seven house beers on tap, a core of five year-round beers, and some rotating seasonals, with the yearly output typically nine or ten beers. The core includes Mad Bug Lager, Wheelhouse IPA, D'Artagna Dark Ale, Wrought Iron Red, and a Blackberry Lager. The Wheelhouse replaced Pot Belly Pale Ale in the regular rotation as drinkers' thirst for more hops increased. Wrought Iron Red has grown over the years to be the bestseller, McClellan said. He and Shane Stahl still brew on the 7-barrel Criveller

Beers brewed: Year-round: Mad Bug Lager, Blackberry Lager, Wrought Iron Red Ale, Wheelhouse IPA, and D'Artagnan Dark Ale. Seasonals: Maibock, Oktoberfest, Stout, and Christmas Ale.

The Pick: Aside from its relatively high alcohol content—6.5 percent—the D'Artagnan Dark has a lot of the hallmarks of an English dark mild, maybe even heading toward a sweet stout. It's rich, malty, and robust, courtesy of six different British malts and roasted barley.

system installed back in 1997. They're making about 350 barrels per year, all served at the bar. "There's no room to grow a bigger brewing system," McClellan said, adding that they don't serve off-premises accounts because "we'd only have the capacity in winter. We're pretty busy here in spring, summer, and fall."

Seafood dominates the menu, along with steak and chicken dishes, and an array of interesting appetizers. There is also a full-service bar. As you're sipping the beers or enjoying the food, take the time to survey your surroundings. Market Street is proud of its renovation work and the fixtures added, and the McClellans won a state award for their preservation efforts. Their handiwork includes a cherry, mahogany, and walnut bar, made from rescued and restored antiques from Philadelphia. The mirror behind the bar was created by master glass engraver Max Erlacher. And check out the antique leaded glass windows, also rescued from Philadelphia. Thinking of all that glass triggers a thought: What's the "gaffer" in the Gaffer District, anyway? It's a master glassblower, of course, a job Corning once offered in abundance.

To get a bird's eye view of the Gaffer District, in nice weather be sure to head up to the rooftop deck at Market Street Brewing. You can imagine what the area looked like in the big flood of '72 and marvel at what it's become. (The Corning campus and museum are a bit to the north and reachable via frequent shuttles.)

Pelham McClellan began his career in the restaurant industry and once owned a legendary restaurant and good beer bar in town called Pelham's Upstate Tuna Co. (now renamed and in other hands). He began serving crafts and imports and launched an early "round the world" beer tour. "I've been in this business, serving beer, for a while," he said. "It's certainly reached another level from where it started."

Market Street Brewing Co. & Restaurant

Opened: 1997.

Type: Brewpub.

Owner: Theresa McClellan.

Brewers: Pelham McClellan and Shane Stahl.

System: 7-barrel Criveller brewhouse.

Annual production: 350 barrels.

Distribution: On-premises only.

Hours: Summer hours: 11:30 a.m. to 10 p.m. Monday to Saturday; noon to 9 p.m. Sunday; call ahead at other times.

Food: Full, somewhat-upscale pub menu.

Parking: Municipal lots or on-street parking.

Naked Dove Brewing Company

4048 State Routes 5 and 20, Canandaigua, NY 14424
(585) 396-ALES • www.nakeddovebrewing.com

Chances are good if you visit the Naked Dove Brewing Company in Canandaigua on a Saturday you'll find co-owner Don Cotter in the middle of a story. It's probably the one about how the brewery got its name. But you might walk in during the middle or the end of the tale. No worries—he'll circle back to it again. I caught the tail end when I entered the brewery on my first visit. ". . . and so it's an anagram of the names," Cotter was saying, pointing to the logo on the Naked Dove T-shirt he was wearing. The start of the story can wait until Cotter comes round to it again. Let's talk about the brewery. Naked Dove opened in November 2010 on the road called Routes 5 and 20, just east of the village of Canandaigua. The owners are Cotter, Dave Schlosser, who also serves as the brewer, and Ken Higgins, whom Cotter calls the "silent partner."

Cotter's credentials include several years in marketing for Constellation Brands, formerly Canandaigua Wine Co. You may never have heard of Constellation, but it's the largest wine and spirits company in the United States, and recently acquired the rights to sell Corona. Later, Cotter worked for Genesee Brewing Company in Rochester, where he was part of a management–employee-led buyout in 2000. Genesee is where he met Dave Schlosser. Dave had brewed at Rochester's Rohrbach Brewpub and at CB Craft Brewers in nearby Honeoye Falls. Dave Schlosser is one of those guys in the beer industry that everyone seems to know. At Genesee, Schlosser became head brewer, and he and Cotter helped that century-old large regional brewery develop and expand its Dundee line of craft beers. Still, Schlosser wanted to open his own brewery, and Cotter signed on, too. "We knew we wanted to do it in Canandaigua," Cotter said.

Canandaigua is a Finger Lakes town that gets a lot of traffic from what Cotter calls "wine tourists"

Beers brewed: Wind Blown Amber Ale, Starkers IPA, 45 Fathoms Porter, and Berry Naked Black Raspberry, plus limited releases and seasonals.

The Pick: A lot of people are afraid of fruit beers, for good reason, but not of the Berry Naked. You can tell there's a real beer—with real hops and malt character—underneath.

and "Rochesterians who summer here." The city is home to the New York Wine & Culinary Center, which boasts a fine restaurant and pub, wine-and-food oriented gift shops, and the home office of the New York State Wine & Grape Foundation. The brewery is in an old truck repair shop on the road just outside of town. In these parts, that road is the junction of State Route 5 and State Route 20. (Route 20 runs from Albany to Buffalo, and is a terrific alternative to the Thruway for those who want a more leisurely and scenic trip across the state.)

With all the wineries, waterfalls, and lake vistas drawing tourists to the area, it might seem more logical to start a brewpub in Canandaigua. Not so, said Cotter. "Our background was in this kind of business, a production company," he said. "I had thirty years in this kind of marketing. Dave had twenty years in this kind of brewing. And none of us knew a thing about running a restaurant." Besides, he said, "We don't want to compete with the restaurants, we want to supply them." They supply about seventy accounts in the Canandaigua–Rochester area. As of July 2013 it was all draft; a bottling line, producing mostly 12-ouncers—was expected to start up before the end of the year.

The brewery building isn't much to look at but it's functional. It's also big, with plenty of room to grow. Schlosser brews on a 15-barrel system, cobbled together from multiple sources. That was a time, Cotter said, when you could find used brewing equipment more easily. "We have more tanks in here than we're currently using, but we'll grow into it," Cotter said. "Dave brewed on a 7-barrel system at Rohrbach's, and 1,000 barrels at Genesee, so he knew the size he wanted . . . 15 barrels is a good place to be."

Now it's about time for Cotter to finish that story about the name. The first choice was Kanandarque, the Iroquois name for the area. "We got a lot of blank looks," Cotter said. "Okay, it was a dumb name." Then they thought of Chosen Spot, which is what Kanandarque means. But the word "chosen" is already in another brewery's name, and they didn't want to tempt legal trouble. Soon, everybody involved in the brewery—including their wives—were brainstorming ideas. One day, someone wrote down the first names of the owners: Dave, Don, and Ken. They played around with the letters. When you mix up the letters, you can spell Naked Dove. "And so it's an anagram of the names," Cotter said.

It's not a bad moniker for attracting attention. "Naked is a 'good' bad word—it makes people . . . interested," Cotter said. "We had a couple one time, a little older, pull in and ask 'What do you do in here?' We gave them some samples. On the way out, the man says to the woman, 'Well I guess we won't have to worry about what they're doing in there anymore.'"

Naked Dove makes four year-round beers, none of them extreme but still interesting nonetheless. (Cotter uses the term "chest-thumpers" to describe the type of beers Naked Dove doesn't brew.) The year-rounders are Wind Blown Amber Ale, Starkers IPA, 45 Fathoms Porter, and Berry Naked Black Raspberry. "Being in wine country, we knew we wanted a fruit beer," Cotter said.

On my summer visit, they had two one-offs, a red ale made for the Red Dove Tavern in Geneva and a Belgian farmhouse ale called A Roll in the Hay. That one was a quenching summer beer at 4.2 ABV. They once did a Belgian dubbel at 8.2 ABV, but that's on the big side for them. Easy-drinking, relaxed beers seem to fit Naked Dove's strategy. "It all depends on the market," Cotter said. "We're planned out for big growth, but we'll take it slow."

Naked Dove Brewing Company

Opened: 2010.
Type: Production brewery.
Owners: Dave Schlosser, Don Cotter, and Ken Higgins.
Brewer: Dave Schlosser.
Type: Production brewery.
System: 15-barrel, custom-built.
Annual production: 2,500 barrels.
Distribution: Finger Lakes area (Genesee to Seneca Falls, plus Rochester).
Hours: Noon to 6 p.m. Monday to Thursday; noon to 7 p.m. Friday; 10 a.m. to 6 p.m. Saturday; noon to 5 p.m. Sunday.
Parking: Yes.

Rogues' Harbor Brewing

Rogue's Harbor Inn, 2079 East Shore Dr., Lansing NY 14882
(607) 533-3535 • www.roguesharbor.com

In 2011, Ithaca-area photographer and videographer Chris Williams visited the Rogue's Harbor Inn in nearby Lansing to pitch a video idea to owner Eileen Stout. They ended up talking about beer. She said she always wanted a brewery. He said he wanted to brew. "I didn't sell her a video," Williams said. "But I did sell her a brewery."

And so Williams set up Rogues' Harbor Brewing, a small (2-barrel) brewhouse in an outbuilding on the inn's property. The brewhouse uses some interesting technology. Williams found that installing standard glycol chillers on his tanks would cost more than he wanted to pay. So he went with an unusual invention, thought up by a New Paltz, New York, farmer with help from some Cornell University engineers. It's called the CoolBot. Simply put, the CoolBot is an upright, insulated case, the size of a small refrigerator, powered by a window unit-style air conditioner attached at the bottom. It cools what's inside (makers say at less cost than standard refrigeration) down to about 32 degrees. It's particularly useful for florists and small farmers selling their wares . . . and, it seems, brewers. Williams has three of the units, each set on casters that he can move into place around the brewhouse to chill his fermenters or his bright tank as needed.

Rogues' Harbor typically has four beers on tap, exclusively at the inn. They include Cayuga Cream Ale, East Shore Pale Ale, and Route 34 Red Ale, plus a rotating brewer's choice. On my mid-summer visit the brewer's choice was an English Bitter. But Williams also let me sample the next one up, a Belgian-style Wit made with orange peel, coriander, and a remarkably low level of Saaz hops. That trace of bitterness? Williams threw in some heather tips, a bittering agent that dates to the pre–hops period of northern European history.

As for the inn itself, it's a restaurant, tavern, and bed and breakfast located just north of Ithaca on the Cayuga Wine Trail's eastern shore. Cayuga

Beers brewed: Year-round: Cayuga Cream Ale, East Shore Pale Ale, and Route 34 Red Ale. Seasonals: a rotating series of Brewer Choice beers, including British Bitter, Black IPA, Unfiltered Wheat, and Belgian-style Wit.

The Pick: The Cayuga Cream Ale is bursting with fruity esters. But you can't beat traditions that date back centuries and are still useful, right? So the Belgian-style Wit, whose bitterness comes largely from the use of heather or heather tips, is the choice. It's a summer seasonal, and the heathery bitterness makes it a hot-season quencher.

Lake's eastern shore is known as a relatively quiet corner of the wine district. But don't be fooled: It still has some fine wineries, including Long Point, King Ferry, and Heart & Hands, all north of Lansing near Aurora. Several members of the Finger Lakes Cheese Trail—dairies making artisan cheese—are in the vicinity, too; the closest is Keeley's Cheese Co. at McGarr Dairy Farm.

The Rogue's Harbor Inn's main building dates to 1830 and is listed on the National Register of Historic Places. The inn is rumored to have been a stop on the Underground Railroad, and later became known as a den of thieves and brawlers— hence the current name. The tavern is rustic, and the dining rooms abound with original woodwork, punched tin ceilings, and chestnut wainscoting. The rooms are decorated with period antiques. The dining menu ranges from pub grub to finer entrées, many with an Upstate New York flavor, like Chicken Riggies and fried haddock with Cayuga Cream Ale batter. Many items are made exclusively with New York-grown or produced ingredients, including nearby cheese and wine.

If there is a house character to Rogues' Harbor beers, it's an assertive fruitiness in the aroma, which Williams admits could be because of relatively high fermentation temperatures. Although he sometimes buys commercial yeasts, Williams is also fond of using homebrewers' supply "smack packs" of liquid yeast and cultivating his own. That leads to some odd hours in the brewery. "I'm not so much a brewer as a yeast farmer," he said. "I have to herd them when they're ready."

Rogues' Harbor Brewing

Opened: 2011.

Type: Brewpub.

Owner: Eileen Stout.

Brewer: Chris Williams.

System: 2-barrel, custom-made.

Annual production: Up to 200 barrels

Distribution: Exclusively at the inn; growlers available for takeout.

Hours: Dinner is served from 4 p.m. to 10 p.m. Monday to Saturday and from 3 p.m. to 9 p.m. Sunday.

Food: Full-service restaurant and bar.

Parking: Yes.

Rooster Fish Brewing/Nickel's Pit BBQ

205–207 N. Franklin St., Watkins Glen, NY 14891
(607) 210-4227 • www.nickelspitbbq.com

The Crooked Rooster Brewpub/ The Wildflower Café

223–301 N. Franklin St.
(607) 535-9797 • www.roosterfishbrewing.com

Stay with me here. Rooster Fish Brewing is located behind Nickel's Pit BBQ, in an old firehouse in downtown Watkins Glen. Up the street, you'll find two more eateries: the Crooked Rooster BrewPub and the adjacent Wildflower Café. All four are owned and operated by Doug Thayer. The brewery began in 2004 inside the Crooked Rooster before relocating to the firehouse in early 2013. Almost all the beer Thayer produces in the 15-barrel brewhouse is sold there, or at the Crooked Rooster and Wildflower Café.

So is this a brewpub or a production brewery with three major outlets? Whatever you call it, it's a sign that Thayer is someone who likes to do things in his own particular style. His first venture was the Wildflower Café; he then branched out to the Crooked Rooster Brewpub. The two are separated by a wall, but share a menu. "I'd say Wildflower is a restaurant with a bar, while the Rooster is a bar with a restaurant," Thayer said. The menu—common to both places—is pub fare, including burgers, sandwiches, and pizzas, and also features three variations on "mussel ale" bowls: Classic, Cajun, and Thai.

With a solid line-up of craft beers, Crooked Rooster began to build a reputation in Watkins Glen before Thayer started brewing, back around 2004. His first attempts were with a 10-gallon system. He soon graduated to a 10-barrel brewhouse. The first two beers were Black Walnut Ale and Butternut Ale, but as he started to look into distributing them, he encountered a problem. "The ATF wouldn't let me

Beers brewed: Firehouse Blonde, Summer Sky Hefeweizen, Original Dark Nut Brown Ale, Mysterious Amber, Dog Tooth Pale Ale, Aspen Wit Ale, Hop Warrior Imperial IPA, Tripel Witch Ale, Wee Heavy Scotch Ale, Raven Black IPA, Salvador Dali Oatmeal-Coffee Stout, and limited releases.

The Pick: The Tripel Witch is a big (9.6 percent ABV) Belgian-style beer, with candi sugar sweetness and a flavor best described as plum-accented.

use those names then because the one didn't contain walnuts or nuts of any kind, and the other contained no butternut [squash]," Thayer said. They remain in the Rooster Fish lineup, rechristened Original Dark Nut Brown Ale and Dog Tooth Pale Ale, and now joined by more than a dozen others, including the light Firehouse Blonde, the strong and hoppy Hop Warrior IPA, the sweetish Belgian-style Tripel Witch, and the Mysterious Amber. That last beer has a mystery ingredient that Thayer challenges you to discover. (The taste profile that comes through for me is caramel.)

Thayer is a self-taught brewer with no formal training, but he has influenced a number of brewers who have come through his operation and moved on to brew elsewhere or even start their own breweries. "I figured out that I'm doing things that a lot of these guys with training say aren't really brew school standards," he said. "But I show them what I do, and I think sometimes my way is more efficient." Thayer initially had plans to distribute outside of his own pub and restaurant, but had trouble keeping up with the in-house demand. The barbecue place opened in the fall of 2012, offering another outlet, and its location inside the old firehouse provided space to expand the brewery side of the business. Even with the 15-barrel brewery, however, it's all Thayer and his brewer, Cory Drake, can do to keep up with demand.

They remain busy in part because Watkins Glen sits near the center of the Finger Lakes wine region, at the bottom of Seneca Lake. Known for its beautiful gorge and state park and the Watkins Glen International Raceway, the city is also perfectly positioned as a base for Finger Lakes travelers. Thayer has watched the wine region grow and has witnessed the boom in the local brewery scene, too. "The growth is great, but I guess I'm also concerned that there continues to be quality as well as quantity," he said. "All these places are great, as long as they are doing things the right way."

Rooster Fish Brewing

Opened: 2004; brewery relocated in 2013.

Type: Production brewery serving three nearby outlets.

Owner: Doug Thayer.

Brewers: Doug Thayer and Cory Drake.

System: 15-barrel Specific Mechanical.

Annual production: 2,500 barrels.

Distribution: Primarily to the three outlets Thayer owns in Watkins Glen.

Hours: Hours vary for the three eateries; it's best to call ahead.

Food: All three locations have full menus.

Parking: On-street parking or a municipal lot.

Scale House Brewery & Pub

23 Cinema Drive, Ithaca, NY 14850
(607) 257-0107 • www.scalehousebrewpub.com

The vibrant little college town of Ithaca doesn't have much in the way of suburbs. But just east of town, in Cayuga Heights, is an area that boasts a modest collection of malls, strip plazas, and local and chain stores and restaurants. Tucked in one of the smaller plazas—called Bishop's Small Mall—are two storefronts: Northeast Pizza and Scale House Brewery & Pub. From the outside they appear to be separate businesses. Inside, they open on to one another. They are linked by owner Steve Fazzary, who has been working for several years to streamline and consolidate the look of both.

The original "brewhouse" is easy to find. Three large tanks, each of which dispenses beer, sit just behind the bar—you'll see all-in-one fermenters, mash tuns, and bright tanks. In 2013, Fazzary added a small all-grain system, a 2-barrel system he expected would produce pale ale, IPA, and a stout, and intended to supplement the extract system, not to replace it. "I fill, ferment, and serve all from the same tank," he said of his original brewhouse setup. Fazarry also started up a manual can filler for 16-ounce cans.

And yet you can get four beers at any one time from these three tanks. Year round, one tank has Red Ale, another has Bock Dark, and one has either Hefeweizen (in summer) or Pilsner (the rest of the year.) You can get four beers at any time is because one of the house beers is a Black and Tan, a combo of the red ale and the bock.

Fazarry's background, like his father's, is in cheese manufacturing, and he once worked for Polly-O. Eventually he bought a laundromat in the small shopping plaza near Ithaca, then purchased the pizza shop in 2006. The shop is a popular place for sit-in and takeout and is a steady enough business, but Fazarry had another plan. He wanted a pub that served its own beers, and opened Scale House in 2007. On the other hand, he worried about getting in over his head. "When I opened the pub, I planned to have microbrews, brewed here," he said. "But I didn't want to go to the expense of getting a big all-grain system and hiring a brewmaster, and then finding

Beers brewed: Extract system: Red Ale, Bock Dark, Hefeweizen, and Pilsner. All-grain system: Pale Ale, IPA, and Stout.

The Pick: The Red Ale seems the best match for the extract system and the yeast. It is, as Steve Fazzary said, refreshing.

that the brewmaster quits and I don't know how to run it. I was afraid of that." He talked things over with Dan Mitchell, owner of the Ithaca Beer Co., a decade-old successful and growing craft brewery on the other side of Ithaca. Mitchell, hearing Fazarry's concerns, recommended starting with something modest, like an extract system.

The extract beers themselves are, in Fazarry's description, "refreshing." He uses the same yeast for all of them. He goes through a 5-barrel batch of each house beer in about a month, or forty-five days for the bock. When he thought about an upgrade, he worried about finding the space. The 2-barrel system seemed to be a good compromise.

In the meantime, his business is good, and the atmospheres at the pub and pizza joint are casual and friendly. The pub serves bar food, such as wings, sandwiches, and burgers, but the Northeast Pizza side has an extensive list of pizzas and calzones, plus wings and even spaghetti and meatballs. Scale House always has a few local guest beers on tap (during my visit, they included brews from Ithaca Beer and Rooster Fish Brewing in nearby Watkins Glen). Fazarry is candid about the nature of his brewing system and his slow buildup to all-grain brewing: "I wanted to keep it simple and consistent," he said. "The beers may not win awards, but this is the model I went with."

Scale House Brewery & Pub

Opened: 2007.

Type: Brewpub.

Owner and brewer: Steve Fazarry.

System: Three 5-barrel, all-in-one extract tanks; 2-barrel, all-grain brewhouse.

Annual production: About 200 barrels on the extract system; no number available for the all-grain system.

Distribution: Draft on-premises only; some cans produced for retail sale at the pub.

Hours: 11 a.m. to 1 a.m. every day.

Food: Pub menu, plus adjoining pizza shop.

Parking: Yes.

Two Goats Brewing

5027 State Route 414, Hector, NY 14818
(607) 546-2337 • www.twogoatsbrewing.com

With his long ponytail, full beard, engagingly cheerful demeanor, and relaxed attitude about most things, Jon Rodgers seems nothing like an accountant. He seems like a guy who makes beer and runs a good-time pub for a living, which is what he is. Still, he *was* an accountant at one time. To gauge just how far he's come since those days, ask him how much beer his 7-barrel brewhouse system makes in a year. "You know, I've never really figured that out," he said. "We just make beer and roll with it." We can assume Rodgers has someone keeping his books (at least for tax purposes). In the three years since he chucked the ledgers for the brew kettle, he's been having the time of his life. "Accounting was boring," he said. "This is not boring."

Rodgers opened his brewpub, called Two Goats Brewing, in March 2010 on the eastern shore of Seneca Lake, a few miles north of Watkins Glen. It's squarely in the area of the Finger Lakes known as the "Banana Belt," the southeast shoreline of Seneca. Experts say it has an average winter low temperature that is 1 degree warmer than the rest of the region.

That may not seem like much, but some wine experts say it makes a big difference in quality. Whether or not you agree, this stretch of the Finger Lakes has a dense collection of highly regarded wineries, like Standing Stone and Lamoreaux Landing, along with some of the area's most noteworthy restaurants. Rodgers knows something about the wine industry, because another of his past jobs was growing grapes. But when he chose the site for his brewpub, on a steep hillside with a gorgeous lake view, he ripped out the vines. (It turns out this particular plot had poor drainage for a vineyard.)

The origins of Rodgers's passion for brewing go back a long way. He said he was just sixteen when he first had a beer at the Chapterhouse, a legendary (but since closed) 1980s-era brewpub in Ithaca, one of the first in the state. And he

Beers brewed: IPA, Redbeard Red Ale, Amber Lager, Head Butt Cream Ale, Goat Mater Ultra Pale Ale, Danger Goat! Blonde Doppelbock, Oatmeal Stout, Brown Ale, and many specials.

The Pick: A good, high-quality cream ale? Yes, here at Two Goats the Head Butt Cream Ale has more body than most, a decent kick between 7 and 8 percent ABV, with a bit of fresh Chinook hops from a nearby farm. Referencing another Upstate cream ale, Rodgers notes: "This is not just another screamer."

remembers his favorite Chapterhouse beer: Blonde Doppelbock. He makes his own version of Blonde Doppelbock today. "That beer changed my life," said Rodgers, who kept the memories into his forties when he decided to brew for a living. He named Two Goats in its honor—the goat is the symbol of bock beer, and two goats, of course, would be the symbol for a doppel, or double bock.

Two Goats beers range from summer quenchers like Goat Master Ultra Pale Ale, which Rodgers calls a "bastardized" Kolsch—and Headbutt Cream Ale, to heavier, richer brews like Doppelbock (10 percent ABV) and Oatmeal Stout. But in his heart, Rodgers is a hop-head: "I'm an IPA guy all the way." And he's found a local source for his hops in a Seneca County farmer named Todd Wyckoff, who inspired Two Goats' harvest seasonal Wyck'd Nuggets IPA, a mighty big beer at 9 percent ABV.

Brewing, of course, is just part of operating a brewpub. Rodgers's pub is a rustic place, with rough-hewn timbers, a high-pitched ceiling, and a patio where people are itching to get outside and drink beer. Sometimes they even do that in the winter. For food, Rodgers keeps it simple. Two Goats offers a version of the western New York favorite beef on weck, inspired by the now-closed Clark's Ale House in Syracuse. That's it. There are always six to seven beers on tap, and often live music. The pub can be quiet and charming at times, but can instantly explode into insanity on a Saturday afternoon when a winery tour bus or two roll in.

Rodgers also has a neat parlor game for the tourists. If you sign a $1 bill, Rodgers will fold it around a couple of coins, imbed a thumb tack in it, and then throw it up to the ceiling. If all works well, the tack will stick the bill to the ceiling while the coins fall back down. Does it work? A quick count on my first visit showed at least fifty bills impaled on the ceiling. Rogers has probably never bothered to count them himself. He's too busy having fun.

Two Goats Brewing

Opened: 2010.
Owner and brewer: Jon Rodgers.
System: 7-barrel brewhouse.
Annual production: N/A
Distribution: On-premises only.
Hours: Check the website before you visit.
Food: A beef on weck sandwich.
Parking: An adjacent lot.

Upstate Brewing Company

3028 Lake Rd., Elmira, NY 14903
(607) 742-2750 • www.upstatebrewing.com

Two guys grow up in the small Upstate New York town of Horseheads and become high school friends. Both move on. One goes to Boston and works in the financial industry. The other heads west, eventually running a contracting business in Los Angeles. Both also become homebrewers. Years pass. One day, one guy said to the other: "Dude, let's start a brewery back in our hometown!"

Okay, that last part may be a bit of a simplification. But it is more or less the story of Ken Mortensen and Mark Neumann, owners of Upstate Brewing Company, which began producing beer in New York's Southern Tier region in July 2012. Mortensen and Neumann attended Horseheads High School and chose a location for their brewery in town, just outside the city of Elmira. "We have an Elmira mailing address so that's our identity," Neumann said. Elmira is a small city known as the one-time home of Mark Twain and the birthplace of football legend Ernie Davis. It also suffered major devastation during the floods of Hurricane Agnes in 1972, and like many Upstate cities, has seen better economic times. But that's where Neumann and Mortensen decided to set up Upstate Brewing.

From the start, it was two guys and two beers. But the two beers aren't exactly ordinary. One is India Pale Wheat, a 6.5 percent ABV. It's a merger of India Pale Ale and American Wheat beers and pretty heavy on the hops, too, at 70 IBUs with Magnum, Zythos, and Nugget varieties. "It has the intense floral-citrusy hoppy bitterness of an in-your-face American IPA, with the light and refreshing flavor of an American wheat beer," Mortensen said. The second beer is even more uncommon. Called Common Sense Ale (5.3 percent), it's a nod to Kentucky Common ale, a popular pre–Prohibition style, said Mortensen. (Not to be confused with California Common Beer.) "In a nutshell it's a dark beer that is also light and refreshing," Mortensen said. "It has a

Beers brewed: India Pale Wheat, Common Sense, and seasonals to come

The Pick: An uncommon style, the Common Sense manages to be dark and creamy, yet somehow refreshing, all at the same time.

little bitterness, a lager type of finish. It's appealing to Yuengling drinkers."

More beers are coming to the lineup, starting with an Oktoberfest, a "big" IPA, and perhaps a Black IPA. In 2013, seasonals included a 3.7 percent Irish Blonde for the spring and a Summer Haze. Expect hops to dominate more of their beers as the Upstate guys get rolling. "We really like hops," Neumann said. "That's going to be our signature." But Mortensen quickly chimed in: "We want beers with broad-based appeal." So they won't go overboard.

Their market is in the lower Finger Lakes and Southern Tier regions, in places like Ithaca, Watkins Glen, Hammondsport, and perhaps Hornell. They also signed deals for distribution downstate in the New York City and Hudson Valley areas. "In our market, Ithaca likes hops," Neumann said. "The rest, they're Bud, Miller, and Coors."

Mortensen said the plan is to grow steadily, so that perhaps within a couple of years he and Neumann could quit their day jobs. That's the plan, anyway. They realize they started Upstate Brewing at a time of rapid expansion in the craft beer industry, both across the country and in New York. They're in the same town, a few miles down the road, from Horseheads Brewing Co. and Birdland Brewing, and are members of the growing Finger Lakes Beer Trail. "I believe a rising tide lifts all boats," Mortensen said. "We're collectively building a market for ourselves." They're built for expansion, with a 7-barrel brewhouse and multiple fermenters and bright tanks. In 2013, they also started canning some of their beer, using a mobile service out of Pennsylvania, with a goal of having half the production in cans. "We want to go slow," Mortensen said. "We want to establish our brands. If you go into a bar and you find the Common Sense, then we want you to go into that bar next time and find it again."

Upstate Brewing Company

Opened: 2012.
Type: Production brewery.
Owners and brewers: Ken Mortensen and Mark Neumann.
System: 7-barrel Ager Tank brewhouse.
Annual production: 500 barrels.
Distribution: Around the Southern Tier and Finger Lakes regions and New York metro area; canning started in 2013.
Hours: The tasting room is open 1 p.m. to 4 p.m. Saturday.
Parking: Yes.

Wagner Valley Brewing Co.

9322 State Route 414, Lodi, NY 14860
(607) 582-6450 • www.wagnerbrewing.com

When Wagner Valley Brewing Co. opened in 1997, it was billed as the East Coast's first "brewery-in-a-winery." Its status as a full-fledged brewhouse within the walls of a winery—in this case Wagner Vineyards overlooking Seneca Lake—remains unusual, at least in New York state. (Several Finger Lakes wineries have craft beers available in their tasting rooms, but those are brewed under contract elsewhere.) That doesn't mean things are unchanged since the 1990s. The Finger Lakes wine trails are now studded with dozens of stand-alone breweries and brewpubs. This wasn't true when Wagner pioneered the beer and wine crossover. In the early days, staff at Wagner were accustomed to welcoming patrons who came for the wine and were surprised to see beer.

Wine trail visitors expect to see beer these days, and their tastes have changed. Wagner's first brewer found that years ago winery visitors recoiled from the idea of hop-heavy beers, and gravitated instead toward big (high-alcohol) and malt-oriented beers. Today, said brewer Brent Wojnowski, the crowd is more adventurous and beer savvy. "We see more people who come for the beer, and they know a lot about it," he said. "They know hops, they know malt, they know the styles. . . . We are definitely seeing the beer tourists."

Wagner Vineyards patriarch Bill Wagner launched the Wagner Valley Brewing Company. Today, his son John and daughter Laura manage things. A couple of different brewers have run the brewhouses, and Wojnowski, who took over in 2010, is looking to work with John Wagner to build on the brewery's reputation. That reputation is due in large part to a beer called Sled Dog Doppelbock, which won some nice awards—at TAP New York and the Great American Beer Fest, to name a few—right out of the box. It is, in fact, one of those high-alcohol and malty beers that appealed to the wine people. It also spawned a seasonal Sled Dog

Beers brewed: Year-round: Mill Street Pilsner, Dockside Amber Lager, Wagner India Pale Ale, and Sled Dog Doppelbock. Seasonals: Grace House Honey Wheat, Caywood Station Oatmeal Stout, Sugar House Maple Porter, Summer Sail Hefeweizen, Coffee Porter, and Sled Dog Trippelbock Reserve. There's also Real Draft Root Beer.

The Pick: You can't go wrong with the warming (8.5 percent ABV), aromatic, and malty Sled Dog Doppelbock (unless you happen to be around when the Triplebock Reserve is available).

Triple Bock. Other mainstays of the lineup include a wheat, amber lager, oatmeal stout, pilsner, pale ale, and ESB. "If you have something as awesome as Sled Dog, why change it?" Wojnowski said. But he pushes on with newer beers. He brought back a former seasonal Coffee Porter, made with coffee from an Ithaca roaster, into the rotation one recent winter. More seasonals are in the planning pipeline.

Something Wojnowski has in common with Wagner's previous brewers is the need to think about—if not outright worry over—the possible mingling of beer yeast and wine yeast, since the two operations fit so snugly together. The brewery, in fact, is entirely enclosed, though not completely airtight, and the brewery–winery has never encountered any issues of contaminated yeast. "If anything, we'd be more concerned about the wild yeasts coming in here," Wojnowski said, pointing down the nearby hillsides covered in vineyards. "To my knowledge, there's no problem."

The potential for other collaborations between the brewery and winery remains open for exploration. For example, the winery has an abundant supply of oak casks for aging its products. As of early 2013, the brewery had never made use of them. But Wojnowski has to pass through the cask wine aging room on his way to his bottling line, so the thought is there.

About 80 percent of the beer made at Wagner is sold at the tasting room, which has no shortage of visitors. You can also order the beers at the winery's on-site restaurant, the Ginny Lee Cafe, which offers a classic Finger Lakes wine country menu.Wojnowski hopes to boost the off-premises sales, and has had some success (like other Finger Lakes breweries) with sales in the New York City area. The Coffee Porter is one that has found tap handles in the city. "It's a beautiful thing to know that people down there are enjoying our beer," Wojnowski said.

Wagner Valley Brewing Co.

Opened: 1997.

Owners: The Wagner family.

Brewer: Brent Wojnowski.

System: 20-barrel HBC brewhouse.

Annual production: 1,200 to 1,500 barrels, including some under contract for other brewers.

Distribution: Kegs and bottles, mostly sold on-site.

Hours: 10 a.m. to 5 p.m. daily. (Tastings don't start until noon on Sunday.)

Food: A full-service restaurant, the Ginny Lee Cafe, on-site.

Parking: Yes.

Brewing Beer

You don't need to know much about beer to enjoy it. After all, you don't need to understand how the electronic fuel injection on your car works to know that when you stomp on the accelerator, the car's gonna go! However, knowing about the brewing process can help you understand how and why beer tastes the way it does. It's like seeing the ingredients used in cooking a dish and realizing where the flavors came from. Once you understand the recipe for beer, other things become clearer.

Beer is made from four basic ingredients: water, hops, yeast, and grain (generally barley malt). Other ingredients may be added, such as sugars, spices, fruits, and vegetables, but they are extras. In fact, the oft-quoted Bavarian Reinheitsgebot (purity law), first promulgated in 1516, limited brewers to using only water, hops, and barley malt; yeast had not yet been discovered.

In the beginning, the malt is cracked in a mill to make grist. The grist is mixed with water and heated (or "mashed") to convert the starches in the grain to sugars (see *decoction* and *infusion* in the Glossary, pages 266 and 268). Then the hot, sugary water—now called wort—is strained out of the mash. It is boiled in the brewkettle, where hops are added to balance the sweetness with their characteristic bitterness and sprightly aroma. The wort is strained, cooled, and pumped to a fermenter, where yeast is added.

A lager beer ferments slow and cool, whereas an ale ferments warmer and faster. After fermentation, the beer will either be force-carbonated or naturally carbonated and aged. When it is properly mature for its style, the beer is bottled, canned, kegged, or sent to a large serving tank in a brewpub. And then we drink it. Happy ending!

Naturally, it isn't quite that simple. The process varies somewhat from brewery to brewery. That's what makes beers unique. There are also major differences in the ways micro and mainstream brewers brew beer. One well-known distinction has to do with the use of non-barley grains, specifically corn and rice, in the brewing process. Some microbrewers have made a big deal of their Reinheitsgebot, proudly displaying slogans like "Barley, hops, water, and yeast—and that's all!" Mainstream brewers like Anheuser-Busch and Genesee add significant portions of corn or rice, or both. Beer geeks howl about how these adjuncts make the beer inferior. Of course, the same geeks often rave about Belgian ales, which have a regular conga line of ingredients forbidden by the Reinheitsgebot.

Mainstream brewers boast about the quality of the corn grits and brewer's rice they use, while microbrewers chide them for using "cheap" adjunct grains and "inferior" six-row barley. Truth is, they're both right . . . and they're both wrong. Barley, like beer, comes in two main types: two-row and six-row. The names refer to the rows of kernels on the heads of the grain. Six-row grain gives a greater yield per acre, but has more husks on smaller kernels, which can give beer an unpleasant astringency. Two-row barley gives a plumper kernel with fewer husks, but costs significantly more. Each has its place and adherents.

When brewing began in America, farmers and brewers discovered that six-row barley did much better than two-row in our climate and soil types. Two-row barley grown the same way as it had been in Europe produced a distinctly different malt. This became especially troublesome when the craze for pale lagers swept America in the mid–nineteenth century. The hearty ales they replaced had broad flavors from hops and yeast that easily compensated for these differences. But pale lagers are showcases for malt character, and small differences in the malt mean big differences in beer taste.

Brewers adapted and used what they had. They soon found that a small addition of corn or brewer's rice to the mash lightened the beer, smoothed out the husky astringency of the six-row malt, and gave the beer a crispness similar to that of the European pale lagers. Even though using these grains required the purchase, operation, and maintenance of additional equipment (cookers, storage silos, and conveyors), almost every American brewer did it. Some say they overdid it, as the percentages of adjuncts in the beer rose over the years. (Is a beer that is 30 percent corn still a pilsner?)

Microbrewers say adjunct grains are cheap substitutes for barley malt. In terms of yield, corn and brewer's rice are less expensive than two-row barley, but they are still high-quality grains. Similarly, six-row barley is not inherently inferior to two-row; it is just not as well suited to the brewing of some styles of beer. Mainstream brewers have adapted their brewing processes to six-row barley. The difference is in the beer those processes produce.

Another difference between micro and mainstream brewers is the practice of high-gravity brewing. The alcohol content of a beer is main-ly dependent on the ratio of fermentable sugars to water in the wort, which determines the specific gravity of the wort. A higher gravity means more alcohol. Large commercial brewers, in their constant search for ways to peel pennies off the costs of brewing, discovered that they could save money by brewing beer at a higher alcohol content and carefully diluting it later. To do this, a brewer adds a calculated extra amount of malt, rice, or corn—whatever "fuel" is used—to boost the beer to 6.5 by volume (ABV) or higher. When the fermented beer has been filtered, water is added to bring the ABV down to the target level of 4 to 5 percent.

How does this method save money? It saves energy and labor costs during the brewing process by effectively squeezing 1,300 barrels of beer into a 1,000-barrel brewkettle. While 1,000 barrels are boiled, 1,300 barrels are eventually bottled. It also saves money by allowing more efficient use of fermentation tank space: 10,000-barrel fermenters produce 13,000 barrels of beer. It sounds great, so why not do that with every beer? Because the high-gravity process can produce some odd flavor and aroma notes during fermentation. That's what brewers aim for in big beers like doppelbocks and barleywines, but these characteristics are out of place in a pilsner. Beer brewed by this high-gravity method sometimes suffers from a dulling phenomenon similar to "clipping" in audio reproduction: The highs and lows are clipped off, leaving only the middle.

With a studied nonchalance, big brewers keep this part of their brewing process away from the public eye. To tell the truth, of all beer styles, American mainstream lager is probably the style least affected by this process. It is mostly a practice that just seems vaguely wrong, and you won't see any microbrewers doing it.

So now you know how beer is made, and a few of the differences in how the big boys and the little guys do it. It's probably time for you to do a little field research. Have fun!

Central New York

Arranging this book was like doing a jigsaw puzzle, where you start on the edges and work in. See that empty space in the middle? When it came to arranging the New York breweries into their different regions, I came to the point where I had empty space in the middle and several pieces still to work in. So this is the big, broad middle called Central New York. It also happens to be the part of the state where I live. It incorporates the Thousand Islands and a piece of the Southern Tier. It encompasses the Mohawk Valley, the remnants of the old Erie Canal, and the Interstate 81 corridor. It even catches a few of the eastern-most Finger Lakes.

It's got the "Salt City" of Syracuse, once a salt manufacturing hub and now home to Syracuse University and the Great New York State Fair. There's Binghamton, the so-called "Parlor City" because of its once fashionable and grand houses, and former home to IBM and Endicott-Johnson shoes. There's Utica, a city that is simultaneously near the start of the Mohawk River and in "the foothills of the Adirondacks," as the ads for Saranac beer have it. And Cooperstown, with the National Baseball Hall of Fame, the gorgeous Otsego Lake, and so much more.

Check out Watertown, with its giant United States Army post of Fort Drum and proximity to the Thousand Islands, a fishing paradise dotted with little isles on which sit grand homes and mansions. The Turning Stone Resort Casino, with its gaming tables and PGA Tour quality golf course, is also located here. The International Boxing Hall of Fame is in nearby Canastota.

And there's farmland—lots of farmland. It's mostly used for dairy production, so it may come as no surprise that the fastest growing company in this area in recent years is the Greek yogurt maker

Chobani. (Other Greek yogurt makers are also nearby.) And this is the region with two of the three largest breweries in the state: Anheuser-Busch InBev's plant in Baldwinsville, near Syracuse, and the Matt Brewing Co. (Saranac) in Utica.

Did I mention snow? Buffalo gets a lot of the national headlines because it's a bigger city, but Syracuse almost always wins the Golden Snowball, topping Upstate's cities with an annual blanket of more than 120 inches. Yet that's nothing compared to Oswego, which can get twice that, or parts of the Tug Hill Plateau, east of Lake Ontario, which often see in excess of 300 inches. But summer is beautiful and fall is spectacular.

So that's it—Central New York, where the state's north, south, east, and west all come together. It is, after all, the crossroads of New York state.

Other breweries and beer companies

Double Barrel Brewing Company (www.facebook.com/DoubleBarrel BrewingCompany) opened in Syracuse in 2013. Several breweries were in the planning stages as this book went to press, including Roots Brewing Company (www.rootsbrewingcompany.com) in Oneonta, Henneberg Brewing Co. (www.hennebergbrewing.com) in Cazenovia, Red Hawk Brewing (www.redhawkbrewing.com) near Syracuse, Erie Canal Brewing Company (www.eriecanalbrewing company.com) in Canastota, Galaxy Brewing Company (www.galaxybrewingco.com) in Binghamton, Binghamton Brewing Co. (www.bingbrew.com) in Johnson City, and FarmHouse Brewery (www.thefarmhousebrewery.com) in Newark Valley.

Other beer sites

The Blue Tusk (165 Walton St., Syracuse); J. Ryan's Pub (253 E. Water St., Syracuse); The Hops Spot (214 W. Main St., Sackets Harbor); The Colgate Inn (1 Payne St., Hamilton); Upstate Tavern (in the Turning Stone Casino in Verona); and The Ale House (3744 Vestal Parkway East, Vestal).

Area Attractions

Oneida Lake (www.oneidalake.com) is the largest lake entirely within New York's border, with shallow water ideal for swimming, boating, and fishing. At its eastern end is Verona Beach State Park and Sylvan Beach Amusement Park. *The Erie Canal Museum* (318 Erie Blvd. East, Syracuse, NY 13202; 315-471-0593; www.eriecanalmuseum.org) is an actual weigh lock building from 1850 restored as a showcase for all things Erie Canal, including a replica packet boat. The **National Baseball Hall of Fame and Museum** (25 Main St., Cooperstown, NY 13326; 888-425-5633; www.baseballhall.org) offers both a showcase of the game's greats, and a museum to the national pastime. The **International Boxing Hall of Fame** (1 Hall of Fame Dr., Canastota, NY 13032; 315-697-7095; www.ibhof.com) includes displays on boxing heroes and history, and an original ring from Madison Square Garden. **Thousand Islands** (www.thousandislands.com), where the St. Lawrence River meets Lake Ontario, offers great fishing and spectacular island homes and mansions, including the famed Boldt Castle.

Sackets Harbor Battlefield (504 W. Main St., Sackets Harbor, NY 13685; 315-646-3634; www.sacketsharborbattlefield.org) is a restored military post near the site of a War of 1812 naval battle. The **Munson Williams Proctor Arts Institute Museum of Art** (310 E. Genesee St., Utica, NY 13502; 315-797-0000; www.mwpai.org) has a permanent collection with more than twenty-five thousand objects, including nineteenth- and twentieth-century paintings and sculptures, and works from the Hudson River School. The **Binghamton area carousels** (www.gobroomecounty.com/community/carousels) date from the 1920s, with two in Binghamton, two in Endicott, one in Endwell, and one in Johnson City. The recently restored carousel in Recreation Park (58–78 Beethoven St., Binghamton) was supposed to be the inspiration for the "Walking Distance" episode of *The Twilight Zone*, written by Binghamton native Rod Serling.

Anheuser-Busch InBev—Baldwinsville Brewery

2885 Belgium Rd., Baldwinsville, NY 13027
(315) 635-4000 • www.anheuser-busch.com

Check out the address of the mammoth Anheuser-Busch InBev brewery just outside the village of Baldwinsville (near Syracuse). Yes, it is on Belgium Road. So you might think, "Wow, when the mighty InBev conglomerate of Leuven, Belgium, took over the world's largest brewer, they put their stamp on everything!" Well, not quite. The road (also known as State Route 31) was called Belgium Road long before there was even a brewery on the site. Moreover, it's hard to tell what impact the hostile takeover heard 'round the world has had on this plant, by far the biggest brewery in New York state.

The A-B InBev takeover in 2008 was the second major ownership change at this plant, which was built in 1976 as a Schlitz brewery. Anheuser-Busch bought it in 1979, reopening it in the early 1980s as one of twelve A-B breweries in the United States. It still pumps out barrels of Budweiser and Bud Light, and Michelob ULTRA and Shock Top, not to mention huge quantities of drinks like Bacardi Silver, Bud Lime-A-Rita, and the Margaritaville line of "5 O'Clock Cocktails." You can see what the plant brews and sample the products, but only if you're there on a special invitation or a community event. The brewery does not allow tours, though it has banquet rooms and a bar where special guests are served.

The plant once had a workforce of more than 800, and came close to its 7-million-barrel annual capacity. That was in the 1990s. By 2013, employment had dropped to about 400, and the production was less than 6 million barrels. But some innovations have begun to stabilize the picture. One is a new 24-ounce canning line. Another was the runaway success of the Lime-A-Rita. "That one really took off," said Nick Mills, who took over as general manager of the Baldwinsville site in 2013, after serving several years as brewmaster.

Longtime veterans at the Baldwinsville brewery tout this plant's flexibility. It has typically been used for specialized packaging—it can do bottles

Beers brewed: About sixty products are made here, from Budweiser and Bud Light to a huge array of "flavored alcohol products" like Bacardi Silver.

The Pick: Shock Top is a great refresher, and Budweiser is an absolute go-to on a hot day at the ballpark or after mowing the lawn. But then nostalgia takes over: When I was at the University of Missouri, just 125 miles west of A-B HQ in St. Louis, I drank a lot of Busch. For me, it's the beer that tastes like college.

and cans in all shapes and sizes, and packages in various arrays, including mixed packs. From "aluminum bottles" to "plastic cans," they do it all. It was the last A-B brewery to make "beer balls," a party keg that is a plastic ball. It has also been used over the years to produce some of A-B's experimental or pilot brands, to see what might be the next big thing.

Another positive for this brewery is its access to an abundant supply of water. It has a direct pipeline from Lake Ontario, about thirty miles to the north. (Lake Ontario also once supplied a nearby Miller brewery that closed in the 1990s.) For a company that has breweries in drought-prone places like Los Angeles, that water line is a source of comfort.

All these are important because of fears following the InBev merger that the company might try to cut costs by closing breweries. A-B InBev pledged not to close any breweries during the term of its existing union contract, so the plants are safe through February 2014 (when the contract expires). The brewery has four 1,000-barrel brew kettles, and Mills said it is laid out for a good "front to back" production scheme. In other words, beer isn't being circulated throughout the brewery in roundabout fashion. It travels in more of a straight line. When you're making upward of six million barrels of beer, that's important.

Of course, many craft beer fans hated Anheuser-Busch, loathed InBev, and consequently, positively despise A-B InBev. As the world's largest purveyor of "fizzy yellow beer," it's an easy target. But I'll repeat here what's been said many times before. Some of the smartest and most skilled people in the beer business work for A-B InBev. They know how to make beer. When they make a Budweiser or Bud Light, it's because that's the beer they want to make, because it sells. They have the technical expertise to make a Bud from Baldwinsville taste just like one from St. Louis, Newark, or Houston, too. That takes brewing know-how.

And say what you want, for example, about a beer like Shock Top, A-B InBev's answer to Blue Moon and domestic Belgian-style wits. Step into the brewery, watch the process, smell the orange peel and coriander that goes into it, and you'll be impressed. Know that it's all controlled from computerized digital screens in a room that resembles NASA's Mission Control, and you might be more impressed. (Or maybe not.)

Anheuser-Busch InBev—Baldwinsville Brewery

Opened: The brewery opened in 1976 as a Schlitz brewery; A-B bought it in 1979 and In-Bev took over in 2008.

Type: National brewery.

Owner: Anheuser-Busch InBev. (Carlos Brito, CEO; Nick Mills, plant manager).

Brewmaster: Nick Offredi.

System: Four 1,000-barrel Pfaudler brew kettles (approximately 930-barrel batch-size each); more than 8 million barrels annual capacity.

Annual production: About 6 million barrels in 2013.

Note: Visits by appointment only. There are no regular tours at this facility.

Brewery Ommegang

COOPERSTOWN N.Y.

656 County Highway 33, Cooperstown, NY 13326
(607) 544-1800 • www.ommegang.com

From the quaint and historic village of Cooperstown, drive a few miles south, then make a left turn and cross a small river. Turn south again and proceed through the rolling countryside until you come to . . . Belgium? Well, not quite. But it's easy to see why you might be confused. You've reached Brewery Ommegang. It is a special place, a brewery like no other in New York state, and one that can generously be described as somewhat off the beaten track.

Brewery Ommegang has a special niche—traditional and innovative Belgian-style beers—and a special pedigree: It's owned by the respected Belgian beer company Duvel Moortgat. It also has a gorgeous rural location that makes it a destination for beer lovers. Want evidence? How about the fact that the annual Belgium Comes to Cooperstown (BCTC) beer festival each summer sells out online in a matter of hours—perhaps even minutes—each April 1. Few New York breweries enjoy such a solid reputation among beer connoisseurs.

The brewery got its start in 1997. Don Feinberg and Wendy Littlefield were a couple who fell in love with Belgium and its beers. They founded a Belgian import company, Vanburg & DeWulf, in Cooperstown in the 1980s. With financial assistance and practical aid from Belgian brewing companies like Duvel and Affligem, Feinberg and Littlefield founded Ommegang on a former hop field south of the village. They built its first building, the distinctive white farmhouse brewery with its central archway, and launched the first three beers: Ommegang Abbey Ale, Hennepin (a saison-style), and Rare Vos (a Brabant-style session beer).

At the time of Ommegang's founding, Duvel Moortgat was still family owned. A few years later, Duvel Moortgat went public and bought out all the partners in Brewery Ommegang, including Feinberg and Littlefield. Their legacy is strong, most notably in the way Ommegang's beers are marketed as pairings with food and in the lavish events that lure visitors to the brewery.

Beers brewed: Year-round: Ommegang Abbey Ale, Hennepin, Rare Vos, and Three Philosophers. Seasonals: Witte, BPA (Belgian-style pale ale), Gnomegang, Adoration, Fleur de Houblon, Art of Darkness, Iron Throne Blonde Ale, Take the Black Stout, and other limited releases.

Although Brewery Ommegang has grown in almost every conceivable way in the past few years—notably through a $13-million investment in buildings, equipment, and more—it's not aiming to get too big for its mission. That mission is to produce classic and innovative beers from what has always been labeled a "Belgian farmstead brewery," steeped in tradition. "What we're not going to do is change into an industrial brewery," said Simon Thorpe, the British-born CEO of Ommegang and its sister business, Duvel Moortgat USA, which imports such Belgian-made brands as Duvel, Maredsous, d'Achouffe, and Liefmans. "We still have a batch-brewing process, with a focus on quality."

Ommegang has increased its capacity to about 100,000 barrels a year, and expected to make about 40,000 barrels in 2013, Thorpe said. That's up from fewer than 5,000 barrels ten years ago. (Duvel Moortgat USA imports about 30,000 or so barrels of its Belgian brands.) It serves what Thorpe calls a "core" market of twelve urban areas, including major cities like New York, Boston, Chicago, Philadelphia, and Los Angeles. Like many Belgian brewers, Ommegang started out packaging most of its beer in bottles, though it has recently transitioned to a ratio of about 55 percent draft to 45 percent bottled.

The Pick: This is my best claim-to-fame moment as a beer writer (and possibly my only one). It's December 1997, and I'm in Cooperstown touring the not-yet-opened brewery with founders Don and Wendy. There's some Ommegang Abbey Ale, the brewery's flagship, sitting in an aging tank, their only beer at this point. Don pours off a little from the tank and lets me have a taste. Here's what I wrote: "Ommegang is 8.5 percent ABV by volume, lightly hopped, with notes of bitter orange and anise. Even a taste straight out of the cellaring tank—some weeks before the first batch was ready to ship—offered hints of the aromas and fruitiness to come. . . ." So there. I tasted and enjoyed the now world-renowned Ommegang before just about anyone.

To stay true to the Belgian tradition, a brewery like Ommegang must take things slowly and deliberately. It can't just crank out beer in a mechanized, industrial way. For example, Ommegang's beers are dosed with a little sugar at bottling, then aged for at least ten days at 80 degrees. This need for warm cellaring space led to one of the first expansion projects at the brewery in recent years. Without a dedicated warm-aging cellar, there would have been a big production bottleneck.

More visible is the visitors center that opened in 2010. It includes a charming cafe, complete with European-style long communal tables, a bar pouring Ommegang's beers and those from the Duvel–Maredsous–d'Achouffe–Liefmans portfolio, and of course, food. The food has a decidedly Belgian flavor: frites (fries) with various dipping sauces, crepes, waffles, sausages, and more. The gift shop sells beer, plus clothing and other mementoes from Ommegang and the rest of the

Duvel Moortgat USA line. Since the new café and visitors center opened, annual visitors to Brewery Ommegang have jumped from fifteen thousand a year to fifty thousand, Thorpe said. And the brewery's celebrated annual events, such as the above-mentioned BCTC, a Waffles and Puppets event, a Christmastime brewery visit by "Sint Niklaas," plus a hugely popular summer concert series, have put Ommegang on the map. Meanwhile, the brewery's original three beers were later joined by the year-round Witte and Three Philosophers (a quadrupel made with a dash of cherry Kriek); and the more recent Belgian Pale Ale, or BPA, a departure from classic Belgian styles.

To aid the creativity, the brewery brought on board some brewers whose jobs include experimentation and pilot batches. They've produced all sort of beers, from the *Brettanomyces*-influenced Ommegeddon Funkhouse Ale, to the rich Art of Darkness BPA, to a collaboration with d'Achouffe called Gnomegang. More specialties and one-offs are constantly under development. "All of our beers have always been Belgian-oriented, but we are experimenting more with what you might call not very Belgian-traditional ingredients and hop varieties," said head brewer Phil Leinhart, who came to Ommegang after working for Anheuser-Busch. "However, at the same time we are doing beers that are very traditional Belgian oriented." One of those, he noted, is Iron Throne Blonde Ale, planned as the first in a series of beers brewed to tie in with the HBO television series *Game of Thrones*.

Brewery Ommegang

Opened: 1997.

Type: Production brewery with on-premises cafe-pub.

Owners: Duvel Moortgat and Simon Thorpe (CEO of Duvel Moortgat USA).

Brewer: Phil Leinhart.

System: 40-barrel Falco-Steineker brewhouse.

Annual production: 40,000 barrels.

Distribution: National, primarily in major markets.

Hours: Noon to 5 p.m. daily.

Food: The pub specializes in Belgian food.

Parking: Yes.

Butternuts Beer & Ale

4021 New York 51, Garrattsville, NY 13342
(607) 263-5070
www.butternutsbeerandale.com

Chuck Williamson is a city boy who wanted to get away from it all and run a farmhouse-style brewery in the countryside. He certainly got away: The native of the New York City borough of Queens lives and operates a brewery in Garrattsville, a tiny bit of rural Upstate about fifteen minutes west of Cooperstown (which is itself not exactly a metropolis).

The brewery, Butternuts Beer & Ale, is housed in a faded yellow barn on an old farm (with a matching yellow farmhouse across the road). As for the farmhouse-style beers, they are going to have to wait until Williamson finishes building his beer empire in the Empire State. Whatever Williamson's original intent, Butternuts has become a robust production brewery, known for packaging its four core beers—a pale ale, a wheat, a milk stout, and an IPA—in cans. All are flavorful but easy-drinking, modest-strength session beers.

Williamson also owns the nearby Cooperstown Brewing Company (page 96) and operates a nanobrewery servicing a nearby golf course clubhouse. In 2013, he was deep into plans to build a 100-barrel production brewery in the town of Cobleskill, in the Mohawk Valley. The plan is to move the big production there and partner with other brewers in need of contract brewing space, while returning Butternuts "to the original concept—a small, farmhouse-style brewery," Williamson said. That means a place making the type of beers associated with the Belgian or French countrysides, like saisons or bières de garde. "We wanted a farmhouse brewery and we were uber geeks about it," Williamson said about the initial concept he and his former partner, Leo Bongiorno, came up with. "We wanted to do everything you could possibly do if you were in Belgium or France. We even considered being a cask-only brewery." Instead of cask-conditioned beers, they ended up with a canning line made by a company called Cask.

Beers brewed: Porkslap Pale Ale, Heinnieweisse Wheat, Moo Thunder Stout, Snapperhead IPA, draft one-offs, limited releases, and seasonals.

The Pick: It's hard to imagine a better fit for a weekend outing than grabbing a six-pack of Porkslap in cans and waiting to be refreshed.

Williamson and Bongiorno found themselves Upstate after having worked in the New York City beer industry for several years. Their experience included stints with the Long Island, Park Slope, and Typhoon companies. Then came Sept. 11, 2001, and their desire to get away from New York. They didn't intend to land quite so far away, but the cost of real estate closer to the big city was prohibitive. The company started on Sept. 12, 2002—a year and a day after 9/11—but they had to do a lot of physical work to the property. They didn't start brewing beer until 2005, and started sales in 2006. During that time, Williamson said, "Dale's Pale Ale [from Oskar Blues Brewery in Colorado] had broken through with craft beer in cans." It was still a relatively novel concept for the craft beer industry, but catching on; it was around the same time that Pennsylvania's Sly Fox Brewing Co. started a canning line. "We thought, 'Why not?'" Williamson said. "It's different. It will make a statement." They already had a lot of the marketing in hand, with farm- and animal-oriented beer names and bright graphics. "We didn't want to go too far against the grain," Williamson said. "We knew cans were going to be a battle. . . . But we felt if there was a beer that was approachable, with good flavor, it could transcend the beer geek and the novice customer. We hedged our bets and went in that direction."

The first Butternuts brew was Heinnieweisse, a German-style wheat, soon followed by Porkslap Pale Ale, whose name is partly a nod to their early days with Park Slope. Within a few years, they added Moo Thunder, a milk stout, and Snapperhead, an IPA. In 2008, they tried to get back to the farmhouse concept by planning to package some beers in 750-milliliter bottles, including a saison-style, under the side label Butternut Valley Farm. But the four canned beers, led by Porkslap, were more popular than they expected, so Williamson rolled with it. (Bongiorno left Butternuts in 2007.) "I never expected Porkslap to take off like it did," Williamson said. It now represents 60 percent of Butternuts' total production. The core Butternuts lineup is sold in fourteen states along the eastern seaboard. "We made beers that are fun to approach so the pretense wasn't there," Williamson said. "It's not a dumbed-down version of craft beer. It's a balanced and flavorful product that you can get used to drinking."

That doesn't mean Williamson won't push some limits with Butternuts beers. He has made some one-off draft beers, and started an imperial draft series called Brutus, with 9 percent ABV-plus versions of such styles as IPA, Scottish Ale, and Doppelbock. On the other side of the spectrum, Williamson will use the 10-gallon system at the nearby golf course to make, among other things, a "light" beer that will appeal to the golf crowd. "I don't want to bring in macro beers," said Williamson, who co-owns the golf course. "We can make our own."

The Butternuts brewery in Garrattsville has had a tasting room for two years, where you can sample its own beers and some of the brews it makes under contract, like Long Island's Spider Bite. If you're visiting and you get to the big yellow barn in the middle of nowhere, you've found it.

The big brewery planned for Cobleskill will let Williamson realize many of his long-held dreams: He'll have a nanobrewery, a packaging brewery, and two micros, one of which will be a farmhouse brewery. He, for one, is not worried about oversaturating the market. "Is there a ceiling?" he said. "There's a ceiling in every business. But beer seems to be something that you can say there just can't ever be enough."

Butternuts Beer & Ale

Opened: 2006.

Type: Production brewery in Garratsville; nanobrewpub on nearby golf course.

Owner and brewer: Chuck Williamson.

System: 14-barrel Pugsley system (open fermentation); a 10-gallon nanosystem at the nearby Butternut Valley Golf & Recreation Club; and a 100-barrel production in Cobleskill is in the planning stages.

Annual production: 8,000 barrels in 2012.

Distribution: Cans and some draft in fourteen eastern states.

Hours: Noon to 6 p.m. daily.

Parking: Yes.

Cooperstown Brewing Company

110 River St., Milford, NY 13807
(607) 286-9330 • www.facebook.com/
CooperstownBrewingCompany

If the Cooperstown Brewing Company did not exist, someone would surely have to invent it. You see, it may or may not be true that Abner Doubleday invented America's pastime in this charming village in the rolling hills where Otsego Lake feeds into the Susquehanna River. But since Cooperstown is home to the National Baseball Hall of Fame and Museum, it makes sense that beer—the beverage of baseball—comes along for the ride.

The Cooperstown Brewing Co., founded in 1995, makes no secret of its baseball connection, with beer names like Old Slugger Pale Ale, Nine Man Golden Ale, and Benchwarmer Porter. Its slightly risqué slogan is "Beer With Balls." It's also true that the brewery is not in the village of Cooperstown itself; it's about ten miles south in the town of Milford. That's because the village wasn't keen on hosting a manufacturing facility, even one that makes beer. No matter. Baseball is still the theme.

Original owner Stan Hall hung a portrait of Golden Era player Nap Lajoie on the tasting room wall when he opened the brewery. It's still there, even if Hall is not. A retired college administrator, Hall installed a 20-barrel system designed by British microbrewing pioneer Peter Austin and put together with the help of Alan Pugsley, of the Shipyard Brewing Company in Maine. (That team also helped create some other New York breweries, like Davidson Brothers Brewing Company in Glens Falls and Middle Ages Brewing Company in Syracuse.) Like all Austin systems, the brewery has a brick-lined kettle and open fermenters. It also uses Austin's signature Ringwood yeast.

But, sort of like the designated hitter and free agency in baseball, change is coming to Cooperstown Brewing Co. First, Hall sold the brewery in 2011 to Chuck Williamson, owner of nearby Butternuts Beer & Ale, about twelve miles away in Garrattsville (page 93). Why buy a brewery just down the road from the one you already own? "It's a

Beers Brewed: Old Slugger Pale Ale, Nine Man Golden Ale, Benchwarmer Porter, Pride of Milford (strong ale), and Backyard IPA.

The Pick: Cooperstown's beer has traditionally been soft and buttery, in an English style. The Pride of Milford is the epitome of that, but as a strong ale (7.7 percent) it can overcome whatever negative perceptions some people might have. In any case, Pride of Milford is a ruby-red, malt-accented, and flavorful beer.

match made in heaven," said Williamson, who also has a 10-gallon nanobrewery and plans for a separate 100-barrel production brewery. "The more I thought it through, the more it made sense."

In some ways, Butternuts and Cooperstown are the yin and yang of breweries. Cooperstown has become an on-premises retail success, selling the vast majority of beer at its own tasting room. Butternuts sells the bulk of its beer in outside markets, with "no retail to speak of," Williamson said. Furthermore, Cooperstown packages in bottles, while Butternuts packages in cans. On the flip side, the brewing equipment is similar (although Butternuts does not use the Ringwood yeast).

Now that he has Cooperstown in his portfolio, Williamson is making other changes. The Austin and Ringwood production meant that all the core beers are English-style, to a certain extent. Old Slugger was intended, way back in 1995, as a knock-off of Bass Ale. But in 2013, Williamson and brewer Wes Nick introduced a plan to switch out the predominantly English-style hops, like Fuggles and East Kent Goldings, and replace them with a more decidedly American hop regimen. In Nick's words, the "softer" English styles are giving way to more "aggressive" American ones. "Baseball is America's pastime, so the beers should have an American character," Williamson said. "That means American hops."

Over the years, the production schedule at Cooperstown led to a selection of year-round beers with no real seasonals. Williamson, at least in his initial stage of brewery ownership, is cutting back on the number of beers. The core beers now are Old Slugger, Nine Man, and Benchwarmer, which are also being gathered and packaged in a Hall of Fame Pack. The Pride of Milford, a strong ale, will stick around, as will the Backyard IPA. Williamson stopped production of the brewery's Strike Out Stout, since it was too similar to Benchwarmer.

The next step is maintaining or boosting the brewery's retail sales, while increasing production for the off-premises and out-of-town market. That's what prompted the rethinking of the Cooperstown beers. "In the '90s, you had these English ales, and people went for that to an extent," Williamson said. "Now you have hops, and the aggressive flavors and brewing styles. . . . For Cooperstown, it would be challenging just to stand by and not make changes."

Cooperstown Brewing Company

Opened: 1995.

Type: Production brewery.

Owner: Chuck Williamson.

Brewer: Wes Nick.

System: 20-barrel Peter Austin.

Annual production: 2,000 barrels in 2012; aiming for 5,000 in 2013.

Distribution: Bottles and kegs, primarily at the tasting room.

Hours: 10 a.m. to 6 p.m. Monday through Saturday, noon to 5:30 p.m. Sunday.

Parking: Yes.

Cortland Beer Company

16 Court St., Cortland, NY 13045
(607) 662-4389 • www.cortlandbeer.com

It's one minute to noon on a Saturday, and the line is already forming outside the Cortland Beer Company, located just off the city's charming Main Street. Brewer and co-owner Tom Scheffler opens up, and within seconds the tasting room is swamped. It seems Cortland, a small city on Interstate 81 between Syracuse and Binghamton, has built up a thirst.

Cortland Beer Co. began brewing its beers under contract at Butternuts Beer & Ale (page 93) in 2008, then opened the doors to its own shop in December 2010. Expansion came quickly, with a sleek new tasting room in an old shoe repair building opening within a year. Awards came, too: Cortland's Flight Level 410, a 10-percent ABV barleywine-style ale, won a prize at TAP New York in its first year (and that wasn't even the bourbon barrel-aged version). "We just keep pushing," said co-owner Dan Cleary, who handles marketing, business, and most of the other aspects of the brewery aside from the brewing.

Cleary's response to the explosion in the number of breweries in New York state—and especially in the nearby Finger Lakes region—is to keep on its course. "Obviously, it's great to see all those breweries, but on the other hand that means you've got to fight for shelf space and tap handles," he said. "So we'll keep being aggressive." For Cortland Beer Co., that means securing as much trade in Cortland as possible, while expanding its reach around other parts of the state. Cortland Beer is on tap at most area bars, about forty tap handles in early 2013. Much of that has to do with local pride and loyalty. "It definitely helps being local," Cleary, who came from Buffalo to attend the local university, said. "We don't have to fight to get into local bars."

Cortland the city is perhaps best known today as the home of SUNY Cortland, a state university

Beers brewed: Naked Lap Lager, Firehouse Pale Ale, Red Dragon Ale, Industrial IPA, Seven Valley Stout, Sunrise Coffee Stout, Heffer Weizen, Pumpkin Ale, Black Widow Stout, and Flight Level 410 (barleywine).

The Pick: I'm a big fan of breweries that do a lot of stouts and porters, and Cortland does these well. But who am I to argue with the Flight 410? It has an aroma of toffee and a sweetish taste combined with a nice modest bitterness.

campus, and as the summer home of the New York Jets. (You may have seen the city in the edition of HBO's *Hard Knocks*, set at the Jets' training camp in 2010.) Aside from the Jets' presence each August, it also boasts theater, music events, festivals, and a connection to the nearby Finger Lakes wine region to boost traffic in the summer. The college helps carry it through the rest of the year. "Cortland does well," Cleary said again, "but we need to grow beyond that. Cortland alone won't sustain us."

Cortland's beers are now distributed, in draft and 22-ounce bottles, in Syracuse and Binghamton, and elsewhere in Central New York state and the Southern Tier. The beers are an eclectic mix, including some solid but not over-the-top beers like a red ale, a lager, and an IPA. Cortland also offers a bunch of stouts, like the milky Seven Valley Stout and the buzz-worthy Sunrise Coffee Stout. The Flight 410, at 10 percent ABV, is alternately called a barleywine-style or an old ale. Some of it is aged in bourbon barrels, which definitely gives it an over-the-top character. They also barrel age some of the Red Dragon Red—named for the SUNY Cortland mascot—to give it some smokiness. "We know we can make good beer," Cleary sad. "We just need to get it out into the market so people can appreciate it."

Cortland Beer Company

Opened: December 2010.
Type: Production brewery.
Owners: Dan Cleary and Tom Scheffler.
Brewer: Tom Scheffler.
System: 20-barrel brewhouse.
Annual production: 1,000 barrels.
Distribution: Draft and 22-ounce bottles, throughout Central New York.
Hours: 2 p.m. to 8 p.m. Tuesday to Thursday; noon to 8 p.m. Friday and Saturday.
Parking: No off-street parking.

Council Rock Brewery

4861 State Highway 28, Cooperstown, NY 13326
(607) 643-3016 • www.councilrockbrewery.com

They say those who can't do, teach. In the case of Council Rock Brewery in Cooperstown, those who teach, brew. In fact, Roger Davidson and his wife, Maureen, prove once again that the old adage is completely wrong: These very capable teachers figured out how to build and run a brewpub with no prior experience.

Oh, and Roger Davidson learned about beer from his college-age son. "My son was home one day and he said, 'Dad, I think we ought to make some beer,'" Davidson said. "And I thought, 'Why? I don't even like beer.'" But Davidson had never really tasted craft or homebrewed beer. It was, as they say, a revelation. "My reaction was, 'Holy Cow!'" Davidson said. "And it built a good father-son relationship."

Like a lot of homebrewers, Roger began with extract, moved to all grain, and then bumped it up from 5 gallons to 10 gallons at a time. "Needless to say, with 10 gallons, you're giving a lot away," Davidson said. "People liked it. So I thought, 'We should be selling this.'"

Nine year after his first homebrew, in May 2012, Davidson opened Council Rock a few miles south of the village of Cooperstown. The brewery is named for an Otsego Lake landmark, a rock located near the mouth of the Susquehanna River. This rock once was a traditional meeting place for local Native Americans. The brewery of the same name is located in a former rehabilitation center that has itself been rehabbed for a different use. It's on Route 28, which takes you from Cooperstown down to Cooperstown Brewing Company in Milford, and also leads toward Brewery Ommegang in one direction and Butternuts Beer & Ale in the other. "There's a real camaraderie here with all the breweries and the brewery staff," Davison said. "We're kind of in the middle of a beer triangle."

There is a Cooperstown Beverage Trail, which includes the local breweries, a winery, and a cider mill. In its first year, Council Rock was a "recommended" stop, just short of being a full-fledged member. Brewers and staff from the other places

Beers brewed: Goldenrod Ale, Vienna Lager, Sleeping Lion Red Ale, All American IPA, Leatherstocking Brown Ale, Wings of Darkness Black Lager, and Sunken Island Scotch Ale.

The Pick: The Sunken Island Scotch Ale certainly has a lot going for it. It was Council Rock's highest-alcohol beer on the day I stopped in for a tasting, but what really sold it was the combination of sweet and spicy tastes and full body.

often hang out at Council Rock, and Cooperstown head brewer Wes Nick has even made beer at Council Rock with Davidson. Their first brew was Wings of Darkness, a 4 percent ABV black lager.

Davidson works on a 3-barrel system, making 50-gallon batches. He thought about opening as a nanobrewery with a tasting room, but he and Maureen decided to go the brewpub route. "We thought it would be advantageous to sell beer by the pint," he said.

The kitchen serves pub fare, including burgers, chicken, and various sausages, from bratwurst to chorizo. The menu also includes "Council Rock's Remarkable Hot Dog," which is "a foot long and half pound" and is served with sauerkraut. And the garlic and pesto French fries have "built a real following," Maureen said.

Council Rock beer selections vary, but early on the Sunken Island Scotch Ale, a 9 percent ABV beer with notes of caramel, developed into a front runner for the flagship. Maureen Davidson calls it her favorite and said "people come in begging for the Scotch." Roger Davidson expected customers to lean toward his lightest beer, Goldenrod, a 4.5 ABV ale with a very dry finish. He has also been happy with the responses to his Leatherstocking Brown Ale, Sleeping Lion Red Ale, and All American IPA. "I'm not really an extreme beer guy," he said. "I think of the flavors I want, then build the beers to meet those flavors."

Council Rock Brewery

Opened: 2012.
Type: Brewpub.
Owners: Roger and Maureen Davidson.
Brewer: Roger Davidson.
System: 3-barrel brewhouse.
Annual production: 300 barrels.
Distribution: Pub-only, as of right now.
Hours: 11 a.m. to 10 p.m. daily.
Food: Pub menu
Parking: Yes.

Empire Brewing Company

empire
BREWING COMPANY

120 Walton St., Syracuse, NY 13202
(315) 475-2337 • www.empirebrew.com

This is probably what happens to all empires: founding, expansion, setbacks, regrouping, and more expansion. It's certainly the story of the Empire Brewing Company, which is well on its path toward conquest, if not of the world than at least of a nice chunk of New York state's beer industry. Empire is, first of all, a brewpub in Syracuse's Armory Square dining and nightlife district. Owner David Katleski is working on plans for a 60-barrel production brewery in the nearby village of Cazenovia. In the meantime, Empire is contracting to have some of its beers made at Greenpoint Beerworks/KelSo (page 221) for the New York City metro area market.

The move from brewpub to production brewery fits Katleski's current vision for his business. "I know that the beer and the brands have appeal outside the Empire [brewpub] walls," he said. But the road has been long, with some twists and turns. The Empire brewpub was started in 1994. Katleski and his then-partner, Mike Hodgdon, won instant success with their combination of eclectic food—with influences from Louisiana to the Pacific Rim—and quality beers. The place also lured in some innovative live music that otherwise passed Syracuse by.

Katleski and Hodgdon took that success on the road, first to Rochester's High Falls district and to then downtown Buffalo. But the Buffalo brewpub quickly foundered, and its closing rebounded back, first to Rochester and then to the Syracuse original. By 2003, all three were closed. After a couple of dark years with no Empire, Katleski returned to reopen the Syracuse brewpub in 2007. He immediately had a new focus: The brewpub would become a leader in local sourcing for food ingredients, beer ingredients, and even power. Empire was among the first companies in the state to operate on 100-percent New York-produced, renewable energy.

Check out the menu and you'll see a note citing the local produce, cheese, and more used in the

Beers brewed: Skinny Atlas Kolsch, Amber Ale, India Pale Ale, Hefe-Weizen, Scotch Ale, Barleywine, Wheat Wine, Smoked Porter, Saison, Golden Dragon, Instigator Doppelbock, many other limited releases, and seasonals.

The Pick: This is one of my hometown breweries, and I've had each of these beers too many times to count. So how am I supposed to pick? I'll go with the one that made my jaw drop on my first sip: the resinous 8.5 percent ABV Wheat Wine, which also has the attraction of being made with 100-percent New York hops and malt.

dishes. There's even a burger made from locally grown elk. The beer is also made with local ingredients, including hops grown on a farm that Katleski owns near his home in Cazenovia, a town just east of Syracuse. This farm will be home to the 60-barrel production brewery that could open as soon as the fall of 2014. It will be a true farm brewery, with hop yards and produce fields, and the design will incorporate the look of traditional hop houses. One of these areas will be devoted to drying and processing local hops.

In the meantime, brewmaster Tim Butler is making more than thirty different beers at the brewpub and overseeing the production of a couple others in Brooklyn. The two bestsellers are beers that have been served at Empire since the start. One is Skinny Atlas Kolsch, usually the lightest beer on tap, and named for Skaneateles Lake, the source of Syracuse's water supply. The other is Empire Amber Ale, a malt-accented pub ale. (The authentic banana-and-clove Hefe-Weizen is also a holdover from the first Empire era.) Butler has pushed forward with many different styles since then, including such varied releases as Local Grind, a Scotch made with locally roasted coffee; Liv and Let Rye, a peppery rye IPA; Golden Dragon, made with locally grown Thai basil; Roasted Pumpkin Ale, made with local pumpkins; Subterranean Ale, a cross between a Belgian farmhouse ale and a tripel; and White Aphro, made with wheat malt, lemon peel, ginger, and local lavender.

Katleski, meanwhile, is a busy guy. In addition to running the brewpub and planning the production brewery, he is the founder and president of the New York State Brewers Association. The group, about a decade old, had its most productive year ever in 2012 when it successfully lobbied the state government for some tax relief, an improved law regulating contracts with distributors, and the New York Farm Brewery law. That last bit is integral to Katleski's vision for the next stage in Empire's development. "We will be a true agricultural enterprise," he said, "growing food for the kitchen and ingredients for the beers."

Empire Brewing Company

Opened: Initial opening 1994 to 2003; reopened 2007.

Type: Brewpub with production brewery in development.

Owner: David Katleski.

Brewer: Tim Butler.

System: 7-barrel Pub Brewing Systems brewhouse.

Annual production: 1,200 barrels at the brewpub; another 3,000-plus under contract at KelSo/Greenpoint.

Distribution: The brewpub system primarily provides beer on-site; the contracted beers serve the New York metro area and about one hundred accounts in the central part of the state.

Hours: 11:30 a.m. to 10 p.m. Monday to Thursday; 11:30 a.m. to 11 p.m. Friday and Saturday; 11:30 a.m. to 9 p.m. Sunday.

Food: Round-the-world cuisine with locally sourced ingredients.

Parking: No off-street parking.

Good Nature Brewing

Brewery: 37 Milford St., Suite 3, Hamilton NY 13346
Tasting Room: 8 Broad St., Hamilton, NY 13346
(315) 824-2337 • www.goodnaturebrewing.com

You've heard of kicking a keg? On its first night in business, Good Nature Brewing almost kicked the whole brewery. Owners Carrie Blackmore and Matt Whalen went all-out from the start. "We were on a 62-gallon [2-barrel] system and we still started with five flagships," admits Whalen, who is also the brewer. "That was ambitious."

They launched the brewery one night in January 2012 with a tap takeover at the Colgate Inn, a place that, as you'll learn, has special meaning for Blackmore and Whalen. "We kicked one third of our inventory in just one night," Blackmore said. "We kicked everything we brought." By midsummer, they had installed a 7-barrel brewhouse and started to get things under a little more control.

The brewhouse, by the way, is powered by electricity, somewhat unusual in the brewing business. Whalen had to hunt down a company, Global Tanks, that would make an electric version. Why, you ask? It's because the village of Hamilton, Good Nature's home, has an electric cooperative, one of those relics of the mid-twentieth century program known as "rural electrification." Rural certainly seems at first glance to describe this village, surrounded by beautiful rolling hills dotted with dairy farms. But there's more to Hamilton than that. And that more is called Colgate University. It's not a big school, just three thousand students or so, but it is big in the affairs of Hamilton, which has a little more than four thousand residents. Many of the quaint, mostly red-bricked buildings in the village's downtown are owned by the university.

Then there's the historic (but not red-brick) Colgate Inn, which is owned by the university and managed by a private company that also operates several of Central New York state's finer

Beers brewed: Year-round: American Pale Ale, American Brown Ale, India Pale Ale, Good Natured Blonde, Chicory Mocha Porter, and The Nor'easter. Seasonals: Great Chocolate Train Wreck, Chamomile Honey Witte, and more.

The Pick: There's a back story to the Chocolate Train Wreck. It was named for a real accident, in 1955, in which a train full of Nestlé products derailed just a few hundred yards from where the brewery is now. The beer, of course, contains chocolate. But I was dazzled by the Chamomile Honey Witte, with its hints of herbs, bountiful honey flavor (it's not completely fermented away), and balance of barley and wheat. It's a beer that enables Whalen's background as a chef to shine through.

restaurants. Blackmore and Whalen decided to start a brewery while having a beer at the Colgate Inn's bar. A patron had come in and asked for a "local" beer. The closest the inn had at the time were from Ommegang (Cooperstown) and Saranac (Utica). Close, but not close enough for Blackmore and Whalen.

Whalen is a native of a Syracuse suburb (about forty miles west of Hamilton). Blackmore had family from Hamilton but grew up in the Bronx, returning to attend Colgate University. They met while teaching school in the Adirondacks, before Whalen went onto a career as a chef. Eventually, they settled in Hamilton. "We began looking for a way to do business that would keep us here," Blackmore said. To pay the rent, they renovated the house they were living in and they homebrewed. "Brewing was a way to heat the place up," Whalen said. Blackmore added that almost all of their beers were perfected in the house.

The name Good Nature came to Whalen while he was working in a garden. He and Blackmore now work to use as many local sources as possible for their ingredients. In Upstate New York, that's a little easier to do with hops than malt. Madison County, where Hamilton is located, was close to the heart of New York's historic pre–Prohibition hop region, at the time the largest in the country. (The county celebrates its heritage every year with the annual Madison County Hop Festival, which includes beer tastings, beer and food pairings, and tours of the old hop kilns that can still be seen in the countryside.) In Good Nature's first year, most of the hops they used came from nearby suppliers like Foothills Hops and Wrobel farms. Growth in the brewery's production, combined with a relatively bad year for hops in the northeast, reduced that percentage as they entered their second year.

Whalen and Blackmore hope to take advantage of the New York Farm Brewery Law, approved in 2012, to win some marketing advantages by using New York ingredients. Unlike some others, they don't plan to operate their own farm. "Our way of doing it will be to buy from local farmers," Whalen said. "It's a lot just to operate the brewery." They did take advantage of a provision in the farm law to open a separate tasting room, in the center of Hamilton at 8 Broad Street. That location, which also offers other New York products and sometimes live music, is closer to the college and easier for visitors to find. Looking ahead, Whalen said he could see them growing into perhaps a 30-barrel brewhouse with a small hop garden and maybe even a modest malting operation.

Spend some time talking to Whalen, and you'll discover a few things about him. One is his love of Black Fly Beer Camp, a get-together to talk beer and make beer, attended by representatives of some of

Upstate's craft breweries. It's held in early summer—black fly season—at Camp Sagamore, one of the region's great camps. You'll also learn that he loves to tinker and make things. That's the inspiration for his "bottling line." It's actually a few pieces of wood knocked together to hold hoses and clamps to bottle 22-ounce beers. It's portable, too. He'll bring it to the next Black Fly Beer Camp to bottle whatever the brewers there create. "That's what this thing is all about," Whalen said, gesturing to the bottling apparatus and the brewery. "Being creative."

Good Nature Brewing

Opened: 2012

Type: Production brewery with a separate tasting room.

Owners: Carrie Blackmore and Matt Whalen.

Brewer: Matt Whalen.

System: 7-barrel Global Tanks.

Annual production: 400 barrels.

Distribution: Primarily draft, with limited releases in 750-milliliter bottles to accounts in Madison County, the Syracuse area, and nearby parts of Central New York.

Hours: Tasting room: 2 p.m. to 10 p.m. Tuesday to Thursday; 2 p.m. to midnight Friday; noon to midnight Saturday.

Parking: No off-street parking.

Gordon Biersch Brewery Restaurant

Destiny USA Mall, 304 Hiawatha Blvd. West,
Syracuse, NY 13290
(315) 478-0990 • www.gordonbiersch.com

Dave Collins spent a few years brewing on the extract system at the Buffalo Brewpub. Now he fires up the gleaming, stainless steel brewhouse at the Gordon Biersch Brewery Restaurant in Syracuse. "It was kind of like going from the 1980 Gremlin, which I used to have, to a brand new Ferrari," Collins said. The owners of Gordon Biersch might have preferred a comparison to a German car, since the brewpub chain's calling card is its devotion to authentic German and European lagers brewed according to the Reinheitsgebot (beer purity law). No matter. This Gordon Biersch, the second in the state, is located inside the Destiny USA Mall, which is owned and operated by the Syracuse-based Pyramid Cos. (For the Buffalo location, also owned by Pyramid, see page 22.) The Syracuse Gordon Biersch opened in late 2012 as part of a major expansion of the mall's dining option, which also included additions of P.F. Changs, The Melting Pot, Cantina Laredo, and a Toby Keith's I Love This Bar and Grill.

Like all Gordon Biersch brewpubs, the standard brews are the light lager Golden Export, a traditional Bavarian Hefeweizen, a malty and mildly sweet Maerzen, a classic Czech Pilsner, and a roasty black schwarzbier. Seasonals are a WinterBock, Maibock, SommerBrau (a Kolsch), and an Oktoberfest. In its first year in Syracuse, marking the twenty-fifth anniversary of the first Gordon Biersch in Palo Alto, California, Collins added an anniversary seasonal, Blonde Bock, between the Maibock and the Sommerbrau. Like other Gordon Biersch brewmasters, Collins also makes Brewer's Select options a few times a year, when time and tank space permit. His first "selects" included a strong pale and a saison, and in his first summer he put out an India Pale Lager made with the Gordon Biersch house lager yeast. That beer allowed him to experiment with more hops than he'd typically used in the malt-oriented German lagers. "It's fun because I'm trying Crystal and Calypso hops, which I've never used," he said.

Beers brewed: Year-round: Golden Export, Hefeweizen, Schwartzbier, Czech Pilsner, and Maerzen. Seasonals: Maibock, SommerBrau (Kolsch), Oktoberfest, Winter-Bock, and some Brewer's Select specials.

The Pick: Malt-accented with a noteworthy hop bitterness, the best-selling Maerzen is indeed the epitome of a well-balanced beer.

"I know the oils [the bitterness levels], but I don't really know how it'll come out." Who says you can't take some risks at a chain brewpub?

The bestseller in Syracuse is the Maerzen, which is similar to the Oktoberfest but a little lighter and hoppier. Maerzens tend to be the bestsellers at most Gordon Biersch brewpubs. "It's a really well-balanced beer and there's something about it that everybody seems to like," said Collins, a Syracuse native.

The system that Collins brews on is a Specific Mechanical design, and the kettle is 15-barrels. The fermenters hold 30 barrels, so he typically brews twice for each batch. Traditional German brewing technique calls for a decoction mash, a more complicated procedure than the English-style infusion method that requires heating up portions of the mash and re-adding it to the tank. The Gordon Biersch brewhouse can achieve the same results, its brewers say, with a steam-jacket heated mash tun. "Our beers are pretty authentic to the German style, and they're made here so they're fresh," Collins said.

The Syracuse Gordon Biersch has found a niche in a city that already has a craft brewery (Middle Ages Brewing Company) and both an all-grain brewpub (Empire Brewing Company) and an extract brewpub (Syracuse Suds Factory).

Coming soon to the Destiny USA Mall and a location near the Gordon Biersch is a World of Beer franchise, part of a Tampa-based, beer-oriented chain that typically offers fifty beers on tap and five hundred or so bottled selections. Collins said he isn't worried about that competition; he even looks forward to stopping in. "It'll be a good place, I'm sure," he said. "It'll add to the beer education that will make us all better. But we make our beer here, and they don't."

Gordon Biersch Brewery Restaurant

Opened: 2012.

Type: Brewpub.

Owner: CraftWorks Restaurants & Breweries, Inc.

Brewer: Dave Collins.

System: 15-barrel Specific Mechanical brewhouse.

Annual production: 1,500 barrels.

Distribution: Mostly on-site at the brewpub.

Hours: 11 a.m. to 10 p.m. Sunday and Monday; 11 a.m. to 11 p.m. Tuesday to Thursday; 11 a.m. to midnight Friday and Saturday.

Food: Upscale, eclectic pub menu, with dishes from most world cultures and an emphasis on German specialties.

Parking: The mall has a huge parking lot.

Matt Brewing Company (Saranac)

811 Edward St., Utica, NY 13502
(315) 624-2480 • www.saranac.com

The Matt Brewing Company in Utica (makers of Saranac) turned 125 years old in 2013. You don't get to that ripe old age in the beer business by standing still. The second-oldest family owned brewing company in the United States has prospered while the vast majority of its one-time peers, the old regional domestic lager brewers, closed or were swallowed up (or vice versa). It takes vision, which the Matt family certainly has.

The critical moment came in the late 1980s, and is an oft-told story in craft beer circles. Matt was known then as the maker of Utica Club and Matt's Premium, two regional adjunct beers with steadily eroding sales. The company's president, F.X. Matt, the third-generation family member to run the brewery, realized something had to change. He recruited two family members—his brother, Nick, and his son, Fred—from their high-powered business careers in bigger cities to return to the family concern. Fred and Nick came because they wanted to help save the family business and keep the operation going for the good of Utica. They bounced around a lot of ideas, but the one that struck gold was an all-malt lager they called Saranac 1888. It was a throwback to the beers the Matt family, whose roots are in Germany's Black Forest region, made when they opened the brewery in 1888. "We like to say we imported that beer from history," said Nick Matt.

From that beer, still sold today as Saranac Adirondack Amber, they built an entire Saranac line, from the bestselling Pale Ale to Pomegranate Wheat, with many seasonals and specialty beers (the High Peaks series). "In the 1980s and '90s, we were getting clobbered by the nationals," said Nick, now the company's chairman (his brother died in 2001). "Now we're back to what our roots were, making full-bodied, really good beer. That's what saved us."

Beers brewed: Saranac Pale Ale, Pilsner, Adirondack Lager, Black & Tan, Season's Best (winter) and other seasonals, High Peaks series, and specialty beers included in seasonal twelve-packs, plus Utica Club (an old-school domestic lager).

The Pick: One of the earliest examples of a Christmas seasonal is Saranac Season's Best, a malt-rich nut brown lager. It's my go-to session beer for Christmas parties because of its malty sweetness combined with crisp finish. In a world of over-the-top Christmas beers, it's a refreshing alternative.

But here's where Matt Brewing Company secured its place in brewing history: While working to build their craft identity with Saranac, the Matt family realized they had quite of bit of unused capacity. This is a brewery, after all, that fires up two 500-barrel brew kettles. So they became the brewery-away-from-home for craft pioneers like Brooklyn Brewery and Harpoon, and incubated some of today's biggest craft beer names. You might say Matt Brewing is the cradle of East Coast craft brewing.

Now, contract brewing takes up about one third of the brewery's capacity. Brooklyn still makes a lot of beer here, with its brewers working on-site. Nick Matt said company policy is not to broadcast the identity of its other contract customers. Meanwhile, the old standby Utica Club is also still around at about 1 percent of total production. That leaves the ever-growing Saranac line. It has its own niche in the craft brewing world, too, hitting what some call "the big meaty middle." Fred Matt sums it up: "At the time we started [in the 1980s], brewers were all in this game to be the first to make water and call it beer," he said, citing the era of light beer, ice beer, and even light ice beer. Saranac caught an early wave of drinkers seeking bolder flavors. "What you get now is an over-reaction—who can blow my head off with the most hops," Fred said. "So it's like politics—the extremists get all of the attention, but the masses are sitting right here in the middle."

Saranac aims for the middle. Almost all of its beers are in the range of 5 or 6 percent ABV, and while some are malt-accented, others are hop-forward, and still more even have fruit and other flavors. They are not envelope-pushing extremists. "Our motto is distinctive and drinkable, and we really believe that's our thing," Fred said. They do make a beer series called High Peaks (the Adirondack Park is about forty-five minutes away, and much of their marketing imagery is tied to the mountains). It includes flavors like Chocolate Orange Porter and Lemon Ginger Saison "because we can," Nick said. And they're working on a pilot brewing system, about 3-barrels, that will allow more experimentation. "It's hard to experiment in a 500-barrel brew kettle," Nick said. Once Saranac had enough different beers in the lineup, back in the early '90s, it also kickstarted the trend of the mixed pack. Its earliest example was the Adirondack Trail Mix, followed later by summer and winter seasonal twelve-packs.

The brewery has surpassed 350,000 barrels a year in total production, and could be at 400,000 soon. That's still under the maximum capacity (perhaps 500,000 to 600,000 depending on the mix), but a lot closer than Nick and Fred ever dreamed. "If you go back ten years, the idea that we'd one day be out of capacity was unthinkable," Nick said.

"We made a lot of progress." That progress has meant a lot of physical changes to the plant, much of which dates back one hundred years or more. Oddly enough, the event that lit a fire under the renovations was, quite literally, a fire. In 2008, a fire damaged the packaging area, including bottlers, fillers, warehouse space, and more. Within a few years, Nick and Fred had replaced and expanded all that equipment, added a canning line, and built more storage and warehouse space. "In a funny sort of way, the fire changed a lot of things here because it gave us the capital to really start improving things," Nick Matt said. "We have continued on that path."

One of their big recent projects was the installation of an anaerobic digester that will clean the brewery's wastewater and generate a big share of its energy. That's an achievement for such an old and sprawling brewery. "To take this monstrosity—and I say that lovingly—and make it something environmentally friendly . . . that's pretty cool," Fred said. And while the brewery itself is something of a phoenix rising out the ashes, so is its surrounding neighborhood. The brewery complex has always made for a great tour, with its old red brick buildings and behind-the-scenes glimpses at the brewing process, ending in the splendidly old school Victorian tavern where you can try some samples (before heading to the charming gift shop).

Saranac also hosts the annual Boilermaker Run road race, which attracts thousands to Utica each June; and a series of Thursday night music concerts, featuring some big-time acts like moe. and Lucinda Williams. All this has helped launch a new generation of shops, restaurants, and bars in the immediate vicinity, particularly on Varick Street, which runs alongside the brewery (see Nail Creek Pub & Brewery, page 116) "We may have helped," Fred Matt admitted. "But really, this is just the American entrepreneurial spirit at work. It's nice to see."

Matt Brewing Company (Saranac)

Opened: 1888; reorganized as Saranac in the 1980s.

Type: Regional brewery.

Owners: Nick Matt (chairman) and Fred Matt (president).

Brewer: Jim Kuhr.

System: 500-barrel central Copperworks brewhouse

Annual production: Approximately 350,000 barrels in 2012.

Hours: Call for tour appointments.

Parking: Off-street lot adjacent to tour center.

Middle Ages Brewing Company

BREWING COMPANY
SYRACUSE, NEW YORK

120 Wilkinson St., Syracuse, NY 13204
(315) 476-4250 • www.middleagesbrewing.com

You've heard of the tortoise and the hare, right? Think of Middle Ages Brewing Company as that tortoise. Not flashy. Not fast. But a winner in the end. Middle Ages has steadily—and I mean steadily—built a strong and loyal following in the Syracuse area since 1995. They didn't try to grow too big too fast. "I always wanted to be the best brewery in Syracuse," said Marc Rubenstein, who opened the brewery with his wife, Mary, in 1995. "I didn't need to be the biggest or the best in thirty states." That's the personality of Marc and Mary Rubenstein, who were nearing their own middle ages (or so they thought) when they opened the brewing company in a former ice cream plant on Syracuse's near-west side. It's an old industrial area that the city and nearby Syracuse University are trying to restore as The Salt District.

The brewery name was meant to conjure up images from the movie *Monty Python and the Holy Grail*, one of the Rubensteins' favorite flicks. That's where they came up with beer names like Grail Ale, Wizard's Winter Ale, and Beast Bitter. To complement that idea, they installed the very British Peter Austin brewery system, with its open fermenters and Yorkshire-born Ringwood yeast.

Most of the beers are still basically in the British style. Middle Ages even does an annual day-after-Christmas beer called Boxing Day Bitter. Yet using the British yeast, they've also made a Belgian-style wit called Swallow Wit and a Belgian-style tripel called Tripel Crown. Most notably, they've got some butt-kicking American beers like ImPaled Ale (an IPA), and Wailing Wench (a double IPA). The ImPaled Ale represents the point in their race—their history—when they started to put a move on the hares of the world. Before then, their beers were nice, with good malt character (Grail Ale), or just a nice hint of hops (Beast Bitter). ImPaled Ale brought a whole new level of hopping,

Beers brewed: Grail Ale, Syracuse Pale Ale, Duke of Winship Scotch Porter, Black Heart Stout, ImPaled Ale, Wailing Wench, Swallow Wit, Old Marcus, Dragonslayer Imperial Stout, Beast Bitter, Druid Fluid (barleywine), and other limited or occasional releases, including a new anniversary ale every year.

The Pick: I lean toward the most English of their English-style ales, the Old Marcus, which Rubenstein originally billed as a "Yorkshire bitter." On cask, it's a trip to a genuine British pub.

although always with a balanced malt underpinning. It turned out Syracuse was a hop kind of town. ImPaled Ale became Middle Ages' bestseller. "I had to be convinced to put that [IPA] in bottles, but boy was it the right thing to do," Rubenstein said. A few years later, the ImPaled was followed by the double IPA called Wailing Wench, which became something of a cult favorite.

Middle Ages makes more than twenty beers, both regular and seasonals, and usually brings out one new offering each year, tapped in conjunction with the brewery's anniversary party, held outdoors at a neighboring city park. As part of its British tradition, Middle Ages also does real ale, cask-conditioned versions of most of its beers for specialty bars, like Syracuse's Blue Tusk and Rochester's Old Toad.

Mary Rubenstein is the company president. In that spirit, the brewery has proudly trumpeted another tidbit of the Middle Ages—the brewster. That's what they called female brewers back in the days when women made most of the beer. The brewery's growlers have the words "Brewster's Jug Ale" on the label.

For most of its history, you'd be hard-pressed to find Middle Ages beers much outside the Syracuse area, except for its deals with the expanding Syracuse-based chain of Dinosaur Bar-B-Que restaurants, in places like Harlem and Newark. The Rubensteins' son, Isaac, has now joined the company and is bringing in new ideas, including opening the tasting room on Sundays and expanding sales beyond the core market of Central New York—maybe even going all the way to Ithaca or Buffalo.

Marc Rubenstein, meanwhile, recently turned over most of the brewing chores to his head brewer, Jess Reaves. "I don't brew as much but I still mash-in, in the morning," he said. "I love to be in the brewery in the morning, open the doors, get some coffee, and go to work."

Middle Ages Brewing Company

Opened: 1995.

Type: Production brewery.

Owners: Mary and Marc Rubenstein.

Brewer: Jess Reaves.

System: 30-barrel Peter Austin brewhouse.

Annual production: 5,000 barrels

Distribution: About 65 percent draft, with some 12-ounce and 22-ounce bottles; mostly in Central New York.

Hours: 11:30 a.m. to 6 p.m. Monday to Friday; 11:30 a.m. to 5 p.m. Saturday; noon to 5 p.m. Sunday.

Parking: Limited off-street parking.

Nail Creek Pub & Brewery

720 Varick St., Utica, NY 13502
(315) 793-7593 • www.nailcreekpub.com

To say that Nail Creek Pub & Brewery lies in the shadow of the Matt Brewing Company (Saranac) is not an exaggeration. It's just simply true. You could throw a pint glass from the Nail Creek's porch (though I wouldn't recommend it) and have a good chance of it landing in front of the Saranac gift shop and visitors center, a few steps down Varick Street in Utica. It's a large shadow, too, when you consider that Saranac brews on two 500-barrel kettles and Nail Creek uses a 3.5-barrel converted homebrew system.

Walk into the Nail Creek bar and you'll immediately spot the tap for Matt's mainstream domestic lager, Utica Club, on the far left. The rest of the taps are an interesting array of craft beers. On my visit, they included three Saranacs, a Brooklyn Brewers Reserve, Victory Hop Devil, Ommegang Rare Vos, and Rogue Hazelnut Brown, among others. Check out the taps dedicated to the house brews produced by owner Chris Talgo and brewer Chris Kogut, and you'll see Nail Creek stepping clearly out of the shadow. Chances are you'll find Belgian- or English-style beers, usually high gravity and tending to the malty side. The Nail Creek house beers are intended to complement the other beers on tap, not repeat them. The first beers Kogut made for the pub give you a pretty good idea of the types of brews he like to make: Breakfast Stout, a rich, hearty, coffee-infused heavyweight; and an 8 percent ABV Belgian Dubbel. "If you can't brew big, you might as well brew interesting," Kogut said.

There's another expression they use at Nail Creek, one you hear frequently from Chris Talgo: "Classy, not fancy." Nail Creek is a comfortable saloon that opened in 2010, built in what Kogut and Talgo swear was a crackhouse on a rundown strip just a few years ago. Today, Varick Street is awash in bars and restaurants, in a revitalized neighborhood. The Nail Creek folks give Saranac and its busy public events schedule credit for much of the turnaround. "I went to the Saranac Thursday concerts [a summer music series], and that's how I found out about this place," Talgo

Beers brewed: Breakfast Stout, Belgian Dubbel, Sour House, and many Belgian- and English-style beers.

The Pick: The Breakfast Stout is my pick here. It may be that it was the first of the day for me (and it was barely after noon), but it went down well with a pair of pulled pork sliders.

said of the Nail Creek building. He also noticed that when Saranac workers left for the day, "they had no place around here to go and hang out." He decided to open a brewpub, even though many people warned him such a venture could not succeed in blue-collar Utica. "Yes, people did say we were crazy, especially when we talked about Belgian beers, sour beers, and that stuff," Talgo said.

Though both are Utica natives, Talgo and Kogut didn't know each other until Talgo posted a sign outside the still-under-construction pub, seeking a brewer. "I couldn't believe it," Kogut said. "I was around the corner, homebrewing and watching this place take shape. All of us [homebrewers] dream that one day we can do a brewery." Said Talgo: "I was still building this place, and Chris comes up and says he'd like to help. I wasn't sure . . . but he brought some of his beer, and it was delicious." Kogut also brought a mechanical sense to the brewhouse—he's an electrical contractor and custom-built the system using his old homebrew equipment as the base. He operates it with commands from his iPhone, and is exploring the idea of building tanks for himself and other brewers.

Talgo and Kogut think alike in terms of beer. "Neither of us are hop-heads, really," Kogut said. But they like to experiment, and Kogut has three French oak casks, each holding 90 gallons, a perfect fit for a 3- to 3.5-barrel system. Sour beers are something of a specialty, and Kogut is playing around with brett (sour yeasts) and lactic fermentation. Kogut is also hoping to start a growler-based bottling operation, and may one day move into a bigger brewhouse.

Can all that succeed in Utica, in the giant shadow of Saranac? "People are really responding to it," Kogut said. "Of course, the business is built on food and having a place to have a good conversation, not just the beer. That helps." Talgo and Kogut are proud to say that visitors to Saranac, along with the workers and even the owners, frequently stop in at Nail Creek. "We get a lot of people who come in here after touring Saranac," Kogut said. "They put on a helluva tour, and then we can offer them something different." Talgo said their big neighbors really want Nail Creek to succeed: "Their brewer has even offered advice. It's not like we're competition—they spill more beer in one day than we make in a year."

Nail Creek Pub & Brewery

Opened: 2010.
Type: Brewpub.
Owners: Chris and Tracey Talgo.
Brewer: Chris Kogut.
System: 3.5-barrel, custom-built.
Annual production: N/A.
Distribution: Brewpub only.
Hours: 11:30 a.m. to 2 a.m. Monday to Saturday.
Food: Full pub menu, served until 10 p.m.
Parking: Yes.

The North Brewery

110 Washington Ave., Endicott, NY 13760
(607) 785-0524 • www.northbrewery.com

Here's a story that will show you how The North Brewery in Endicott rolls. Zach Pedley and his father, Eric Pedley, decided to challenge each other to devise single-hop, single-malt beers. Eric Pedley made a beer called Perle of Pleasant Mountain, with only Perle hops and pale ale malt. Zach made a beer with New Zealand's Nelson Sauvin hops and Irish stout malt. Now, if this were a story about a father-and-son team of homebrewers (which they are), or about a father-and-son owned homebrew supply shop (which it has been), you might not think it all that unusual. But this is the philosophy they bring to the commercial production brewery they opened in Endicott in February 2013. "We have some beers that we'll have on most of the time, but our real goal is to constantly do new and interesting beers, across all styles, and variations on styles," Zach Pedley said. "If we could do a new beer every day, we would." Indeed, they made more than fifty different recipes in the first six months of operation.

The brewery opened in a space that had been the Pedley's homebrew supply shop for several years. The shop still exists, but as the brewery-grown Zach said, "We'll probably minimize the homebrew stuff." The shop is located in downtown Endicott, a small city just west of Binghamton that was once home to the Endicott-Johnson Shoe Company and the launching point for the company that became IBM. For much of 2013, the Pedleys and their associate, Joey Biscardi, brewed on a 1.5-barrel, 3-vessel brewhouse, with 2-barrel fermenters. Between double-batching and frequent brewing, Zach said they were making as much beer as a 7-barrel system. By the end of 2013, they hoped to install a new 3-barrel brewhouse, and

Beers brewed: A constantly rotating selection, including Blondie (pale ale), False Prophet (rye IPA), American Dream (East Coast IPA), Blood Wheat (cherry wheat), Toxic (black IPA), Black Donald (porter), Cerberus Prime (stout), Watershipdown (carrot and ginger IPA), Mesmerize (Double IPA), Warrior (old ale), Inspirational Beer Breakfast (hopped stout), and many more.

The Pick: A tough call, because I'd like to have tried a bunch of the beers they told me about but weren't available on my visit. The Mesmerize, a 9 percent ABV Double IPA, was loaded with Sorachi Ace and Simcoe hops, balanced by a healthy addition of Maris Otter malt for a big, bold, and pinewoods-aroma experience.

beyond that, either a bottling or canning line. For the guys at North, size doesn't seem to matter as much as the adventure in beer making. Their website identifies the two Pedleys and Biscardi as "Jedi Brew Mastas."

They sell much of their beer through the tasting room, where there are five beers on tap, but are building some off-premises accounts. One of those accounts is the kind of bar "that will take whatever our lightest beer is," Zach said, but the others will take what comes. "They know they're getting new beer all the time," he said. "That's how our [tasting room] customers are too. They come in and ask: 'What do you have today?' That works for us."

The lighter beers on the spectrum range from Blondie, a 5 percent ABV pale ale that is usually available, to the less-frequent 3 percent ABV saison. Much of the rest accelerates through the alcohol level and flavor profile, from False Prophet, a 6.7 percent ABV rye pale ale, to Cerberus Prime, a 7 percent ABV chocolate oatmeal stout. As with many of their beers, these often have variations: There's a bigger stout, called Cerberus Hellfire, at 10 percent ABV. There's another set of beers with the names Isareal Bitter (an English bitter), Wasareal Bitter (an English IPA), and Notareal Bitter (an Imperial IPA).

When asked if he likes to brew Belgian styles, Zach Pedley initially answered, "My favorite beers to brew are porters and stouts." Then he expanded: "I have Belgian styles, but we kind of resist classifications," he said. "We'd rather do styles, or start with a style, maybe a stout, and then play around and see where it goes." What you get, in that formula, are endless variations on a theme. At The North Brewery, you never know what you're going to get next.

The North Brewery

Opened: 2013.

Type: Production nanobrewery.

Owners: Eric and Zach Pedley.

Brewers: Eric Pedley, Zach Pedley, and Joey Biscardi.

System: 1.5-barrel Blichman; plans to install a 3-barrel brewhouse by late 2013.

Annual production: 500 barrels.

Distribution: Mostly growler sales through the tasting room; some off-premises accounts.

Hours: 3:30 p.m. to 7:30 p.m. Tuesday to Thursday; 3 p.m. to 9 p.m. Friday; 11 a.m. to 8 p.m. Saturday; noon to 5 p.m. Sunday.

Parking: No off-street parking.

Sackets Harbor Brewing Company

212 West Main St., Sackets Harbor,
New York 13685
(315) 646-2739 (BREW)
www.sacketsharborbrewpub.com

Tom Scozzafava has a theory about doing business: "You gather your acorns and your nuts and you put them away for the winter," he said. "If you don't, you can be in peril in a hurry." It seems an appropriate adage for a business—in this case, a brewpub—that operates on the frequently frosty shores of Lake Ontario in northern New York.

So it was that one of Scozzafava's first steps when he and his wife took control of Sackets Harbor Brewing Company in 2010 was to embrace winter. Instead of closing for extended periods in the winter months, as the pub used to do, Scozzafava and his wife, Pearl Ashcraft, decided to keep it open year round. "You can't run a restaurant if people are never sure if you're open or not," he said. "It's worked. We do good business year round."

In summer, of course, Sackets Harbor Brewing Co. takes full advantage of its position alongside the beautiful blue lake. In 2013, it built a major expansion of the deck. This is a waterside pub, and in Upstate New York the same factors (in this case the lake) that make winters so rigorous also make summers delightful. Inside, the brewpub is cozy, housed in a former New York Central Railroad depot that dates back to the mid-nineteenth century, when a young Ulysses S. Grant was stationed nearby. Now, Sackets Harbor Brewing Co. attracts the summertime-by-the-lake crowd as well as the snowmobile-and-winter-sports folks in the colder months.

Sackets Harbor is one of New York's oldest continuously operating brewpubs, dating back to 1995. It was originally owned by the Flynn family,

Beers brewed: Year-round: War of 1812 Amber Ale, Thousand Islands Pale Ale, Grant's Golden Ale, Saint Stephen's Stout, and Sunrise Pale Ale. Seasonals: Saison de Sackets, Ontario Oktoberfest, Munich Helles, Featherhammer Maibock, and many more, including limited releases such as the Revelations big beer series.

The Pick: I loved the Thousand Islands Pale Ale when it debuted as a crisp and citrusy classic American pale. On my visit, a warm and breezy day on the lake, I also really liked the Munich Helles, a traditionally biscuit malt-inflected German light lager, with classic Tettnang and Hallertau hops.

who also owned other properties in the Sackets Harbor and Watertown areas. The businesses had started to suffer and the brewpub was nearing foreclosure when Scozzafava took over, "but the Sackets Harbor brand was strong around here," said Scozzafava, who had a career in finance in New York City before returning to his northern New York home. "So there was some equity in the place and the brand that we want to build back up."

Surprisingly, Sackets Harbor remains, as of 2013, the only brewery or brewpub in the Thousand Islands region, a spectacularly beautiful area where the St. Lawrence River and Seaway opens into Lake Ontario. Besides the lake and the islands, Sackets Harbor has one other nearby asset: It's just west of the small city of Watertown, on whose northern edge you'll find Fort Drum, one of the country's largest army bases and home to the famed 10th Mountain Division. When it opened, the brewpub attracted a strong following among soldiers who had become accustomed to good beer overseas, especially German brews. "They're good guys and good supporters of us," Scozzafava said of the army crowd.

From the start, Sackets Harbor's beers were malt-oriented, perhaps from that German beer association. But brewer Andy Gersten, who started at Empire Brewing Company in Syracuse, has brought a much more varied approach in the years since he took over the brewhouse. Gersten operates a 7-barrel DME brewhouse, and production was up to 1,000 barrels in 2013. There are ten house-brewed beers on at any time, as well as a couple dozen that Gersten brews during the course of a year. In 2012, to demonstrate his creativity, Gersten launched a series called Revelations, with four beers based on the Four Horsemen of the Apocalypse. Each beer was based on the horses mentioned in the Bible—one black, one red, one brown, and one white. Black, for instance, was represented by Dark Horse IPA, a 7.1 percent ABV black IPA, brewed with pale and dark crystal malt and hopped with Galena, Warrior, and Columbus. The flagships remain War of 1812 Amber Ale— a naval battle took place in the harbor during that war—and the West Coast-hopped Thousand Islands Pale Ale. Rotating beers include the rich and malty Saint Stephen's Stout, a Maibock called Featherhammer, a session ale (4.9 percent ABV) called Barstool Bitters, and a cream ale called Grant's Golden Ale.

Both the 1812 Amber Ale and Thousand Islands Pale Ale have been brewed and packaged under contract for off-premises sales in the past, most recently by Genesee Brewing Company. But contract brewing ceased, at least temporarily, in 2012. Scozzafava is exploring the possibilities of resuming contract brewing or eventually opening the area's first production brewery. "We've got revenues on the right track and business is good," Scozzafava said. "So the future is looking up."

Sackets Harbor Brewing Company

Opened: 1995.
Type: Brewpub with off-premises production planned.
Owners: Tom Scozzafava and Pearl Ashcraft.
Brewer: Andy Gersten
System: 10-barrel DME brewhouse.
Annual production: 1,000 barrels.
Distribution: On-premises only.
Hours: 11:30 a.m. to 10 p.m. daily.
Food: Traditional to slightly upscale pub fare.
Parking: Yes.

Syracuse Suds Factory

320 S. Clinton St., Syracuse, NY 13202
(315) 471-2253 (AALE) • www.sudsfactory.com

Occupying one of the most prominent corners in Syracuse's Armory Square nightlife and entertainment district is the place that also brought brewing back to the city in 1993: Syracuse Suds Factory. Owner Al Smith actually started his brewpub a few blocks north of Armory Square, in a roomy red-brick downtown building. The second location, to which Smith moved in 1998, is also spacious, with its main bar and dining area, and side and backrooms. You don't get much closer to the heart of the Armory than this.

The brewing system is extract. It's a 7-barrel Pub Systems brewhouse, a little dinged here and there from its several moves, first from the defunct Chapter House brewery in Ithaca, and then from one spot in Syracuse to another. The original and longtime brewer at Suds was Norman Soine, an extremely smart and dedicated beer guy whom many homebrewers in town remember as being an ardent proponent of all-grain brewing. He had worked as a brewer at the Schlitz (later Anheuser-Busch) plant near Syracuse and at Matt Brewing Company (Saranac) in Utica. Yet Soine made the Suds system work to his liking, even though it was an extract system, and could often be seen in the brewhouse after hours from his regular job at a local candle company. If you asked him about beer and brewing, you'd better have had a few hours to spare. Soine died in 2011, and the Syracuse Suds Factory soldiered on, with Smith doing the brewing whenever he found himself short a brewer.

Beers brewed: Pale Ale, Irish Red, Weizen, Sweet Stout, Black Cherry Lambic, Honey Light Ale, Pale Ale, and Brown Ale.

Suds is a fully stocked bar, with lines dedicated to both mainstream and craft beers, plus a full liquor selection. (Its bartenders frequently win the mixed drink contests at the annual Syracuse Winterfest.) Smith acknowledges that his house brew may not suit all of his customers, and makes sure he has a beer for every taste. Suds is the sort of place that has something for everyone. That goes for the food, too. The chilis and chowders are

The Pick: Sentiment leads me to the Pale Ale, which once was made with the hops that the late brewer Norm Soine grew at his home. The Pale Ale is still a hop-accented beer, whatever their source.

exceptional, again winning Syracuse Winterfest awards with regularity. Suds is also home to a fine array of burgers and other pub fare, prime ribs specials, and the Friday fish fry. (Something you should know about Syracuse: The fish fry here is almost always haddock, not cod or catfish or any of the other fish you might find elsewhere.)

Smith has always been proud of the fact that Suds Factory returned brewing to the city—that's the city limits, so I don't count the Anheuser-Busch plant in nearby Baldwinsville. (Smith opened a second pub, Suds Factory River Grill, in Baldwinsville in 2012 under the shadow of the A-B plant, but this location does not brew its own beer.) Syracuse, particularly its north side, had once been home to dozens of breweries, back in the late 1800s up until Prohibition. Most were German, with the odd English- or Irish-owned brewery thrown in (with names like Greenways and Moore & Quinn). The last old-time brewery, Haberle Congress, closed in 1962. The Suds beer lineup reflects those traditions. The bestsellers, Smith said, are the hop-accented Pale Ale and the malt-forward Irish Red.

Syracuse Suds Factory

Opened: 1993; moved to its current location in 1998.

Type: Brewpub.

Owner: Al Smith.

Brewers: Matt Benjamin and Evan Wayton.

System: 7-barrel Pub Brewing Systems brewhouse.

Annual production: About 300 barrels.

Distribution: House brews are sold here and at Suds Factory River Grill in Baldwinsville.

Hours: 10:30 a.m. to midnight Monday to Saturday; noon to close Sunday.

Food: Full menu, from pub fare to more upscale entrées.

Parking: No off-street parking.

Water Street Brewing Company

168 Water St., Binghamton, NY 13901
(607) 217-4546 • www.waterstreetbrewingco.com

After the short-lived Parlor City Brewing Co. went out of business in the late 1990s, it took more than ten years for Binghamton, the leading city in New York's "Southern Tier" region, to land another craft brewery. Several were in the pipeline by 2011, but Water Street Brewing Company got there first, opening as a downtown brewpub that March. John Bleichert brought an electrical engineering background to the project, while his wife, Michele, brought business savvy. They were precise in what they wanted their brewpub to be. No TVs. "We don't even have one at home," John Bleichert said. "We read." No chicken wings. "Never while we own the place," he said. And no beers that knock you over with hops. "I'm not a hophead," he said.

Is that a turnoff at Water Street? Not at all. This is a comfortable place, with creative food and interesting, mostly malt-forward beers. There is no table service: You order drinks at the bar and your food at the service station at one end, and pick up your food when the flashing pager says it's ready. "Here we keep it simple," John said. "People come in here to enjoy the beer and food, have a conversation, and even play games." Water Street's motto is "Fresh. Local. Uncomplicated."

John Bleichert grew up in Albany, went to school in Rochester, and got an electrical engineering job with IBM that took him to Binghamton. (IBM still has a presence in Binghamton, but its heyday as a major employer in town is long over.) The Bleicherts decided to open a brewery, and for business reasons chose to begin with a brewpub, saving the possibility of a production brewery for the future. "This is a business that has to pay the mortgage, and so far it does," John said. "Some people see this first as a brewery," he continued, "but we have to think of it first as a restaurant." As a restaurant, it puts an emphasis on local sourcing of ingredients—much of its produce and quite a bit of the meat come from local suppliers. The menu includes a large

Beers brewed: Muenchener Helles, Sweet Summer Rye, Weizenbock, Harvest Ale (a brown ale), IPA, Thousand Year Porter, 3BB (English ordinary bitter), and many others.

The Pick: The 3BB is everything you want in an English-style session bitter, only a little lighter in color. You could wile away long hours in the pub with this one.

number of vegetarian and vegan options, from a hummus sandwich, to a taco salad with a choice of soy crumbles, to a version of the Binghamton classic spiedie (a type of marinated meat sandwich) made with tempeh, a meat substitute.

John Bleichert is also interested in local sources for his beers, but within reason. He has no plans to apply for the state's new farm brewery license, saying he will use local ingredients when he can. On my visit, there was an English-style ordinary bitter called 3BB, made from malt produced by FarmHouse Malt in nearby Newark Valley, one of the first modern malting operations in the state. Malt is certainly the key to Bleichert's beers. A refreshing Muenchener Helles has a solid biscuit-malt character, and the Thousand Year Porter has a robust, roasted malt highlight. Even the beers you might expect to lean toward the hop side of the equation show off their malt. The Harvest Ale is an American Brown, with bitterness supplied by Northern Brewer hops, while the IPA is characterized as a "British-style" with a clearly identifiable malt balance.

Bleichert brews on a 7-barrel Premier system, and produced 300 barrels in 2012. He can do up to 600 barrels, but has only brewed for a few limited off-premises accounts. Most of his beer, a rotation of about twenty, is served straight from the serving tanks, which are visible across from the bar.

The Bleiciherts have been warmly received in Binghamton thus far, both by those seeking a comfortable pub dining atmosphere and by beer geeks, including the active local homebrewing club. Off-premises sales and potential production brewing are possibilities for the future, but it is in the Bleicherts' nature to be careful as they grow.

John Bleichert attributes Binghamton's long craft-brewery drought to the loss of population after big companies like IBM shed jobs. And it didn't help that Water Street and other potential craft brewers started the process in 2011, at a time when the city was besieged by some devastating floods along the Susquehanna and Chenango rivers, which run through or near downtown. "We helped bring this part of downtown back, and we're proud of that," John said. "We will grow, but it will be cautious growth. I'd rather be at maximum capacity before taking the next step. That's the way we are."

Water Street Brewing Company

Opened: 2011.

Type: Brewpub.

Owners: John and Michele Bleichert.

Brewer: John Bleichert.

System: 7-barrel Premier Stainless system.

Annual production: More than 300 barrels.

Distribution: Almost exclusively at the brewpub; limited off-premises accounts.

Hours: 4 p.m. to 11 p.m. Tuesday to Thursday; noon to midnight Friday and Saturday; noon to 7 p.m. Sunday.

Food: Full, eclectic menu with many vegetarian offerings.

Parking: There's a big parking garage across the street.

Brewpubs, Microbreweries, Nanobreweries, and Craft Breweries

When the new brewing movement started in America in the 1970s, no one knew what to call these little breweries. "Brewery pub," "boutique brewery," and "microbrewery" were all terms used. By the early 1980s, two words had settled into general use: microbrewery and brewpub.

At the time, the industry's pundits defined a brewpub as a brewery that sold most of its beer in an in-house taproom. They defined a microbrewery as a brewery that produced under 15,000 barrels a year. These terms gained legal recognition in some states, as deals were struck to allow the new businesses to start up and as tax rates were determined. The federal government acknowledged the special nature of small breweries in the early 1990s, granting a substantial tax break to those with an annual production under 50,000 barrels.

Eventually the industry itself came up with a whole set of labels. "Brewpub" continued to be used for breweries that sold the large majority of their beer on-premises by the glass. "Microbrewery" referred to packaging breweries whose production was less than 50,000 barrels. "Regional" brewery applied to smaller breweries established before 1970 that did not distribute to all of America. Nationally distributing giants like Anheuser-Busch, Miller, and Coors were dubbed "national brewers" or "megabrewers."

But the growth of some successful microbreweries has made even 50,000 barrels an uncomfortable fit. Southern Tier Brewing Company in Lakewood, for example, will produce more than 70,000 barrels in 2013, and Blue Point Brewing Company on Long Island will top 60,000 barrels, yet many people might still think of them as microbreweries. Nationally, many micros, like Sam Adams, are larger. Clearly some of these are no longer microbreweries, yet their beer is exactly the same as it was. To be called a microbrewery has a cachet to it—implying that it's not mass-market beer—that most microbrewers don't want to surrender. And then there are the really small "nano" breweries that are exploding on the scene.

What to call these varied breweries? The term you hear more often these days is "craft brewery." This implies that the beer is somehow crafted rather than produced in a factory. Craft breweries are different, the brewers explain, because the beer is made in single batches, not in several that are then combined in one huge tank or blended after fermentation to ensure consistency.

Putting a label on a brewery these days is not as easy as putting a label on a bottle. For example, what do you call a place like Matt Brewing Company (Saranac), a regional brewery that brews the very mainstream Utica Club, a dying line dwarfed by the company's powerfully delicious and varied Saranac line of beers? Brooklyn Brewery has their bottled beers brewed up at Matt's, but they also put a lot of beer out of their own brewery in Brooklyn. Then there's CB Craft Brewers in Honeoye Falls, where most of the beers they produce are made for other companies . . . and then sold in their own tasting room as well. These breweries aren't readily pigeonholed. The fact is, microbrewery has always been a code word, as has craft brewery, but they mean the same thing. Both describe a brewery that makes beer in an authentic manner—using ingredients and techniques appropriate to a given style of beer or brewing—and that brews beers other than mainstream American-style lager.

The Boulder, Colorado-based Brewers Association (www.brewers association.org), representing more than one thousand mostly "craft" brewers, has come up with a definition built around the words "small, independent, and traditional." They define small as producing fewer than 6 million barrels per year (which covers most of the breweries in this book). Independent breweries can't be more than 25 percent owned by a non-craft brewer. Traditional means that either the brewery's flagship beer, or at least 50 percent of its total production, must be all malt (no adjunct grains).

So that's a start. You can call them craft breweries or you can call them microbreweries. Or you simply call them breweries. To differentiate a brewery based on the kind of beer it makes seems to be missing the point. Categorizing them by size penalizes the ones that succeed and outgrow the class. Call them breweries, and then let the beer do the talking.

In this book, you'll see that we categorize most of the breweries as either a brewpub or a production brewery. In this sense, production brewery sells most of its beer off-premises, while a brewpub sells most of its beer on-site. As you'll discover, with many companies doing a lot of both, those lines are getting blurred, too.

Albany Capital Region —Adirondacks

This is two regions joined as one, but you could argue they are connected by Interstate 87, the Adirondack Northway.

Let's start with Albany, a city founded by the Dutch back in the seventeenth century. In the immortal words of a character in *His Girl Friday*, a classic film in the genre known as screwball comedy, "They've got the state capitol up there." The skyline is dominated by the historic state capitol building and the towering state government office buildings built in the 1960s by former governor Nelson Rockefeller. (Hence the name "Rocky's Rockpile.") And don't forget The Egg, a state-operated entertainment center shaped like—you guessed it— an egg.

But Albany is just one of several cities clustered in the capital region. There's Troy, located across the Hudson River, a former industrial city (where they used to make shirt collars, of all things) that has seen a bit of a downtown resurgence in recent years. And Schenectady, founded by the Dutch even earlier than Albany, was a long-time hub for General Electric.

A little to the north is Saratoga Springs, a.k.a. "The Spa," a haven for sporting types and pleasure seekers for more than a century, and home to the famed Saratoga Thoroughbred Race Course. Keep heading north and you'll reach Glens Falls, a little city just outside the Adirondack Park's "blue line" boundary. And then you get to the 'dacks. Be prepared for incredible views of pristine lakes and mountains. Also be prepared, depending on the season, for black flies and mosquitoes. Not to mention bears and occasional moose.

The Adirondacks are protected by the state constitution as "forever wild," which means regulations that chafe at some residents and business owners. That's not to say there hasn't been development. A big boost came in 1980, the second (and last) time Lake Placid hosted the Olympic Winter games. (You may recall that Olympics—Eric Heiden won five speed-skating medals and the United States Men's Hockey team scored a little "miracle" by beating the Soviets and winning the gold medal.) If you're fit, the best way to see the Adirondacks is by climbing a mountain. There are 46 of them, with summits over 4,000 feet: That's why the people who make it to the top of all of them are called "46ers." But there are plenty of less rigorous—yet still spectacular—hikes throughout the region.

Beyond the capital region and the Adirondacks is the region of Lake Champlain, which serves as the border with Vermont and leads, at the top, to the French-speaking province of Quebec. It's good beer territory, especially if you've built up a thirst by climbing an Adirondack high peak.

Other breweries and brewing companies

In Plattsburgh, the brewpub formerly known as Bootleggers and more recently as Legends was transitioning to a new company called Plattsburgh Brewing Co. Several small breweries were on track to open sometime in late 2013: BarkEater Craft Brewery (www.barkeaterbrewingcom) in Lowville, west of the Adirondack Park; St. Lawrence Brewing Co. (www.stlawrencebrewing.com) in the far northern college town of Canton; and Paradox Brewery (www.paradoxbrewery.com) in Schroon Lake.

Other beer sites

The Bier Abbey (613 Union St., Schenectady) has a chalkboard full of choices, many of them Belgian. Stop by the English-accented Man of Kent (4452 State Route NY 7 in Hoosick Falls, east of Troy). Mahar's Public House (14 S. Main St. in Castleton-on-Hudson, south of Albany) has a wide array of draft beer (a sister pub in Albany has closed). Wolff's Bier Garten (895 Broadway) and The Olde English Pub & Pantry (683 Broadway), both located in downtown Albany, specialize in German and British beers respectively. Also stop by Liquids and Solids at the Handlebar (6115 Sentinel Rd., Lake Placid).

Area Attractions

Tours are available of the ***State Capitol*** (State St., Albany, NY 12230; 518-474-2418; www.assembly.state.ny.us/Tour). The ***New York State***

Museum (222 Madison Ave., Albany, NY 12230; 518-474-5877; www.nysm .nysed.gov/information/general/) has exhibits preserving the Empire State's legacy, from art to history to environmental artifacts.

The racing season at the *Saratoga Race Course* (267 Union Ave., Saratoga Springs, NY 12866; 518-584-6200; www.nyra.com/saratoga) lasts from late July to Labor Day. Be sure to also check out the *National Thoroughbred Hall of Fame* (191 Union Ave., Saratoga Springs, NY 12866; 518-584-0400; www.racingmuseum.org). "Taste the waters" at *The springs of Saratoga Springs* or "take the waters" at the Roosevelt bath houses in Spa State Park. (518-584-2535; www.nysparks .com/parks/saratogaspa).

For a taste of local history, explore the *Saratoga National Battlefield* (648 Route 32, Stillwater, NY 12170; 518-664-9821 ext. 224; www.nps .gov/sara/index.htm), a turning point in the Revolutionary War. *The Fort William Henry Museum & Restoration* (48 Canada St., Lake George, NY 12845; 518-668-5471; www.fwhmuseum.com) is a living history museum and restoration dedicated to the French and Indian War. The *Stockade Historic District* (www.historicstockade.com), located in Schenectady, is the oldest residential district in the United States, with more than forty homes that are over two hundred years old.

Lake Placid Olympic Sites (www.whiteface.com/facilities) is home to Olympic history, from the downhill slopes of Whiteface Mountain, to the bobsled run at Mt. Van Hoevenberg, to the ice where "USA, USA" defeated the Russians. The *Adirondack Museum* (9097 State Route 30, Blue Mountain Lake, NY 12812; 518-352-7311; www.adkmuseum.org) explores the heritage and history of the Adirondack region. Or drive the mountain roads of *The Adirondacks* (www.adirondack.net/hiking), where you can't miss the trailheads that take you to the top of peaks or just across the rugged landscape.

Adirondack Brewery and Pub

33 Canada St., Lake George, NY 12845
(518) 668-0002 • www.adkpub.com

The Adirondack Brewery and Pub in the southern Adirondack town of Lake George used to close for weeks at a time in the winter. Not anymore. "Beer season is all the time," said owner John Carr.

Carr is a nonstop beer guy. Watch him bound up the steps in the three-level packaging brewhouse he installed in 2010 (behind the brewpub he opened in 1999), and you'll sense the energy he brings to all things beer. "I just want beer that tastes good," he said. "Easy to drink. No machismo about it." He is adamant about several beer-related topics, and one of them is that as his business grew, he was going to keep everything in house. That's why he built the addition in 2010, with more tanks and a bigger bottling line. "I do not believe in contract brewing at all," he said. "If you're a brewer, you should brew it yourself. People need to know where it comes from." Walk into the pub on Canada Street, the lively main thoroughfare leading into the town of Lake George, and you'll immediately see both a greeting station for the bar and restaurant, and a gift shop where you can buy growlers, six-packs, and brewery merchandise. So is this place a pub or a packaging brewery? The answer is yes.

Beers brewed: Bear Naked Ale, Bobcat Blonde Lager, Beaver Trail Brown Ale, Adirondack IPA, Black Watch IPA, Dortmunder, Black Rye Saison, Dirty Blonde, seasonals, and brewer's specials.

Adirondack Brewery and Pub opened in 1999 and eventually made up to 2,000 barrels a year, with some off-premises accounts starting in 2000. Carr said he wants to get to a "comfortable" production of 15,000 barrels a year, even though his capacity is probably closer to 22,000. That has a lot to do with the 12-head bottler he installed in 2010. He'll still sell a lot of beer at the pub, which does a thriving growler takeout business along with the restaurant and bar service and the bottled beer sales. In 2013, Carr changed his registration to be a microbrewery, even though he operates a busy and successful brewpub in a

The Pick: I've had enough flights of brewpub beer to know that the first one on your left, the lightest offering, is almost never worth your time. Not here. The Bobcat is a real German-style light lager, refreshing with a malty character. At the other end of the spectrum, the Black Rye Saison is smoky and just a little intense.

tourist town. He anticipated half his sales to be at off-premises accounts by 2014. The beers are already in more than half the counties of New York.

Carr throws himself into the brewing process with enthusiasm. He'll talk at length about his brewing water, which comes from Lake George—easily one of the most beautiful of the New York's many beautiful lakes—and needs no treatment, except for chlorine removal. The water resembles that of the Czech region of Pilsen.

Carr's brewery makes beer in all styles, but is especially adept at German and Czech-style lagers, with their reliance on soft, clean water to accent the flavors of malt and hops. "You don't need to over-hop to get that really nice hop flavor, because it just floats on top," he said. "You can get those delicate flavors." One of his beers that showcases this effect is the Dortmunder, which has a characteristic German malt breadiness with a fine layer of aroma hops and a soft bitterness. And yet this is an American craft beer: It is lightly dry hopped with Cascade. "It's Dortmunder, and it fits a lot of the Dortmunder profile, but it's different," Carr said.

The bestseller is Bear Naked Ale. Although some people might buy a beer just because it has the work "naked" in it, this beer needs no gimmicks—beyond the fact that it's a German-style *altbier*, of course (a relatively rare German ale). "I like to think of it as the Fat Tire of the East Coast," Carr said, citing the flagship brew from Colorado's New Belgium Brewing Company. "It's a good Tuesday night beer."

Carr bills himself as founder-brewer, and members of his brewhouse team are jacks-of-all-trades. "It's kinds of a socialistic system," he said. "Everybody brews, everybody bottles, everybody washes kegs." Despite all the beer emphasis, the pub is serious about being kid-friendly, as it should be in a town that was just meant for the good old family vacation. Adirondack Brewery and Pub is just across the road from historic Fort William Henry, and other lake and mountain destinations dot the local landscape. The menu is famous for its big, juicy burgers with beer-battered fries and other pub fare like prime rib, chicken dishes, pasta, and seafood. "It's all fun," Carr said. "Beer is fun."

Adirondack Brewery and Pub

Opened: Brewpub opened in 1999; production brewhouse opened in 2010.

Type: Brewpub with an attached production brewhouse.

Owner and Brewer: John Carr.

System: 15-barrel Bohemian brewhouse.

Annual production: 15,000 barrels.

Distribution: Bottles and draft; on tap at pubs in more than half the counties in New York state.

Hours: Seasonal hours; check the website.

Food: Full pub menu, noted for its burgers.

Parking: A small off-street parking lot.

The Beer Diviner and Bly Hollow Brewing

Brewery: 241 Bly Hollow Rd., Cherry Plain, NY 12040
Tasting room: Corner of State Routes 22 and 43, Stephentown, NY 12168.
(518) 658-0299 • www.thebeerdiviner.com

Jonathan Post's goal was to build a brewery in the West African country of Burkina Faso, where a traditional form of low-alcohol beer has deep cultural significance. Instead, he built a nanobrewery that makes oatmeal stout, American IPA, and other high-alcohol beers in a small corner of the Taconic Mountains, near the New York–Massachusetts border. There's a good story here, and Post, a former college English professor, will tell it in a memoir he's calling "The Beer Diviner." In the meantime, his 2-barrel brewery, Bly Hollow Brewing (aka The Beer Diviner), qualifies him for inclusion here.

The brewery opened in April 2012 in Cherry Plain, on a remote and steeply inclined section of Bly Hollow Road, about forty-five minutes east of Albany. In 2013, he launched a Kickstarter drive to outfit a separate tasting room in the nearby crossroads town of Stephentown. He's operating the tasting room under the state's Farm Brewery law, which offers several benefits, including the right to open as many as five off-premises tasting rooms, and the right to sell beer, wine, and cider instead of simply handing out samples. And Post is taking the farm brewery concept a step further: He's using the model of Community Supported Agriculture (CSA) and applying it to beer. In a typical CSA, customers pay to buy a "share" of a farm's produce, usually picking up their share once a week. Post is selling monthly shares of his beer for $325 for six months, and $600 for a year.

But let's get back to that African story. Post was working as an English professor at the State University of New York at Albany, and homebrewing was a hobby. At work, he met a colleague who was from the West African nation of Burkina Faso. He joined his friend on a trip to the friend's home

Beers brewed: Ancestral Red Ale, Got Your Back (Coffee Oatmeal Stout), Ancient Gruit Ale, New York State IPA, Very! Brown Ale, Getcha Honey Wheat Ale, and Oak Aged Vanilla Porter.

The Pick: Post didn't have the Gruit on tap when I visited, although I did sample an extraordinary blended-in-the-keg sample of the Gruit mixed with the oatmeal stout. But my favorite was the Very Brown, a clean, malt-forward beer with local and Maris Otter barley malt, and Post's own Cascade and Centennial hops.

village of Dan No. There, Post discovered the rich culture and tradition of beermaking practiced by the local people, who call themselves Dagara. They produced a low-alcohol, uncarbonated and unrefrigerated beer using millet and sorghum. The villagers eventually asked Post to help them build a modern brewery in Dan No.

"I spent many times sitting in a circle, drinking the millet beer from a calabash [a hollowed-out gourd used as a drinking vessel]," Post said. On that and subsequent trips, Post learned that beer typically is brewed by the oldest woman in each village, and the practice is accompanied by traditional rites and incantations. Long story short: The Dagara legend has it that thousands of years ago, the gift and instruction of beer making were given to the people, possibly before they even learned to make bread. That coincided with their transition from hunter-gatherers to an agricultural-based society, with villages in fixed places. This struck a chord with Post, who had grown up the son of an American Foreign Service officer and lived in about eighteen different countries by the time he was twenty-four. "I thought maybe there was something to what these villagers were saying," Post said. "I'm kind of like the hunter-gatherer. There's something about beer that makes sense for me—the idea of staying in one place and living in a fixed community."

In Post's telling, the story is more detailed and nuanced than space permits here. There did come a point where he was invited to a "divination" ceremony, accompanied by a new batch of village beer, and was tagged with the title "The Beer Diviner" by the people. "I said, 'What the heck does that mean?' and they said, 'We don't know; you'll have to figure it out.'" Today, his company is officially Bly Hollow Brewing, but another African friend who heard Post's story suggested marketing and branding using the name The Beer Diviner. The brewery also uses the slogan "Mystical Ales."

The important thing for the purposes of this book is that a major restructuring of SUNY Albany occurred around this time and left Post without a job. So, he put the idea of building a West African brewery on hold and set to work on one much closer to home. "I had never heard of a nanobrewery," he said, "but I got the idea of a nano in a small village in West Africa." Post built his brewery on the foundation of an old farmhouse on Bly Hollow Road. He started in April 2012 with a $1/2$-barrel system, which he outgrew by that fall. He set up his 2-barrel system and opened a tasting room. In 2013, Post was looking to push distribution into the New York City area.

Oddly enough, Post used no millet or sorghum in his beers in the first few years. The closest thing is probably his Gruit, a barley malt-based beer that uses herbs like yarrow and wormwood in lieu of hops.

His lineup also includes an all-New York state IPA (with his own hops and barley grown in the state and malted in Massachusetts). He also brews a coffee oatmeal stout (which won a medal at the 2013 TAP New York festival) called Got Your Back, and a beer he calls Ancestral Red Ale. All of his beers are fairly high in alcohol, with big, bold flavors. "Because my niche is so small," he said, "I can get away with high alcohol, expensive beers."

His eventual plan is to open more tasting rooms around the Albany area, and even put his 2-barrel kettle on wheels so he can use it to fill fermentation tanks at each outlet. In the back of his mind, however, there is still that project in the African village, whose name Dan No means "good beer" in the Dagara language. "I think we'll get there," he said "but we have some work to do here first."

The Beer Diviner and Bly Hollow Brewing

Opened: 2012.

Type: Production brewery with off-site tasting room.

Owner and Brewer: Jonathan Post.

System: 2-barrel brewhouse.

Annual production: 310 barrels.

Distribution: Kegs and 2-ounce bottles; a tasting room and outlet in Stephentown, plus selected accounts in the Albany area.

Hours: The tasting room is open from 1 p.m. to 8 p.m. Friday to Sunday.

Parking: Yes.

Blue Line Brewery

SARANAC LAKE

BLUE LINE BREWERY
MADE IN THE ADKS

555 Lake Flower Ave., Saranac Lake, NY 12983
(518) 354-8114 • www.bluelinebrew.com

Inside the blue line, things are different. They are certainly more relaxed. Take the sign outside Blue Line Brewery in Saranac Lake. A set of hours are listed. But under them, it reads: "If you see the yellow jeep or someone inside, please stop by. We will be happy to serve you."

The owner of the yellow jeep and of Blue Line Brewery is Mark Gillis, who moved to Saranac Lake in 2010, and opened the 3-barrel nanobrewery in December 2012. The blue line refers to the boundary of the Adirondack Park, the 6-million-acre forest preserve created by New York state in the 1890s. It is protected by the state constitution, which declares its forests, mountains, and waterways "forever wild." Saranac Lake is one of the largest towns inside the park. Gillis and his family moved there from Westchester County, lured by the town's pitch as an "All-America city."

Gillis had worked in the financial services industry, but increasingly found it wasn't necessary to be in New York City. He had been a homebrewer, but he didn't expect to run a brewery when he moved. "I always figured that Saranac [Matt Brewing Company] was in Saranac Lake," said Gillis, referring to the 125-year-old large-scale brewing company that is actually in Utica, an industrial city that's about a forty-five-minute drive outside the blue line. Gillis quickly sized things up in Saranac Lake. "So there wasn't a brewery and I said, 'Why not? Why not open a brewery here?'" The brewery is in an old car wash (with a great floor drain already installed), along Route 86 (Lake Flower Drive), the road that connects Saranac Lake and the tourist-oriented city of Lake Placid. "It's the busiest road in the Adirondacks," Gillis said, adding that a business class teacher had once given him a piece of advice: "You don't need marketing—just open next to a McDonald's or a Burger King." Sure enough, the golden arches are visible just across the parking lot.

Beers brewed: APA, 6'er Pale Ale, Red Skin Red Ale, Ice-Out Brown, Forest Home Black Lager, and Maple Porter.

The Pick: I actually had the Black Forest Home Black Lager at a Lake Placid pub the night before visiting the brewery, and came away impressed. Gillis said it's his favorite, too.

It was in the early days of the brewery when I visited, but Gillis was starting to establish some patterns. He had five beers on tap at the tasting room (which still looks a little like a car wash, but with a doorway punched through the side and a nice finished wood bar along one wall). All of his beers were between 4.5 percent and 6 percent ABV, but you'll find they're not always exactly "regular" beers, either. Gillis takes his core lineup and throws something extra into a portion of the batch, on occasion. On my visit, for example, the Forest Home Black Lager was infused with rosemary and honey. The Red Skin Red Ale had hints of real ginger, and the Ice Out Brown Ale had something about it that gave a rich, warm, earthy flavor—you know, that taste they call umami. Yes, it was bacon. Gillis baked some bacon, crumbled it up, and put it in a mesh bag, then dropped that into a 25-gallon fermenter (the other 25 gallons of the batch were bacon-free). It didn't taste at all like bacon, yet there was something about it. . . .

The thing is, at that point, Gillis was still lamenting that he hadn't yet had time to "play around" with his beers. So we'll see what happens next. The brewery has more than a dozen bar accounts in the Lake Placid and Saranac Lake areas, and Gillis said he's "pounding the pavement" to secure more. (Around here, that probably should be pounding the hiking trail.) The bestseller at his bar accounts is his pale ale, which he originally called Pisgah Pale, after the local mountain near his home. Renamed 6'er Pale Ale, it's balanced and malty enough to have a touch of sweetness. The term "6er" refers to someone who climbs the six peaks in the immediate Saranac Lake area. (It's a play on "46er," which is someone who summits all forty-six of the Adirondacks' high peaks.)

In the tasting room, his early bestseller was Maple Porter, a beer he intended only as a winter seasonal. It proved too popular to take off the rotation. "There's one lady, she must be seventy, she comes in every week or so, pounds four samples, then takes home a growler of the maple porter," Gillis said. "I guess that's an Adirondacker for you."

Blue Line Brewery

Opened: 2012.
Owner and Brewer: Mark Gillis.
System: 3-barrel brewhouse, mostly used equipment.
Annual production: 150 barrels.
Distribution: Tasting room and more than a dozen local accounts; draft only.
Hours: 1 p.m. to 5:30 p.m. Monday to Wednesday; 3 p.m. to 7 p.m. Thursday and Friday; noon to 6 p.m. Saturday; noon to 4 p.m. Sunday.
Parking: Yes.

Brown's Brewing Company
Walloomsac Brewery

50 Factory Hill Rd., Hoosick Falls, New York 12090
(518) 273-2337 • www.brownsbrewing.com
Taproom: 417 River St., Troy, NY 12180

If you want to start a successful production brewery, it might help to have a successful brewpub as your launching pad (and money source). On the other hand, if your brewpub is so successful that it occupies all your time, it can keep you from fulfilling the brewery dream. That, in a nutshell, is the dilemma that had been facing Garry Brown for nearly twenty years.

Brown's brewpub, now called Brown's Brewing Company Taproom, overlooking the Hudson River in downtown Troy, has been going strong for twenty years. So strong in fact, that it's the largest brewpub, by volume of beer sold, in New York state and one of the largest in the Northeast. The brewpub makes about 2,800 barrels a year, of which at least 75 percent is sold at the pub. There are also off-premises keg accounts and a bottling line. But the pub brewery, a 15-barrel system, is at capacity.

Since its founding, the brewpub has helped to revitalize downtown Troy, an old industrial city once known as Collar City (back when men's collars were detachable). The city's legacy as the home of "Uncle Sam" also gave the brewpub one of its former names, Troy Pub & Uncle Sam Brewery. (The place started as Brown and Moran's, before original partner Jim Moran left.) Now it's simply Brown's. For years, Garry Brown dreamed of a freestanding brewhouse that would allow him to sell more off-premises beer. "But, you know, running a restaurant is a big job," said Gregg Stacy, who handles marketing for Brown's. "Now there's a good team running the restaurant and brewpub, so Garry had the time to put this in motion."

Beers brewed: Pale Ale, Brown Ale, Hefeweizen, Porter, Tomhannock Pilsner, Oatmeal Stout, Imperial Stout, Cherry Raspberry Ale, Irish Amber Ale, Harvest IPA, Oktoberfest, Pumpkin, Rauchbier, Dunkelweizen, Dunder and Blixem Strong Ale (Christmas seasonal), Belgian Strong Ale, Whiskey Porter, Hoodoo Voodoo Ale, and other seasonals and specials.

The Pick: The Oatmeal Stout is the flagship, and it's a good one. But a good brown ale is sometimes hard to find, and the beer known as Brown's Brown Ale is better than good. I'm tempted to say it's dependable, too. It's boldly flavored, with lots of nuttiness and a fine balance of hop bitterness (courtesy of Mt. Hood hops) and lingering sweetness.

Brown and brewer Peter Martin spent a good deal of the winter of 2012–2013 building the production brewery themselves. It's a 50-barrel brewery with kettles and other equipment once used by Magic Hat Brewing Company in Burlington, Vermont, located on the Walloomsac River in a town called Hoosick Falls. That's about a forty-minute drive from Troy and just a stone's throw from the Vermont border. The brewery is in an old industrial mill, which dates to circa 1810. The mill has housed many businesses in the past; the longest-lasting was a wallpaper manufacturer. There's a piece of irony in that, Stacy said. "They made wallpaper using oatmeal in the process," he said. "Our best-selling beer is Oatmeal Stout."

The new brewery has room for storage, tanks, and other brewing equipment. It has one unusual feature: Martin and Brown installed four large open fermentation squares in addition to some smaller closed fermenters. And there's a spectacular view of the Walloomsac Falls in the back. Old-time mills used the falls for power, not their beauty. In that tradition, the folks at Brown's are intent on getting the brewhouse running first, with a tasting room—possibly making use of the scenery—as an afterthought. The brewery property will also have a hop yard. Brown's Brewing has been a pioneer in the use of New York grown hops and is exploring the use of New York barley (and malt houses). Garry and Kelly Brown's farm supplies other ingredients, such as the beechwood that is smoked to make Brown's Rauchbier.

The production brewery will concentrate first on filling the unmet demand within the capital region. (Stacy estimates that market has been only half the size it should be.) Then they expect to branch out with distribution in southern Vermont, western Massachusetts, and New York City, and across to the other cities of Upstate New York.

Brown's marketing tagline is "Dependable Ales & Lagers." That could imply solid, not spectacular, but that's not the case here. There are high-quality staples like Pale Ale, Brown, and Hefeweizen, and also a host of engaging seasonals. The Christmas seasonal, Dunder and Blixem Strong Ale, pays homage to another not-well-known Troy claim to fame: Clement C. Moore's 'Twas the Night Before Christmas was originally published in a Troy newspaper, and Dunder and Blixem were the original names for Donner and Blitzen.

The brewpub was producing about twenty-two beers in 2013, and typically has twelve on tap. The brewpub brewhouse will remain in service after the production brewery opens, for small batches and experimentation. The menu is an inventive take on pub fare, from burgers and sandwiches to steaks and pasta, and both New Orleans- and south-of-the-border-influenced entrées.

It may have taken Garry Brown a long time to realize his dream of a big production brewery, and the task of converting an old paper mill into a state-of-the-art brewery is daunting, but he's been there before. "Garry had the vision to create a business that helped bring new life to Troy in 1993," Stacy said. "The same kind of thing is happening here."

Brown's Brewing Company

Opened: Brewpub in 1993; production brewery opened in 2013.

Type: Brewpub in Troy; production brewery in Hoosick Falls.

Owners: Garry and Kelly Brown.

Brewer: Peter Martin.

System: 15-barrel (brewpub); 50-barrel (brewery).

Annual production: 2,800 barrels in the brewpub; the brewery will open with 20,000 barrels, and a 60,000-barrel eventual annual capacity.

Distribution: The current brewpub system supplies 75 percent of its output to the on-premises pub. The production brewery will boost off-premises sales in the Northeast.

Hours: 11:30 a.m. to 11 p.m. Monday to Thursday; 11:30 a.m. to midnight Friday and Saturday; 11:30 a.m. to 10 p.m. Sunday.

Food: Full restaurant menu at the brewpub.

Parking: There is off-street parking behind the block, along the river.

C.H. Evans Brewing Company (Albany Pump Station)

19 Quackenbush Square, Albany, NY 12207
(518) 447-9000 • www.evansale.com

Spend any time at a brewery and you'll realize that much of what happens there involves moving large volumes of liquid from one place to another. In other words, plumbing. So perhaps it was inevitable that a 200-year-old building in downtown Albany that helped pump millions of gallons of Hudson River water to a reservoir would one day house a brewery. (It still looks a lot like the engineering marvel it once was.) Check out the 20-ton overhead cranes dangling from the 40-foot-high ceilings. The Albany Pump Station, and the C.H. Evans Brewing Company it now hosts, pumps a lot of liquid these days in the form of beers like its highly successful Kick Ass Brown and Pale Ale.

This brewpub venture was started by Neil Evans in 1999, a fifth-generation member of a family that began brewing in Albany back in 1786. He simultaneously resurrected the family business and jump started a renaissance of bars and restaurants in the downtown area, particularly from its location on Quackenbush Square and up Pearl Street. "When we started, we really were the anchor down here," Evans said. "Now there's lots going on." That is, lots of bars and restaurants, but just the single brewpub in Albany itself. "I wish there were more brewpubs down here," Evans said, citing Portland, Oregon, which has similar demographics but thirty brewpubs. "I'd like not to be the only brewpub, but certainly would want to be the best."

In 2012, Evans said goodbye to his longtime head brewer, George de Piro, who moved to Druthers Brewing Company in Saratoga Springs, and welcomed Ryan Demler. He has kept the pace going. Demler had experience at production breweries like the Olde Saratoga Brewing Company's Mendocino brewery in Saratoga Springs, but prefers the fast-paced brewing at a brewpub. He does more than fifty beers a year at the Pump Station, although the core brown, pale ale, and

Beers brewed: Capitol Light, Quackenbush Blonde, Evans Wit, Kick Ass Brown Ale, Knickerbocker Lager, Maibock, Empire State Bitter, Pump Station Pale, Poor Soldier Porter, Breakfast Stout, and many limited releases.

The Pick: The Kick Ass Brown Ale is legendary, for good reason. It's a malty brown all right, but that kick in the pants comes from hops. Lots of hops. You may have to drink this one standing up.

hefeweizen make up about 40 percent of the total volume. "I wouldn't want to say we're conservative in what we make, because we're not," Demler said. "We did a spiced Belgian strong ale, for example, with anise, but we're probably not going to go out and do a big pepper and lavender beer—not soon anyway."

The Pump Station attracts a crowd that ranges from business people and political types from the nearby capital to dedicated craft beer fans. "We do such a huge volume and a lot of our customers are looking for approachable beers," Demler said. "But then we get a lot of the beer geeks who are looking for something interesting. So we give them something to look for." The range goes from Capitol Light and Quackenbush Blonde on one end to an Imperial American IPA, Poor Soldier Porter (and its barrel-aged brother), and a Breakfast Stout. The pub has twelve beer lines and only infrequently puts a guest beer on tap (usually from a nearby craft brewery). Demler puts one beer in a real ale cask each Friday. And there's lots of good beer food here, from Louisiana-style jambalaya to British fish 'n chips to Polish golabki to a German-influenced wurst platter. Evans describes the food menu as "eclectic American," with an emphasis on the beer-and-food combo.

Despite its relative lack of brewpubs, the Albany region is seeing a major explosion in local production breweries, some of which are quite large. But Evans is happy building the Pump Station as a beer-and-food destination. That leaves enough room to grow. "When you think about it, ten years ago people said this wouldn't be able to keep going, and now we've more than doubled [our production]," he said. "So we just keep going, and we have an aggressive young brewer—we'll keep getting better."

C.H. Evans Brewing Company (Albany Pump Station)

Opened: 1999 (although the logos cite the original Evans brewery as opening in 1786).
Type: Brewpub.
Owners: Neil Evans (managing partner).
Brewer: Ryan Demler.
System: 10-barrel New World System brewhouse.
Annual production: 1,200 barrels.
Distribution: At the pub and some off-premises accounts (mostly restaurants) in the Albany area; limited number of 750-milliliter bottles of specialty beers sold at the pub.
Hours: 11:30 a.m. to 11 p.m. Monday to Thursday; 11:30 a.m. to midnight Friday and Saturday; noon to 8 p.m. Sunday.
Food: Full "eclectic American" pub menu.
Parking: Its own parking lot off Pearl Street.

Cooper's Cave Ale Company

2 Sagamore St., Glens Falls, NY 12801
(518) 792-0007 • www.cooperscaveale.com

Cooper's Cave Ale Company in Glens Falls used to bill itself as the smallest brewery in New York—or at least as the smallest "non-brewpub" brewery. In today's age of nanobreweries, however, even Cooper's Cave Ale Company's original 2.5-barrel (10 gallons at a time) brewing system might not qualify as the smallest. Besides, Cooper's Cave has not only graduated to a 7-barrel brewhouse, but also is no longer a "non-brewpub." Instead, it has gone in quite the opposite direction. It added a pub and restaurant in 2008, and that portion of its business has now taken over, representing the vast majority of the beers it sells.

How did that happen? "For nine years, we had a lot of good loyal customers," said Adrian Bethel, who manages the place and is the son of founders Edward and Patty Bethel. "A lot of them just wanted to come in here and sit down and have a beer and a burger." The tasting room was a friendly sort of place where the regulars would hang out despite Patty's limit of three samples per visit. (When the brewery started, its production was so small customers had to sign up for growlers, to be picked up when ready.) If you've read the first edition of this book, you may remember a quote from Patty Bethel making something clear: "I don't want a pub." And yet, nine years after Cooper's Cave opened—on St. Patrick's Day in 1999—Cooper's Cave added a brewpub. Adrian Bethel, who studied restaurant management at SUNY Cobleskill, clearly had a role in that. "We're very happy with the pub," he said. "You get more return on the beers. We should've done it earlier." No need to go into the family dynamics there.

A walk around Cooper's Cave reveals that it is actually several kinds of businesses rolled into one. There's the brewery, the gift shop, the pub and restaurant, the ice cream shop, and the soda company. Cooper's Cave makes an extensive line of soft drinks, and its ice cream setup produces

Beers brewed: Tavern Ale, Radeau Red, IPA, Pathfinder's Porter, English Pale Ale, Bluesberry Ale, Sagamore Stout, Bumppo's Brown Ale, and other seasonals.

The Pick: I liked the Bluesberry Ale, and then the bartender recommended mixing it with the stout, the way many customers like it. And that was indeed a terrific idea. But I'll go with the Tavern Ale, whose earthy British flavor belies its extra light color.

dozens of hard, soft, and yogurt flavors. All of this is located on the edge of downtown Glens Falls. Luckily enough, it's right along a popular bike trail that stretches from Fort Edward in Glens Falls to Lake George.

Glens Falls is a busy little city, right off Interstate 87 (the Adirondack Northway). Mountains are visible from the city, but it sits just outside the Adirondack Park. With Fort Edward nearby, and a real Cooper's Cave featured in *Last of the Mohicans*, you can see where the brewery and brewpub gets their Colonial-era themes. Edward Bethel's interest in writer James Fenimore Cooper and French and Indian War reenactments shows in the beer names: Bumppo's Brown Ale, Radeau Red, Sagamore Stout, Pathfinder's Porter, and so on.

The beers are produced in a self-designed 7-barrel system made from old dairy equipment. The brew kettle is rectangular. Adrian Bethel refers to it as a "Franken Brewery," although he described its 2.5-barrel predecessor that way, too. "Maybe one day we'll buy a brewhouse," he said. There's an earthy, mineral character to many of the Cooper's Cave beers that likely comes in part from its use of a Burton Ale yeast. "Our beers are mostly English in style," Bethel said. There are usually twelve beers on tap, which rotate seasonally. Bluesberry Ale—a beer with a solid malt base that tempers the berry—is the pub's bestseller.

The food menu features an eclectic array of sandwiches, salads, burgers, and entrées, with several varieties of steaks and seafood options. A specialty item is the boule, a ball-shaped, French-style bread served with soup or chili. The place has a main dining room and a smaller room for private parties, but don't forget to check out the patio alongside the bike trail. It's used year round—there's an overhead heater, and the space is sealed in clear, removable vinyl. "It can get pretty toasty in the winter, and people actually like coming out here and watching blizzards," Bethel said, though in the summertime, when bikers are stopping for ice cream, that's hard to imagine.

Cooper's Cave actually produces less beer in its new format than it did before it opened the pub. It dropped from about one hundred off-premises accounts to just a handful. Perhaps that will grow again, but for now Adrian Bethel is happy with the way things are going. "This has been pretty successful for us, so we'll see how it goes," he said.

Cooper's Cave Ale Company

Opened: 1999.

Owners: Edward, Patricia, and Adrian Bethel.

Brewer: Edward Bethel.

System: 7-barrel, self-built.

Annual production: 400 barrels.

Distribution: Mostly on-site, with some off-premises accounts; mostly draft, with a few 22-ounce bottles sold at the tasting room.

Hours: The tasting room, brewpub, and ice cream shop all have different hours. Call before you visit.

Food: A full brewpub menu with steaks and seafood options.

Parking: No off-street parking.

Davidson Brothers Brewing Company

184 Glen St., Glens Falls, NY 12801
(518) 743-9026 • www.davidsonbrothers.com

You'll probably never find anyone in the beer world who's as passionate about his brewhouse system or as devoted to his distributor. But that aptly describes Rick Davidson, the "brewing brother" in the business that has operated a brewpub in downtown Glens Falls since 1996. And his passion is the driving force behind an ambitious plan he and his brother and partner John launched in 2013: Davidson Brothers is building a 50-barrel production brewery just outside of Glens Falls, in the town of Queensbury.

That's another thing—Davidson is passionate about and devoted to his hometown, too. "The reason we opened this place [the brewpub] was to make our community a better place," Rick Davidson said, citing the brewpub's role in helping revitalize the city's downtown core. "We're going all-in on the brewery, putting up everything we have," he said. "Why would we do that? Because it's going to be something that we hope makes this community better."

Now, you may ask, why did it take so long to expand from the original 7-barrel brewpub and add the good-sized production brewery? Rick Davidson will tell you it had a lot to do with the type of brewing system he operates. Davidson Brothers was an early example of the British-style brewing system first designed by Peter Austin in Yorkshire, England. This system was then spread to various corners of North America in the 1990s by Alan Pugsley of Maine's Shipyard Brewing Company, who consulted on those projects.

Davidson will tell you that Pugsley was not initially impressed with the guys from Glens Falls, who had never homebrewed or operated a business before. "Alan actually told his wife: 'This is going to be the first one that fails,'" Davidson recalls. Yet it persevered. Rick Davidson, who works in the pub while his brother has an outside job, became an advocate of the system, which

Beers Brewed: The pub typically offers a mix of core, seasonal, and Brewer's Choice beers, including Ryley (light rye ale), Brown Ale, Red Ale, IPA, Dacker (light Scotch Ale), Smoked Porter, Oatmeal Stout, Scotch Ale, Amber Ale, and I-87 (a bigger IPA).

The Pick: I was disappointed on my visit not to find Dacker, a light Scotch ale made from a recipe handed down for four generations to an Adirondack resident named Duncan Kincaid. But the bigger (8.3 percent ABV) and darker Scotch Ale, sweet and malty, satisfied my Highland cravings.

uses a brick-lined, direct fire kettle and a quirky British yeast called Ringwood.

Over the years, some of the original Austin operations closed, or at least modified the way they work. Not Davidson Brothers. "Alan came back not too long ago and said, 'This place is like a living history exhibit of how an Austin system looked in the 1990s,'" Davidson said.

Staying true to the system didn't mean sacrificing success. The brewpub, housed in a circa-1865 building, thrived as a comfortable lunch, dinner, and beer spot in Glens Falls, with an eclectic pub menu and solid, mostly British-style beers, led by an enormously popular IPA. Along the way, Davidson Brothers decided to share the beers with others around New York state. But first, they needed to find a contract brewer who could be true to the style. "It had to be an Austin system or we wouldn't go there," Rick Davidson said. "We thought eventually there would be one close by with capacity, but that never happened. So we went up to Shipyard."

With Pugsley's Shipyard Brewing Company making the IPA and some of their other popular beers in bottles and kegs, Davidson Brothers expanded its market to seventeen counties of eastern New York state. This is where Rick Davidson starts singing the praises of his distributor, Saratoga Eagle, operated by the Vukelic family. "We couldn't ask for better distributors," he said. "They know that what's good for their business is good for ours, and vice versa. I know that may not be true of all breweries and distributors, but it's been true for us."

By this time, the brewery shakeout of the late 1990s and early 2000s had happened, and business for the brewpub was thriving. But Shipyard was running out of room for contracts, and newer Peter Austin breweries weren't coming online. "The brewery we're doing now wasn't on our radar," Rick said. "But John and I got to thinking, 'You know, this Alan Pugsley/Peter Austin system of brewing is dying, dying a slow death of attrition, and the guys that started with it aren't doing it anymore.' So we said, 'We'll do it.'"

The brewery, expected to open in early 2014, will be the second-largest Peter Austin in the country, at 50 barrels (after the 100-barrel Shipyard brewhouse). They're planning a full retail shop and a well-designed tour, making use of a second mezzanine overlooking the brewhouse. Even with the new brewery, Rick Davidson doesn't see his company becoming a national—or even a regional—behemoth. "We believe in offering our beers to the accounts that we know will keep them on and support them, and we know we have the distributor who can help us do that," he said. At the brewpub, meanwhile, you'll still be able to enjoy what Davidson Brothers has always been about: beer, food, and atmosphere that are solid and comforting.

Davidson Brothers Brewing Company

Opened: Brewpub opened in 1996.

Type: Brewpub; production brewery expected to open in 2014.

Owners: Rick and John Davidson.

Brewers: Jason Kissinger and A.J. Davidson.

System: 7-barrel Peter Austin brewhouse.

Annual production: The brewpub currently produces 1,000 to 1,200 barrels. Shipyard produces more than 2,000 barrels; that will shift to the new production brewery.

Distribution: Throughout seventeen counties in eastern and northern New York; more than half the distribution is draft.

Hours: 11:30 a.m. to 10 p.m. Monday to Friday; 11:30 a.m. to 11 p.m. Saturday and Sunday.

Food: Full restaurant menu, pub style.

Parking: On-street parking and municipal lots.

Druthers Brewing Company

381 Broadway St., Saratoga Springs, NY 12866
(518) 306-5275 • www.druthersbrewing.com

As you might expect, a place called Druthers Brewing Company is all about choices. Co-owner and brewmaster George de Piro made his choice, and it all started in 2012 with the opening of Druthers Brewing Company in downtown Saratoga Springs, the spa and resort town best known for its mineral springs and thoroughbred race course. It's the first—and for now the only—brewpub in what de Piro hopes will be a brewpub "empire." Why start there? "Because it's the only town in Upstate New York that's growing," he said. "It's a small city, but it thinks of itself as a big city."

Druthers has an address on Broadway, the city's main street, which is lined with historic hotels like the Gideon Putnam and a collection of both locally owned and high-end chain retailers, but it's really off-Broadway. You enter through a gate that opens onto an outdoor patio, with the new purpose-built brewery and restaurant set back behind the other buildings on the street. It had been a vacant lot, which is somewhat surprising in the center of a city that, as de Piro said, is actually growing while much of the state lags behind.

De Piro has five partners in the project, including Chris and Brian Martell. But he's the face of the place, mostly because of his background as the highly visible head brewer at the C.H. Evans Brewing Company and Albany Pump Station brewpub in downtown Albany. He left there on good terms but wanted to strike out on his own. De Piro thought about opening a production brewery, but decided against it. "I prefer brewpubs," he said. "I'm a staunch believer that beer is best when it's fresh. Almost everything we serve here was made within twelve to eighteen days."

The Druthers brewhouse is located on a level above the bar and dining area. A glass window lets customers looking up from their beers see the action. De Piro operates a 10-barrel JV Northwest system—"It should have been twenty [barrels]," he said a year after opening—and makes all styles of beer, including porters, wits, barleywines, pale

Beers Brewed: Golden Rule Blonde, Brevity Wit, Simple Truth Barleywine, Druthers Stout, Fist of Karma Brown Ale, All In IPA, Vienna Lager, seasonals, and specials.

The Pick: A difficult choice, but during my warm-weather visit I thoroughly enjoyed the fresh spiciness of the Belgian Wit. And you gotta love a wit named Brevity.

ales, and Vienna lager. One of his best-known beers at the Pump Station was a multiple-award-winner called Kick Ass Brown, and he makes a similar version at Druthers, called Fist of Karma. The menu uses the words "kick ass" in the description, if not the name. "It is my beer after all," de Piro said.

It was hard to get a good read in the first year, but de Piro thinks the top-selling beers seem to be the Golden Rule Blonde (a Kolsch) and the All In IPA. He keeps those on most of the time, while rotating others beers on the pub's seven taps. (The only guest draft is a hard cider; de Piro plans to serve only his beers.) But he likes to play around, so even his regular beers might show some variations occasionally.

The pub prides itself on fresh food, locally sourced whenever possible. There are pastas, burgers, and sandwiches. Many items are made with some of de Piro's beers, particularly the blonde, which finds its way into the beer-battered fish 'n chips and the marinated grilled salmon.

Druthers' motto is "You are your choices," a quote from the Roman philosopher Seneca. De Piro keeps that in mind when deciding what to brew. "My philosophy has always been that when a customer comes in they should be able to find a beer that they like," he said. "I don't expect that everybody is going to like every beer, but I do expect that everybody can find something they like. That should be everybody's philosophy."

Druthers Brewing Company

Opened: 2012.

Type: Brewpub.

Owners: George de Piro, Chris Martell, Brian Martell, and other investors.

Brewer: George de Piro.

System: 10-barrel JV Northwest.

Annual production: Capacity is about 1,200 barrels; production expected to be about 1,000 barrels in 2013.

Distribution: On-premises only.

Hours: Open daily from 11:30 a.m. to 12:00 a.m.

Food: Eclectic pub menu.

Parking: No off-street parking, but municipal lots nearby.

Great Adirondack Brewing Company

2442 Main St., Lake Placid, NY 12946
(518) 523-1629 • www.adksteakandseafood.com/brewery

Around Lake Placid, the place on Main Street with the red clapboard siding and green roof is usually known simply as "Steak and Seafood." But that doesn't mean you should forget about the beer. The restaurant is officially known as the Great Adirondack Steak and Seafood Co. The brewery, in a smaller red and green building out back, goes by the name of Great Adirondack Brewing Company. Both have been owned and operated by the Kane family since the 1990s.

The brewhouse opened in 1996 and has had several head brewers over the years, all of them enthusiastic, passionate keepers of the Great Adirondack's tradition—hearty, rustic beers to go along with the hearty, rustic food and décor. The latest brewer is Frank Koester, who first came to Lake Placid from his home base on Long Island to shoot photos for the *New York Daily News* and other publications. In the mountain spirit, Koester is something of a jack-of-all-trades—he's trained as a chef and can handle electrical wiring pretty well. His craftsmanship as a woodworker can be seen in the custom tap handles, carved from cedar, in the Steak and Seafood bar. They're his tap handles, and since early 2013, when he took over as head brewer after a year and a half as assistant, they're his beers, too. He operates the brewery's original 7-barrel JV Northwest brewhouse (with fermenters and bright tanks added over time to increase capacity). He also has a 15-gallon pilot brewery, complete with a 14-gallon steel conical fermenter. "After I stopped needing to buy new camera equipment, I found new toys," Koester said.

Beers brewed: Whiteface Black Diamond Stout, Adirondack Abbey Ale, Farmhouse Pale Ale, Ausable Wulff Red Ale, Haystack Blonde Ale, John Brown Pale Ale, and many seasonals.

Almost all the brewhouse's 500-barrel annual output is made for the brewery. (There are also a handful of off-premises accounts in the Lake Placid area, and that part of the business may grow over time.) The beers are served directly to the restaurant from the tanks, through connections that were installed from the brewery to the bar after a fire in 2002. And there's another story associated with that fire. That year, Great Adirondack Brewing

The Pick: The Smoked Porter wasn't on during my most recent trip, but the Munich Helles German lager was a fine, easy-drinking replacement for summer. But I'm still in awe of the roasty, toasty, deep flavor of the Ausable Wulff Red Ale.

Company had won the TAP New York festival's Matthew Vassar Brewers' Cup for the best brewery in the Hudson Valley. (The contest's definition of Hudson Valley is obviously a little elastic.) The winning brewery keeps the cup for a year, and then hands it off to the next winner. When the fire broke out, the head brewer at the time made sure to grab the cup. It was returned mostly undamaged.

Over the years, Great Adirondack's beers have won several TAP New York awards, and a handful of Great American Beer Festival medals, too. These are the beers that brewer Koester now has under his watch—beers like Whiteface Black Diamond Stout and the Belgian-influenced Adirondack Abbey Ale. His personal favorite among the legacy beers he has inherited is the malty Ausable Wulff Red Ale, named for a famous fishing fly. "That's the one I'm most likely to take to drink at home," he said.

But even with his pilot system, Koester isn't content simply to make the core beers and regular seasonals. In his first few months, he made an authentically German biscuity Munich Helles and an Oatmeal Stout. The Oatmeal Stout, meant to provide an alternative to the big Whiteface stout, was launched in late spring of Koester's first year. "Only in Lake Placid would an oatmeal stout be a summer seasonal," he said.

Another thing about Lake Placid: Many of the hotels, shops, dining areas, and tourist attractions are densely clustered, so walking is often the most convenient way to get from one place to another. With this in mind, Great Adirondack offers a number of seasonals that run into the high 9 to 12 percent ABV range, for those who aren't driving anywhere after a few. Koester's own tastes lean toward sessionable beers with solid, earthy flavors (he is a fan of the classic European hops). "We want to make sure there are beers that you can have [more than one]," Koester said. "You know, when you're having pint after pint."

The Steak and Seafood menu is chock full of steaks and seafood, of course, plus some pastas and other pub fare, served in a classically rustic Adirondack dining room with cabin-style wood décor. When I mentioned that one of my favorite food-and-beer pairings of all time is the Steak and Seafood restaurant's prime rib with the brewery's Smoked Porter, Koester got a gleam in his eye. Working up to some more seasonals and specials that complement the menu is another step for him, Koester said. "That will be fun. I feel like I'm just starting to play around and develop some good stuff."

Great Adirondack Brewing Company

Opened: 1996.

Owners: The Kane family.

Brewer: Frank Koester.

System: 7-barrel JV Northwest.

Annual production: 500 barrels.

Distribution: Mostly on-premises, with a handful of off-premises accounts.

Hours: 11:30 a.m. to 9 p.m. Sunday to Thursday; 11:30 a.m. to 10 p.m. Friday and Saturday.

Food: Rustic, hearty fare.

Parking: None on-site, but several downtown municipal lots.

Lake Placid Pub & Brewery/Lake Placid Craft Brewing Company

LAKE PLACID
pub & brewery
REAL TOWN. REAL BEER.

813 Mirror Lake Dr., Lake Placid NY 12946
(518) 523-3813 • www.ubuale.com

No matter how big or successful it gets—and it is fairly big and quite successful already—the Lake Placid Pub & Brewery (LPP&B) never forgets its roots. Check out the happy hour crowd at the bar on the first floor of the three-story pub and you'll still find the regulars who've been coming here for thirty years, since back when it was just a "regular" bar called PJ O'Neill's. They still order bottles of Bud and Coors Light. The craft beer boom happened around them. The evidence is close at hand: LPP&B boomed, too.

But owner Chris Ericson made a commitment to those regulars, even as he built a company that makes more than 1,500 barrels of beer each year at the pub in Lake Placid and another 7,000 through a sales and distribution deal with Matt Brewing Company (Saranac) in Utica (page 111). Ericson and a partner started the brewpub in 1996, and Lake Placid Craft Brewing came along in 2002 (more on that later). Today, the pub-brewery caters to locals and tourists on three different levels. The second floor has offered Lake Placid house beers and pub food since 1997. The third-floor Hop Loft came along in 2013 and features something I've never seen in another brewpub—a dedicated play room for the kids.

The flagship beer on which all this is built is Ubu Ale, a strong (7 percent ABV) and dark beer that will never be mistaken for a Bud Light. Ubu, a dark ruby red English strong ale, has been "legendary" since its debut. Adding to its reputation is the tale of how it was once special-ordered for the White House by President Bill Clinton.

Beers brewed: Ubu Ale, Lake Placid IPA, Moose Island Ale, 46'er Pale Ale, Frostbite Pale Ale, Dr. Fogg's Oatmeal Stout, Bruce's Brown Bag Ale, Ectoberfest Lager, Twice Bitten Barleywine, and many more.

The Pick: There are lots of good beers to choose from here, but I can remember in great detail the first time I had an Ubu Ale. It was at a beer festival in Syracuse in the late 1990s, when Lake Placid was new and a ripple went through the crowd every time someone tried it. I made my way over. Sure enough, it's a warming, rich, and tasty beer to remember.

Ericson and his head brewer, Kevin Litchfield, are now also making about fifty different styles each year to cater to the crowds who increasingly come for full-flavored craft beer. "That's really why we did this expansion," Ericson said of the work that happened during the winter of 2012–2013, when they added tanks, doubling the brewhouse capacity, and a new cold storage, kitchen, and the third-floor area. "This really gives us permission to brew and brew," Ericson said. "One of our goals is to be one of the only brewpubs that always has a lager on, and we couldn't do that before." Ericson has become something he probably never imagined at the start: a brewing company executive. But he still yearns to get back in action at the brewhouse. "I want to get the boots back on," Ericson said. "Right now, though, I'd probably get in the way."

LPP&B's beers run the gamut from light to heavy, from Wolf Jaw Wit to the annual release of Twice Bitten Barleywine. In between are beers like 46'er Pale Ale, Nippletop Milk Stout, Fade to Black IPA, Golden Rye Ale, Ectoberfest Lager, KB's Wee Heavy, Bruce's Brown Bag Ale, and many more. "We'll pretty much always have a golden and pale, but they might change now and then," Ericson said. "There's lot in the rotation."

LPP&B's menu is basically pub fare, with burgers and fish 'n chips, but Ericson has ambitions. In 2013, the restaurant added a line of flatbread pizzas. People come for the beer, but the food keeps them for a while. "We had a philosophy from the start with the food that if we couldn't do it well the majority of the time, we wouldn't do it," Ericson said, noting the stiff competition for fine dining in Lake Placid. "We didn't want to get too far over the tips of our skis, foodwise."

But that's enough about the pub. Ericson, the executive, also doubles as the owner of the Lake Placid Craft Brewing Company. It's kind of a long story. In a nutshell, in 2002 Ericson bought a failed brewery in Plattsburgh, a city at the northern tip of New York, across Lake Champlain from Burlington, Vermont. He ran it for ten years—about one year too long, he now admits—before deciding that it was the wrong business model to use in his effort to get beers like Ubu, IPA, and 46er Pale Ale into the wider marketplace. Enter the Matts, Nick and Fred of Utica's Matt Brewing Company (Saranac). The Matts' excess brewing capacity and Ericson's need for a place to make and package his bestsellers was a match that couldn't be passed up. But Ericson makes one thing clear: He is the "100-percent owner" of Lake Placid Craft Brewing. "I won't say it's all been perfect all the time," he said. "But I'm really happy with how it turned out."

He also makes it clear that he and Litchfield come up with the recipes—usually on at the pub first—and then work with Saranac to scale them up, from a 7-barrel brew kettle to one of Saranac's 500-barrel kettles. "Lake Placid is positioned as a bigger [high alcohol] brand, while Saranac is distinctive and drinkable," Fred Matt said. "Lake Placid Craft is going to go in that direction." And don't be surprised to see Chris Ericson pull his brewer's boots back on to help it get where it's going.

Lake Placid Pub & Brewery/Lake Placid Craft Brewing Company

Opened: 1996 (Lake Placid Pub & Brewery); 2002 (Lake Placid Craft Brewing Company).

Owners: Chris and Catherine Ericson.

Brewer: Kevin Litchfield.

System: 7-barrel McCann brewhouse (at the pub).

Annual production: 1,500 to 1,800 barrels at the pub; 7,000 to 10,000 through Lake Placid Craft Brewing (brewed at Saranac).

Distribution: At the pub and a handful of local accounts served there; beer sold in bottles and draft in northeastern states through the Saranac distribution network.

Hours: 11:30 a.m. to 10 p.m. Monday to Saturday; noon to 10 p.m. Sunday.

Food: Pub menu includes flatbread pizzas.

Parking: Limited in the immediate area.

Mad Jack Brewing Company (The Van Dyck Lounge)

237 Union St., Schenectady, NY 12305
(518) 348-7999 • www.vandycklounge.com

The Stockade neighborhood in Schenectady is, according to many historians, the second-oldest continuously inhabited area in the country. The history of the Van Dyck Lounge, located in the Stockade district and home to Mad Jack Brewing Company, is anything but continuous, especially when it comes to its status as a brewery. It brewed and then it stopped, and then it brewed again. Now you can say "brewing continuously since 2011." New owners reopened the place in 2009 and restarted the dormant brewery two years later, bringing in a brewer, Drew Schmidt, with a long Albany-area beer pedigree. And this time, it looks like the brewery is here to stay.

In fact, said manager Mike McDonald, a member of the clan that owns both the company and lounge, brewing might be the thing it becomes known for. "Mad Jack may become the name for everything," he said. "The brewery is what could make this a destination." But that's getting ahead of the story. And this story really starts way, way back in 1661, when Dutch settlers established a trading post on the Mohawk River. The buildings today may not be quite that old, yet the National Park Service says the Stockade has the nation's highest concentration of houses two hundred years old or older. The Van Dyck Lounge inhabits two of them—side-by-side houses that are now united in one restaurant, bar, and music club. The brewery is in a separate building out back.

The Van Dyck opened in 1947 and was known for decades as a great club to see live jazz. Famous musicians who played there include Coleman Hawkins, Chick Corea, Dave Brubeck, and Thelonious Monk. Today the upstairs music room still hosts live music—primarily jazz and rock—as well as comedy acts. The high-vaulted ceiling and woodwork interior boast spectacular acoustics. McDonald said the rock and comedy performers

Beers brewed: Year-round: Brodey'O Blonde, Pinhead Pale Ale, Fightin' Irwin IPA, and Tub's Stout. Seasonals: Stockade Saison, Dutchman Ale, Bonnie Brown, Mad Jack Frost Winter Ale, Mad Jack's Irish Red, and more.

The Pick: The 2025 Hefeweizen is one of the most boldly banana-and-clove influenced unfiltered wheats I've had in a long while. It also has a nutty character that gives it the backbone to become a year-rounder (it almost is already).

lure more beer drinkers today than the jazz acts, but jazz will stay a part of the Van Dyck's legacy.

Schenectady is a General Electric town, and the giant GE plant still dominates the cityscape. So where does that leave the Van Dyck and Mad Jack Brewing in beer terms? As a blue-collar industrial town, Schenectady always had its share of Bud, Miller, and Coors drinkers. "The people here aren't beer geeks, but they are beer drinkers," McDonald said. "But the trends here like a lot of places are moving in the direction of the quality of beers we make."

McDonald's uncle, Jack McDonald, is the "Mad Jack" of the brewery's name and the principal behind the family properties, which include two other nearby places: the fine-dining Stockade Inn and the Irish pub-influenced Pinhead Susans. Jack McDonald bought the Van Dyck at auction after it had been closed for a few years, then had to buy the fixtures and the brewing equipment in separate auction lots. The family took two years to renovate and rehabilitate the place.

Drew Schmidt, the brewer, previously worked the brew kettle at the Big House Brewing Co. (now closed) in downtown Albany. He was out of brewing for a few years before being lured back at the Van Dyck. The brewery is a 10-barrel HDP system from Canada and is squeezed into the building across the rear courtyard. Mad Jack produced 400 barrels in 2012, probably a little more than half its capacity. About 80 percent is sold in the Van Dyck, with about a dozen other accounts in the Schenectady–Albany region. Not surprisingly, the Stockade Inn and Pinhead Susan's are the two biggest off-premises accounts.

All the beer is draft, for now. The brewery building isn't big enough to handle bottling, but expansion could come down the road, Mike McDonald said. The beers run the gamut, from pale ales and lagers to porters and stouts. The most popular is the 2025 Hefeweizen, McDonald said. It has a classic and profound "banana-and-clove" aroma associated with German hefeweizens. Drew Schmidt said the yeast he uses for the hefeweizen produces lots of phenols, which enhance the clove character. "People come in and ask for the 'banana beer,'" McDonald said. Other notable beers include Tub's Stout, brewed to a higher gravity and sweeter character than the more typical dry Irish stout, and Jack Frost, a spiced winter lager.

McDonald and Schmidt hope to continue building on the reputation of the beers. "As long as we can continue making the high quality beers we're making now," McDonald said, "we'll keep growing."

Mad Jack Brewing Company (The Van Dyck Lounge)

Opened: Restaurant reopened in 2009; brewing restarted in 2011.

Owners: Jack McDonald and Mike McDonald (manager).

Brewer: Drew Schmidt.

System: 10-barrel HDP.

Annual production: 400 barrels (2012).

Distribution: Mostly on-premises; some off-premises draft accounts.

Hours: 4 p.m. to 10 p.m. Monday to Thursday; 11:30 a.m. to 11 p.m. Friday; noon to 11 p.m. Saturday.

Food: Steaks, seafood, and more.

Parking: Its own parking lot at Union Street and Erie Boulevard.

Olde Saratoga/Mendocino Brewing Company

131 Excelsior Ave., Saratoga Springs, New York 12866
(518) 581-0492 • www.oldesaratogabrew.com

Nor'wester. North Country. Ten Springs. Mendocino. UB. Kingfisher. Olde Saratoga. Spanish Peaks. Harlem. Ringside. And remember Funny Cide Light? These are the names that are—or have been—associated with the large brewing operation on Excelsior Street, at the north end of the city of Saratoga Springs.

The 125-barrel brewery, at this point the fifth largest in the state, has had a lot of identities and still does. Its primary focus is brewing Kingfisher Premium Lager for distribution to Indian restaurants across the United States and Canada. It also makes Mendocino beers, like Red Tail Ale and Eye of the Hawk, for East Coast distribution. It also has its own line, called Olde Saratoga, sold mostly in New York state. And it solicits many other beers to be made under contract for other brewers.

Let's start by sorting out the ownership. The brewery was founded in 1997 by Nor'Wester, a pioneering West Coast beer company out of Portland, Oregon. Nor'Wester commissioned an oversized brewery to handle its East Coast distribution—and remember this was in the 1990s, long before that idea caught on. To make a long story fairly short, Nor'Wester got a loan to help build the brewery from the United Breweries (UB) Group, a large beer company (makers of Kingfisher, among others), based in Bangalore, India. Nor'Wester defaulted on the loan, and UB took control of the Saratoga brewery, which then was going by the name North Country.

Around that time, UB also took control of Mendocino Brewing Company, a well-regarded brewery in Hopland, California. And so, UB rebranded the Saratoga brewery as Mendocino and gave the brewery the contract to make Kingfisher for the American market. It produced the Mendocino line for the East Coast and had a short-lived local label

Beers Brewed: Kingfisher Premium Lager; Mendocino's Red Tail Ale, Eye of the Hawk Select Ale, Black Hawk Stout, White Hawk Original IPA, and Blue Heron Pale Ale, plus an Imperial series, the Talon (Double) series and seasonals, Olde Saratoga's Saratoga Lager, Saratoga IPA, seasonals, and several contract beers.

The Pick: I first had the West Coast version of Red Tail Ale in 1991 in the lodge at Yosemite National Park. It's one of those beers that you remember your first taste of. The current Red Tail still takes me back to the time when American craft brewing was in its early days.

called Ten Springs. With its large brewhouse, it also began seeking contracts. It produced beers for the big Brooklyn Brewery for a while and for smaller brewing companies like Sackets Harbor and Harlem, along with another West Coast brand, Spanish Peaks. Contract brewers come and go, of course. Brooklyn and Sackets Harbor both pulled out, leaving the brewery's primary business (other than Kingfisher) to be found in a company called Shmaltz Brewing Company (page 167), makers of the He'Brew line and Coney Island Craft Lagers.

In 2013, Shmaltz had grown large enough to open its own brewery in nearby Clifton Park, taking its beers and some Mendocino employees with it. So, at the time this book was going to press, Olde Saratoga/Mendocino was in another sort of transition period. The brewery hired veteran Luke Erdody as its head brewer in 2013, which turned out to be a good match. He's up to the challenge of producing a light-tasting and light-bodied lager like Kingfisher, a difficult skill to master. "I actually like brewing Kingfisher," Erdody said. "It's a true lager."

With Kingfisher a fairly solid anchor, the focus is on boosting Mendocino east of the Mississippi, said Max Oswald, the brewery's northeast regional sales manager. The flagship continues to be Red Tail Ale, one of those classic West Coast pale ales (like Sierra Nevada Pale Ale) that helped spur the craft beer boom in the first place. "People talk about all the West Coast brewers opening in the East, but this is really where that started," Oswald said.

But Mendocino is not riding Red Tail alone. Its beers are grouped into various series, such as the Select collection that includes Eye of the Hawk, Black Hawk Stout, and White Hawk Select IPA; and the Imperial collection, featuring a barleywine, a stout, and an IPA. A new series, called Talon, will be mostly double or stronger versions of beers like IPA, packaged in 22-ounce bottles. Creative seasonals include the Black Orange IPA for spring and White Ale with Key Lime for summer. The Olde Saratoga line includes Saratoga Lager, at 5.5 percent ABV with Czech and German hops; and Saratoga IPA, at 6.8 percent ABV with Cascade and Fuggles hops. The summer seasonal is a Kolsch. "Olde Saratoga is a grassroots brand," Oswald said. "The thing is to grow it in the local market and move it on from there."

Olde Saratoga/Mendocino is a production brewery, about a mile north of the downtown Saratoga Springs business district, but it has a well-appointed tasting room that features beers from several of its lines on tap. That part of the business is supported by local customers, "and the beer adventurers who come in to see what we're about," Oswald said.

Olde Saratoga/Mendocino Brewing Company

Opened: 1997.

Type: Production brewery.

Owners: Mendocino Brewing Company (owned by the UB Group, India).

Brewer: Luke Erdody.

System: 125-barrel Santa Rosa brewhouse.

Annual production: About 50,000 barrels (70,000 barrels capacity).

Distribution: Kingfisher Premium Lager is sold throughout the United States and Canada. Mendocino brands are distributed east of the Mississippi, and the Olde Saratoga line in eastern New York state and parts of New Jersey and Connecticut.

Hours: 5 p.m. to 10 p.m. Monday to Friday and noon to 10 p.m. on Saturday. Growler fills and packaged beer for sale.

Parking: Yes.

Shmaltz Brewing Company

Est. 1996

6 Fairchild Square, Clifton Park, NY 12065
(518) 406-5430 • www.shmaltzbrewing.com

You could say that Shmaltz Brewing Company was established in 5757. But it didn't start brewing its own beers in its own brewhouse until 5774. That would be according to the Jewish calendar, of course. The dates could also be recorded as 1996 and 2013.

Here it's important to get something straight. Shmaltz, makers of He'Brew Beers, is not just for a Jewish audience. "People who aren't Irish drink Guinness," Shmaltz CEO Jeremy Cowan likes to say. "People who aren't Jewish drink our beers." That's why in 5774 . . . or rather 2013, Shmaltz opened a 50-barrel brewery to make He'Brew beers for a market that spans forty states.

The brewery is in the Albany suburb of Clifton Park in Saratoga County, not far from the Olde Saratoga/Mendocino Brewing Company (page 164) where Cowan had his beers made under contract for years. After seventeen years in the wilderness of contract brewing, Cowan finally found his own promised land. If you think this piece is a little long on the Jewish shtick, by the way, you probably haven't been exposed to Cowan and his marketing. They're loaded with a Borscht Belt mentality, as seen with the beer originally called Messiah Bold—aka "The Beer You've Been Waiting For."

He'Brew is trademarked as "The Chosen Beer." We're talking about a company with beers known as Funky Jewbelation and ReJewvenator, as well as Hop Manna and David's Slingshot. It's run by an owner who wrote a memoir a few years back called "Craft Beer Bar Mitzvah: How It Took 13 Years, Extreme Jewish Brewing, and Circus Sideshow Freaks to Make Shmaltz Brewing Company an International Success." But, as Cowan said, the shtick is for everyone, of all persuasions. So are the beers, none of which are mainstream, and some of which push the edge, even bordering on extreme.

Cowan launched the He'Brew brand in San Francisco before moving east and setting up the

Beers brewed: He'Brew Beers: Genesis Dry Hopped Session Ale, Messiah Nut Brown Ale, ReJewvenator, Funky Jewbelation, Hop Manna IPA, Bittersweet Lenny's R.I.P.A., Origin Pomegranate Ale, David's Slingshot (summer lager), limited releases, and seasonals.

The Pick: Dubbel, doppel, or double—it doesn't matter for a beer as complex as the ReJewvenator. Fig, molasses, nut, and raisin flavors (and more) are found in this brew.

company headquarters in New York City. Tireless marketing paved the way for a successful brand, and the success of that brand paved the way for the brewery. Shmaltz production, which then included both He'Brew and Coney Island Lagers, finally topped 10,000 barrels per year and headed toward 15,000. Cowan called that the breakeven point for opening a brewery, especially on such a large scale. But it didn't happen without worry. "This is a scale of investment that is terrifying and unheard of in my entire life," Cowan said. "But this is where you're able to start covering the expense and a save of efficiencies." He has solid support, however. He brought former Olde Saratoga/Mendocino general manager Bob Craven and head brewer Paul McErlean to Shmaltz when he started up.

Craven and McErlean were integral in building up the Shmaltz beers and brands during the contract days. They set up a state-of-the-art brewhouse in the spring of 2013, and not without some seemingly divine last-minute intervention, sort of like the parting of the Red Sea. Cowan had been in long-term negotiations with a landlord elsewhere, but that deal fell through late in the process. "We suddenly needed a place to go," Cowan said. He managed to locate and seal the deal on the warehouse space in Clifton Park rather quickly. "The folks here, the town, everybody, couldn't have been more cooperative," he said. The space is huge, with room to grow. "We're going to grow, but carefully," Cowan said. The tasting room is also spacious.

Now it's on to the beer. He'Brew started with Genesis Ale and Messiah Bold, which have now evolved into Genesis Dry Hopped Session Ale and Messiah Nut Brown Ale. Those were followed by beers like Hop Manna IPA and Bittersweet Lenny's R.I.P.A (a rye double IPA). After that, Cowan's He'Brew line starts to seem like bringing chaos out of order. Take ReJewvenator, a "double dunkel" that is a combination Belgian dubbel and European doppel bock. Or Funky Jewbelation, a beer that changes from year to year and is a literal a blend of other brews in the He'Brew line. And Origin Pomegranate Ale may not be the only craft-brewed pomegranate beer out there, but it's likely the only one with a label that name-checks pomegranate from the Bible's "Song of Songs." It all makes David's Slingshot summer lager—He'Brew's first lager—seem rather tame, despite the somewhat unusual use of Vienna malt in a summer lager.

And speaking of lager . . . in 2007, Cowan founded a second beer line, called Coney Island Lagers, which ditched He'Brew's Biblical icons in favor of garish images from the beachfront playground, such as Sword Swallower India Pale Lager and Human Block Head America Imperial Bock. Not long after opening the Clifton Park brewery, Cowan sold the Coney Island line to Alchemy & Science of Burlington, Vermont. Cowan was to be a consultant for the Coney Island beer, while retaining full ownership of Shmalz and He'Brew.

At this point, there's just one thing left to say: *L'chaim*!

Shmaltz Brewing Company

Opened: Company started in 1996; brewery opened in 2013.
Type: Production brewery.
Owner: Jeremy Cowan.
Brewer: Paul McErlean.
System: 50-barrel JV Northwest.
Annual production: Up to 20,000 barrels.
Distribution: Thirty-six states; bottles and draft.
Hours: Check the website or call for hours.
Parking: Yes.

Ales and Lagers

If you're going to visit the breweries in this book, you'll have to know how to speak the language of beer to talk shop with the bartenders and tour guides and not embarrass yourself on the tour. First off, beer is any fermented beverage made from malted barley, usually with an addition of hops. The two main types of beer are ales and lagers.

What's the difference between the two? It's quite simple: two different yeasts. These have a number of small differences, the most important of which is that the optimum temperature for fermentation and aging is higher for ale yeasts (in the 60 degrees Fahrenheit range) than for lager yeasts (in the 40 degrees Fahrenheit range). That's more than just a thermostat setting. The warmer operating temperature of ale yeast encourages a faster, more vigorous fermentation that creates aromatic compounds known as phenols and esters. These can give ale-fermented beers fragrant aromas such as melon, banana, raisin, clove, and vanilla. (Lew Bryson invented a useful term for these aromas: "alefruit.")

On the other hand, the cooler lager fermentation produces a very clean aroma and flavor palette. Lagers generally have purer malt and hop characteristics. A lager brewer will tell you that there's nowhere to hide when you make lager beer; the unadorned nature of the beer makes flaws stand out immediately.

Think of the two yeasts in terms of jungles and pine forests. Warm ale fermentations are like lush jungles with exotic arrays of flavors, splendid in their diversity. By comparison, cold lager fermentations are more like northern pine forests—intense, focused, and pure.

For much of the history of the American craft brewing movement, ale brewers outnumbered lager brewers, often by as much as ten to one. Given that lagers are by far the most popular beers in the world, how did this come to be? In a few words: Ale can be easier, cheaper, and faster to produce.

After lagers are fermented, they undergo an extended aging period of at least three weeks at low temperatures. The cooling and the tank time required add energy costs and decrease turnover. In the same amount of time, it would be possible to put twice as much ale through those tanks. Add the energy and labor costs of the more complicated decoction brewing process used for lagers, and you wind up with a product that costs substantially more to brew than ales, but has to be priced the same. No wonder there have been more ale brewers!

When it comes to lager, New York is blessed with several brewers making deliciously varied lagers—for example, Matt Brewing Company (Saranac), Brooklyn Brewery, and Greenpoint Beerworks/KelSo. (The New York City metro area seems especially welcoming to lagers, despite the added expense and space requirement.) Meanwhile, many craft brewers who didn't have the expertise or the space for lagering ten years ago have brushed up on the technique and added tanks to accommodate the process.

And of course these craft lagers are, for the most part, full of body and flavor (unlike the pale yellow, fizzy, mass-produced domestic examples). So, yes, the number of ales still exceeds the number of lagers, in New York as well as elsewhere. But watch out—the lagers are gaining.

Hudson Valley—Catskills

A lot of people like to talk about whether or not the Hudson River is really a river, at least south of the Albany–Troy area. The Hudson is tidal up to the dam north of Troy; south of the dam, it's an estuary. Given the steep banks along most of its length through this area—the Palisades, the Hudson Highlands, and Storm King Mountain—you could even call it a fjord. But don't miss two important points: It's historic and it's beautiful.

History happened because with no current and no waterfalls, navigation was a breeze. This provided Henry Hudson with an easy route to explore, even though it wasn't the Northwest Passage he'd been hired to find. That ease of navigation made the Hudson an important battleground in the Revolutionary War.

The area was settled first by the Dutch, then the British, and finally by the Americans. Sailboats regularly plied the wide waters all the way to Albany. Towns grew up along the Hudson, leading to rich trade up- and downriver with fruit, produce, furs, and meat. The Roosevelts—a family that gave us two presidents—made their money this way. In later years, the wealth would come from the factories that lined the Hudson, though these factories would dump their waste into the estuary and create problems for generations not yet born. Starting in the 1970s, a cleanup of the Hudson began, first with an end to dumping, and later culminating in the massive PCB dredging project.

Different kinds of stories and histories happened here too. This is the land of Rip Van Winkle, Ichabod Crane, and the Headless Horseman. The Borscht Belt, now long since faded away, launched stand-up comedy nearby. And in 1969, thousands and thousands of young, long-haired, flower-adorned young folk gathered over the course of a rainy few days in 1969 for the original Woodstock festival (not, however, in Woodstock itself).

Today, the charms of the Hudson Valley make it a magnet for affluent or mobile New Yorkers seeking to leave their city troubles behind. They're the types who patronize the many boutique shops and farmers markets, and the craft breweries, too.

It sometimes seems the Hudson Valley has two kinds of towns: The ones that have been "re-discovered," and the ones that are still waiting for their chance. Up to about Poughkeepsie, the commuter rail lines make many of the towns into bedroom communities for city workers. Elsewhere, there's the feel of a more rural small town.

And while the river is the region's main street, don't forget the mountains. The Catskills march away to the west and north (along with sub-ranges like the Shawangunks near New Paltz) and the Taconics form a line down just off the eastern side of the river.

In a state filled with beautiful scenery, the Hudson Valley could well be the most impressive. Come on up and enjoy the fjord.

Other breweries and brewing companies

Sloop Brewing (www.sloopbrewing.com) in Poughkeepsie is a part-time nanobrewery with a growing reputation but no tasting room of its own. Yonkers Brewing Co. (www.yonkersbrewing.com), located at the point where the valley ends and New York City starts, was transitioning from contract to nanobrewing as this book went to press.

Other beer sites

The Hop (458 Main St., Beacon) is a combination retail store and craft beer bar; Golden Rail Ale House (29 Old North Plank Rd., Newburgh) is modeled on an English pub; The Country Inn (1380 County Road 2, Krumville) hosts many taps and legendary bottled beer selection; The Craftsman Ale House (235 Harrison Ave., Harrison) boasts draft and bottled beer, and Half Time Beverage (2290 South Rd., Poughkeepsie) is the region's best-known beer retailer.

Area Attractions

The **Walkway over the Hudson** (845-454-9649; www.walkway.org) is a spectacular pedestrian-and-bike friendly use of a former railroad bridge spanning the Hudson River between Poughkeepsie and Highland. It's 212 feet high and 1.28 miles long. **The Catskills** offer more than 300 miles of hiking trails, many with marked trailheads off the main road (www.catskillmountaineer.com; www.visitthecatskills.com, and www.backpacker.com [search for Catskills]).

Historic venues include ***Washington's Headquarters State Historic Site***, (84 Liberty St., Newburgh, NY 12551; 845-562-1195; nys parks.com/historic-sites/17/), just behind Newburgh Brewing Company. Gen. George Washington spent more time at this headquarters site than at any other during the war, and planned strategy for the Saratoga campaign here. The ***United States Military Academy at West Point*** (845-938-2638; www.westpoint.edu/Visiting/SitePages/Home.aspx), America's oldest military academy, offers a gorgeous setting. There is a visitors center at the Thayer Gate, off Route 218, and the West Point Museum houses a wide variety of war paraphernalia. The ***Franklin Delano Roosevelt National Historic Site*** (4097 Albany Post Rd., Hyde Park, NY 12538; 845-229-9115; www.nps.gov/hofr/index.htm) includes Springwood, FDR's home, and his presidential library. Also nearby are Eleanor Roosevelt's home, Val-Kill, and the Vanderbilt Mansion. ***The Old Rhinebeck Aerodrome*** (42 Stone Church Rd., Rhinebeck, NY 12572; 845-758-8610; www.oldrhinebeckaerodrome.com) stages World War I-era dogfights and aerial demonstrations. ***The Museum at Bethel Woods*** (200 Hurd Rd., Bethel, NY 12720; 866-781-2922; www.bethelwoods center.org/museum) is a multimedia exploration of Woodstock and the Sixties. ***The Thomas Cole Historic House*** (218 Spring St., Catskill, NY 12414; 518-943-7465; www.hudsonriverschool.org/introduction) is the restored home and studio of the artist and founder of the Hudson River School. The Hudson River School Art Trail maps sites where visitors can see the views that inspired Cole, Frederic Church, and other Hudson River School Artists.

Andean Brewing Company (Kuka)

300 Corporate Dr., Unit 2, Blauvelt, NY 10913
(646) 450-5852 • www.kukablog.com

The taste is earthy but subtle. That subtlety is matched on the labels by the small (quite small) print indicating "brewed with maca root." There is maca root in all the Kuka brand beers brewed by the Andean Brewing Company, located in a corporate park in Blauvelt, Rockland County.

Maca is a root vegetable shaped like a radish and eaten like a potato, with a taste you begin to perceive as you progress through the beer lineup. It doesn't whack you over the head. But it catches up to you. "It's earthy, nutty, and creamy," said Andean Brewing founder Alireza Saifi. "It's there in the background. Too much tastes like dirt, so we don't use too much." It also tends to mask the alcohol, he said, so a 6 percent ABV beer might taste more like a 4 percent session beer, and a near-barleywine-strength 10 percent beer might taste more like a 6 or 7 percent beer. That, of course, can be a little dangerous. Otherwise, these beers, whether an IPA, a Brown, or a Belgian Tripel, taste like the beers you'd expect in those styles. In fact, they are all surprisingly authentic.

So why put maca in there at all? It's not a gimmick, Saifi said, pointing out that maca is both a traditional food of Peruvians living high in the Andes Mountains and a source for their traditional, low-alcohol beer. It grows well at 4,000 feet and above. It's Saifi's goal to make beers using such traditional ingredients from around the world. He just happens to be starting with maca root. Of course, it helps his products stand out from the crowd. He's certainly aware that maca root has reported health benefits—including its alleged power to balance the hormones and, by the way, stimulate the libido. But you won't find any of that on the label of Andean Brewing's Kuka beer. And even though the federal Alcohol and Tobacco Tax and Trade Bureau says it's okay "to talk about it," Saifi is not comfortable doing

Beers brewed: Pale Ale, American IPA, Imperial Rye IPA, Belgian Blonde Ale, Belgian Golden Ale, Belgian Tripel, Banana Nut Brown Ale, and Imperial Stout.

The Pick: This one's hard. The Banana Nut Brown Ale is superb, and with all that flavor, who can tell there's maca root in it? The Rye IPA is an extraordinarily smooth beer for 9.4 percent ABV, confirming the "masking" effect of the maca additive.

so. He's more interested in making sure customers know they're getting authentic beers.

He's coy about saying how much goes into each beer, but it seems clear it's not a major ingredient. Some beers—the ones that are heavier with more alcohol—have more than the lighter beers. Saifi said each brew has "enough" to give it a maca character. The maca root comes in powdered form and is added to either the mash or the kettle, depending on the beer. "If you like our beers and can appreciate the interesting profile, you'll come back to them," he said.

Saifi is an Iranian immigrant raised in New York City. He's such a New Yorker he considers Blauvelt, just minutes from the Tappan Zee Bridge, to be Upstate. A few years before launching the brewery, he tried making an iced tea from coca leaves. The tea was produced in Italy, but the idea fizzled when he found it hard to get it through customs. His first beer venture ran afoul of problems with the brewery he had contracted with, so he built his own, a 20-barrel Crivaller brewhouse. The corporate park space, which includes a tasting room, has room for expansion. The fermenters are each 20-barrels, and Saifi said he intends his batch size to stay that way. That means—at least for now—no double-batching in a 40-barrel fermenter. "We are an artisanal brewery, so we believe in small batches and making room for more types of beers," Saifi said.

The brewery started in February 2013 with seven fulltime beers and more in the pipeline. Despite that one quirky ingredient, some beers are relatively straightforward, such as the American Pale Ale and Imperial Rye IPA. Then there are the innovative brews. The Belgian Golden Ale, for example, is made with Blue Agave (although the Tripel version uses the more traditional Belgian candi sugar). And there's a Banana Nut Brown Ale, with real fruit, that tastes like a mouthful of banana bread in liquid form. And there's an Imperial Stout made with chocolate, coffee beans, and piñon nuts. Notice all the South American flavors? "There's a big world of ingredients out there," Saifi said. "Right now we're focused on South America, but of course that's a big place with a lot of foods."

Kuka is a word derived from "coca"; in the Andean language it can mean "food as a gift from the gods." That will cover a lot of the brewery's experimentation. In the future, Saifi said, Kuka may experiment with a commercial version of the traditional beer made exclusively from maca root, as the Andean people brew it. "But we need to establish our brands first, establish ourselves as brewers," he said. "We want to build a level of trust with our customers and then see where we go."

Andean Brewing Company (Kuka)

Opened: 2013.

Type: Production brewery.

Owner: Alireza Saifi.

Brewers: Alireza Saifi and Alon Hochman.

System: 20-barrel Crivaller brewhouse.

Annual production: About 1,200 barrels.

Distribution: Lower Hudson Valley, New York City, and Long Island. All beers are available in draft; the low-gravity beers (under 8 percent ABV) are in 12-ounce bottles and high-gravity beers come in 22-ounce bottles.

Hours: Call for tasting room hours.

Parking: Yes.

Brewery at Dutch Ale House

255 Main St., Saugerties, NY 12477
(845) 247-2337 • www.dutchalehouse.com

A brewer at another Hudson Valley brewpub advised: "Don't miss the Dutch Ale House—it's a lot of fun." He got that right. The Dutch Ale house is a friendly bar, with good food, lots of kitsch, and an adjoining "party room" and art gallery. Oh, and there's that little brewhouse in the backroom. What more could you want from a brewpub in the lively little Hudson River community of Saugerties?

It's all set in motion by the warm welcome from co-owner and Saugerties native Karyn Pavich, and the slightly more boisterous greeting from Johnny Pavich, her husband and the brewer. Once he starts talking, you learn two things: He has an enthusiasm for beer and he's not from Upstate. He's from Queens. Moreover, unlike almost every other beer maker in this book, he didn't start out as a homebrewer—he taught himself. "I learned to brew before I brewed here," he said. "I thought, 'I'm going to make beer and hopefully people will enjoy it.' And they tell me they do."

A bar has occupied this location for a long time, though exactly how long is hard to say. "It's been a bar since the day Prohibition ended, and it opened the day Prohibition ended, so it was probably a bar before then, if you know what I mean," Pavich said. Past names include Coby's and the Dutch Tavern. Pavich likes to tell people "the first TV in Saugerties was in this bar," as he points to a spot now occupied by a sleek flat screen showing ESPN. Until Johnny and Karyn Pavich bought it in 2009, it had been a "good beer" bar for a while. The cards Pavich hands out still say "One of the Hudson Valley's Best Beer Bars." Today you'll find beers like Ommegang, Troegs, Lagunitas, KelSo, Bronx, and Long Trail on tap. Like many an old bar, the main room is narrow but deep. There's a mural over the bar, and a pair of Dutch wooden shoes hangs on the wall.

It took Pavich until February 2012 to get the brewhouse going. "It's small—really small," he said. It's a 2.5-barrel system (not the smallest in New York), and Pavich gets 5 kegs at a time, brewing about twice a month. That makes his annual

Beers brewed: Dutch Colonial Summer Wheat, LX Porter, and Karyn's Pale Ale (KPA).

The Pick: There was only one beer on tap during my visit—the Porter. It was rich and satisfying, a little on the sweet side. A sessionable dark beer for a place you'd like to spend a session in.

production about 60 barrels a year. His beers include Dutch Colonial Summer Wheat, brewed with Cascade hops (5.25 percent ABV), LX Porter, and Karyn's Pale Ale (KPA). "I'm only making beer for [the bar] now," he said, "but I have ambition to do distribution and maybe even bottling."

His regulars join a "mug club," with stoneware mugs adorned with the ale house logo and members' numbers on them. They are made locally by Wardell Pottery. The brewpub's food menu is pub fare with salads, sandwiches, burgers, and some main courses. There are a few signature twists, like the Mahi-Mahi Ceviche and Ginger Shrimp Wontons appetizers, a Ropa Vieja (shredded Lain-style beef) entrée, and fried plantains as a side dish.

Saugerties is a Hudson River town not far from Woodstock (though if you're looking for the site of the famous 1969 music festival, it's about 70 miles away in Bethel). Pavich said 90 percent of Dutch Ale's customers are locals, but more and more tourists are coming to enjoy the river and mountains. "And more of them are interested in enjoying good beer," he added, "so that's what we try to do."

Brewery at Dutch Ale House

Opened: 2011.

Type: Brewpub.

Owners: Johnny and Karyn Pavich.

Brewer: Johnny Pavich.

System: 2.5 barrels, self-built.

Annual production: 60 barrels.

Distribution: On-premises only.

Hours: Bar: 11:30 a.m. to 11 p.m. Monday to Saturday; noon to 11 p.m. Sunday.

Food: Full restaurant menu.

Parking: No off-street parking.

Captain Lawrence Brewing Company

ELMSFORD, NEW YORK

444 Saw Mill River Rd., Elmsford, NY 10523
(914)-741-BEER • www.captainlawrencebrewing.com

Where would Scott Vaccaro and Captain Lawrence Brewing Company be without the four-year fermentation science degree offered by the University of California, Davis? Vaccaro could have been a Villanova-educated accountant instead of the owner and brewer at Captain Lawrence. But that seems doubtful. It's not just that Vaccaro learned brewing at Davis. The four years he spent learning how to brew beer *and* getting a real four-year degree also made his Villanova-educated accountant dad a little happier with the career choice. "I convinced my parents that I could get a degree in a subject that I wasn't yet old enough to drink," he said.

Dad's smiling now: Captain Lawrence exploded out of the box in December 2005 and within eight years had outgrown its first brewery, moved into a second in the Westchester County town of Elmsford, and was on track to make 20,000 barrels in 2013. That puts Captain Lawrence in the top echelon of New York craft brewers. "I did not expect it to get this big," Vaccaro said. "I was just hoping to do what I loved."

Not bad for a brewery named after a street, either. "I grew up on Captain Lawrence Road [in South Salem] and that's where I made my first batch," said Vaccaro, who homebrewed while still a high school senior. Vaccaro then embarked on a storybook brewing odyssey: He landed an internship at the respected Adnams Southwold Brewery in England, then got a job after graduation at Sierra Nevada Brewing Co. in California. After a while, he was lured back to the East Coast and discovered that if he wanted a job in a brewery near home, he would have to open it himself. The original Captain Lawrence was in Pleasantville and had a 20-barrel JV Northwest system. It quickly hit its maximum 8,700-barrel-per-year capacity. "The day we knocked out the walk-in cooler with the forklift was the day we said, 'We need to get bigger,'" Vaccaro said.

Beers brewed: Year-round: Freshchester Pale Ale, Liquid Gold, IPA, Captain's Kolsch, Smoked Porter, Brown Bird Ale, and Imperial IPA. Seasonals: Sun Block, Pumpkin Ale, and Winter Ale. Limited releases: Smoke from the Oak barrel-aged series; Hops N' Roses, Nor'Easter, Xtra Gold, Espresso Stout, St. Vincent's Dubbel, Saison, and more.

The Pick: Liquid Gold is fermented at a high 84 degrees and has hints of lemon, orange, and banana. My tasting notes describe it as a "light" Belgian, but there's nothing light about the flavor.

The new brewery opened in late 2011. It has a 40-barrel Newlands system, although Vaccaro admitted that at times he wishes for a 50-barrel system. He also installed a 7-barrel pilot system for experimenting and small releases. Using that system and a 12-ounce bottling line, he serves a market that includes parts of New York, New Jersey, and Connecticut. His sales are 75 percent draft and 25 percent bottles. "Our big market is New York City," he said. "Our home market is a draft market."

Captain Lawrence grew on the strength of a few core beers, notably the flagship Freshchester Pale Ale, Kolsch, Smoked Porter, and a spiced Belgian light ale called Liquid Gold. These remain in the year-round rotation along with the IPA (hopped with Citra and Centennial), Imperial IPA, and Brown Bird Ale. The big system is running all-out to fill orders for those beers and for the popular seasonals like Sun Block (American wheat) and Pumpkin Ale. There are also about a dozen limited-releases. Barrel-aged beers include the Smoke from the Oak series, and the sours include Hops N' Roses, made with rose hips, hibiscus, and elderflower. But making time and space for those can be a challenge—"We grapple with the production side versus the creative side," Vaccaro said.

Vaccaro lets his assistants play around with some of the limited releases. Brewer assistant Anthony Perillo made a Coffee IPA, for example, and assistant Mike Coulehan came up with Monkey Madness, a Belgian golden brewed with mango purée. Vaccaro himself tinkered with the Pale Ale for five and a half years after it debuted. "I still drink more Pale Ale than anything else," he said.

The new brewery is located in one of Westchester County's ubiquitous corporate office and industrial parks, but that doesn't mean that Vaccaro (or his mom, to be more precise) didn't work to make the tasting room inviting. It even has an outdoor bocce ball court.

Captain Lawrence Brewing Company

Opened: Original location 2005; new location in 2011.

Type: Production brewery.

Owner and Brewer: Scott Vaccaro.

System: 40-barrel Newlands brewhouse, with a 7-barrel pilot system.

Annual production: 20,000 barrels.

Distribution: New York metro area, and parts of Connecticut and New Jersey.

Hours: 4 p.m. to 8 p.m. Wednesday to Friday; noon to 6 p.m. Saturday; noon to 5 p.m. Sunday.

Food: The Village Dog hot dog cart is at the tasting room Wednesday through Saturday.

Parking: Yes.

Cave Mountain Brewing Company

5359 Route 23, Windham, NY 12496
(518) 734-9222 • www.cavemountainbrewing.com

The Catskill Mountains may not be as grand—or as high—as the Adirondacks, and the heyday of the Borscht Belt hotels may be long gone. But drive up to Cave Mountain Brewing Company in the ski resort town of Windham, and you'll be reminded of the grandeur of the mountain range and the nearby Hudson River Valley vista. When you step inside the brewpub, you'll also be reminded that entertainment in a mountain resort carries with it a certain sort of vibe: You're here to escape. You're also high—that is, in the sense that Cave Mountain Brewing is probably the highest-elevation brewery in New York state. The town of Windham is about on par with the town of Lake Placid, at more than 1,800 feet, but the Cave Mountain brewpub is nearer to the local ski runs. (It certainly seems higher.)

Cave Mountain has another marker: It's probably the smallest brewhouse operating in any brewpub in New York. Owner Timothy Adams is quite aware of that claim to fame because he has clearly reached the capacity of what he can brew on his 1-barrel system. "We could use more capacity, but we just don't have the space under this roof," Adams said. He's thinking about building a production brewery close by in the near future. In the meantime, Adams, who describes himself as "owner-brewer-chef," and his brewer, Jamie Caligure, do their best to keep the beers coming and to keep them creative. The brewpub generally has twelve beers on tap, all of which are house brews unless the little brewhouse can't keep up. The bestsellers are Belgian White, American IPA, and Blueberry Wheat. These beers are always on tap, as are other core brews like Irish Red, Honey Blonde, and Oatmeal Stout.

After that, Adams and Caligure get to play around. Sometimes they come up with a variation on the core beers, like a Smokin' Hot Blonde, and other times they think a little more outside the box. One such limited release was a Patersbier Ale, or "Father's Beer," based on the Belgian Trappist monks' tradition of a beer made for their own

Beers brewed: Hefeweizen, Belgian White, Sweet Oatmeal Stout, American I.P.A., West Coast Red, and Blueberry Wheat. Seasonals: Blueberry Stout, Wedel Weiss, California Common Lager, Peach Wheat, Chai Milk Stout, Guru Gluten-Free Pale Ale, seasonals, and limited releases.

The Pick: What better way to warm up after a day on the slopes than with the rich and flavorful Oatmeal Stout—a chairlift in a glass.

personal stashes. Others have included a California Common Lager (a lager fermented at ale temperatures) and a Chai Milk Stout. "These beers follow the folly and the fancy of the brewer, so he can flex his muscles and have fun," Adams said.

Adams, who had worked as a chef in restaurants around New York state, launched Cave Mountain Brewing in 2008. "I'd been cooking and working as a chef, and when I decided to do my own place, it seemed like a brewery—a brewpub—was the right way to go," he said. The building has something of a mountain-chalet, ski-lodge feel to it, and the menu offers upscale pub food. "It's all relatively comfort-based," Adams said. "We have a small open kitchen so we're not able to do everything I'd like to do as a chef." Still, you'll find grilled fish and steaks, sandwiches, burgers, wraps, and more.

All of this keeps the brewpub hopping most of the year, not just during ski season. "Summer and winter are neck and neck a far as volume of sales," Adams said, listing downhill mountain biking as one of the warm-weather draws. "In the summer, there's more apt to be families and tourists on week days because school's out. In the winter we're slammed every weekend."

Cave Mountain Brewing Company

Opened: 2008.

Type: Brewpub.

Owner: Timothy Adams.

Brewer: Jamie Caligure.

System: 1-barrel brewhouse.

Annual production: 300 barrels.

Distribution: On-premises only.

Hours: The pub opens at 5 p.m. Monday, Thursday, and Friday; it opens at noon on Saturday and Sunday.

Food: Upscale pub menu.

Parking: No off-street parking.

Chatham Brewing

30 Main St., Chatham, NY 12037
(518) 697-0202 • www.chathambrewing.com

Chatham is a small town offering a rural escape for city dwellers. Some come from nearby Albany, about forty minutes away, and others drive more than two hours from New York City to their weekend homes in the area. It's the kind of place where folks like to buy fresh, local produce from farmers, try the cheese made at local dairy farms, and otherwise embrace the concept of "buy local."

"It's a very supportive community for small artisanal producers like ourselves," said Chatham Brewing co-owner Tom Crowell on a Saturday morning while he helped to pour beers at the indoor farmers market that has been hosting the brewery's tasting room. Since opening in 2006, Chatham Brewing has become part of the fabric in this town. It's located just off the Taconic Parkway, which connects the capital region and the big city.

Crowell and James "Jake" Cunningham started as homebrewers, as did so many other small brewers. They've always preferred—and now specialize in—British-style ales like IPAs and porters. They began brewing on a 3.5-barrel system that once served the Big House Brewing Co., a downtown Albany brewpub. As of early 2013, Chatham Brewing was housed in an old carriage house in an alleyway off Chatham's Main Street, hence their slogan: "Imported From Main Street." But Cunningham and Crowell are moving that little brewhouse to the building farther down Main Street that has been hosting the indoor farmers market. It was a former grocery store, among other things. They're also installing a new, custom-built 20-barrel brewhouse in that building. The 3.5-barrel system will brew pilot and small batch experiments—or what Crowell calls "more esoteric brews"—and will be the centerpiece of the new tasting room.

It's worthwhile at this point to talk a little about Chatham's unusual downtown geography. The streets join at odd angles, and some turns are so

Beers brewed: Blonde, Amber, IPA, 8 Barrel Ale, New Belgian Tripel, Maple Amber, many seasonals, and some one-offs.

The Pick: I'm really, really tempted to pick the Tripel, which has some wonderful caramel notes. But that 8 Barrel is the beer that really defines the brewery's character, with an excellent balance of malt and hops.

sharp you double-back on yourself. The reason: Chatham was once a major railroad junction where five different railroads met and crossed. That explains the odd blocks and the occasional flatiron-style buildings. (It also explains the railroad-symbol design in the company logo.)

Combined, the 23.5-barrel setup will be operated primarily by Matt Perry, who joined Chatham as its head brewer a few years after Crowell and Cunnigham started. In 2013, both owners still had their "day" jobs but hoped to transition into fulltime brewery guys after the new production brewery was up and running. Although their first brewing system was a hand-me-down, they custom-ordered the 20-barrel system. "We couldn't stomach the idea of buying a system that we're going to be working with and not seeing it first," Crowell said. "This way, we get what we want."

That could describe the thirty or so different beers Chatham makes, too. Take the one they call 8 Barrel. "This is our own favorite," Crowell said. "It's not hoppy enough for an IPA or a Double IPA, which is what we were shooting for. We had some judges taste it, and they said it doesn't meet the style guidelines for a Double IPA. But we like it the way it is. So, for now, we don't even put a style in the name. I guess you'd say it's like a strong amber." They also brew a special beer, an amber, that is the house beer at The Dive Bar in New York City.

Until they get the new brewhouse installed and ramped up, Chatham is selling much of its beer from farmers markets, including the tasting room in Chatham, and at off-premises accounts in places like Troy, Hudson, and Rhinebeck. The brewery's reputation in those areas was enhanced when it won the Matthew Vassar Brewers' Cup for the Hudson Valley's best brewery in 2012. Chatham Brewing sells beer in growlers and various sizes of kegs, including pony and Cornelius kegs. Crowell and Cunningham have a state grant that will allow them to buy a bottling line, but until then they do small-scale bottling in 22-ounce sizes of just a handful of their beers, including a barrel-aged brown ale, an Imperial Stout, and a Tripel. For a brewery that specializes in British styles, how'd they end up with a Tripel? "Matt [the brewer] wanted something he could take to Belgium Comes to Cooperstown," Crowell said, referring to the phenomenally popular summer fest at Brewery Ommegang.

The whiskey barrels that Chatham uses come from the Hillrock Estate Distillery in the Hudson Valley, another example of the type of local sourcing of which the brewery is so proud. "We get people who are traveling up the river doing beer tastings, looking for what's local," Crowell said. "So we're looking for that synergy with the local producers around here, for hops, and maybe even barley some day."

Chatham Brewing

Opened: 2006.

Type: Production brewery.

Owners: Tom Crowell and Jake Cunningham.

Brewer: Matt Perry.

System: 3.5-barrel Specific Mechanical (pilot system); 20-barrel Specific (coming in 2013).

Annual production: Under 500 barrels in early 2013; expected to increase to 1,500 or 2,000 after the new brewhouse installation.

Distribution: Primarily at the local farmers market and tasting room.

Hours: 11 a.m. to 5 p.m. Saturday.

Crossroads Brewing Company

21 Second St., Athens, NY 12015
(518) 945-2337 • www.crossroadsbrewingco.com

In 2010, Crossroads Brewing Company opened its brewhouse and tasting room. Then it opened a bar in an adjoining space in 2011. It added a kitchen in 2012. The next step, which may take a while, is renovating and reopening the upstairs performance space in its building, once known as the Brooks Opera House.

Crossroads Brewing is located in the first floor of the 1890s-era opera house building that sits two blocks from the Hudson River in Athens, a former industrial and river port town about forty minutes south of Albany. Both the business and the building are owned by Ken Landin and Janine Bennett. Hutch Kugeman has been the brewmaster from the start, overseeing Crossroads in its move from a production brewery with a tasting room to a combination brewery and brewpub. "It was great when we got that bar open and said, 'Hey, please come over and buy a pint.'" Kugeman said.

With its 7-barrel brewery (formerly used at Defiant Brewing Company and with enough tanks to brew some double batches), Crossroads now has forty off-premises accounts, from Albany down through the Hudson Valley and as far as Brooklyn. It serves a growing customer base in Athens with its ten rotating beer taps. In 2013, it was the only bar in town. (While it has a full liquor license, it only offered beer and wine at that time.) The renovation that Landin oversaw resulted in a brewpub dining area that mixes vintage woodwork and fixtures with some new installations, including a massive bar that easily accommodates a flight of Crossroads beers—and the notebook that a visiting beer writer is carrying—with room to spare.

Kugeman, an enthusiastic brewer, is right at home offering tastes of his beers, and leads tours on Saturdays. "I can't wait to see what you think of this one," he said before almost every pour. He

Beers brewed: Lighthouse Wheat, Outrage IPA, Angry Pete's Pale Ale, Brick Row Red Ale, Brooks Brown Ale, Brady's Bay Cream Ale, Abbey Road Belgian, Athens Mill Amber Ale, and seaonals.

The Pick: Abbey Road is a particularly fruity and spicy Belgian, but why argue with the popular choice? Outrage IPA is a liquid journey through the American hop landscape (without being over the top). You can't beat that.

learned to brew at the Pelican Pub & Brewery in Oregon, then spent eight years at Great Adirondack Brewing Company brewpub in Lake Placid. He also had a brief stint at Ithaca Beer Co. while he worked to start up Crossroads.

One of the first beers he brewed in Athens, the Outrage IPA, is still Crossroads' bestselling beer. "I really was going for a hop forward, West Coast pale," he said. "That was a new thing around here." He didn't expect it be the bestseller. It has 90 IBUs (a measure of hop bitterness, and a pretty high one at that), and is heavily dry hopped. Hop additions include Cascade, Centennial, Citra, Simcoe, Amarillo, Galaxy, and Falconer's Flight. "For a flagship beer, it's pretty tough to do," Kugeman said. "It's complicated."

He also launched First Pitch Pils early on, intending it to be a year-round beer. But lagering takes up too much needed tank storage space, so it was dropped to a seasonal. Then there's Homewrecker Imperial Double IPA. If the Athens customers were unsure of an IPA at first, imagine what the imperial version meant. "It took a while for some folks to realize you can't really drink five of these without some consequences," Kugeman said. And just to show his across-the-board skills, Kugeman also adds beers like Abbey Road, a 6.7 percent ABV Belgian, Brady's Bay Cream Ale, and Black Rock Stout.

Kugeman even makes his own root beer and cream soda, and the brewpub's wine list includes a generous number of New York state wines. The menu, overseen by chef Paul Parillo, puts heavy emphasis on local ingredients from Hudson Valley farms, orchards, and food producers. It's a pub menu, but a farm-fresh one. It's seasonal, too. Our spring visit found us ordering some wild rice cakes and a polenta served with spring pea shoots. It'll make you rethink pea shoots.

Athens is in a part of the growing Hudson Valley trend that combines artists, farm-to-table foodies, and weekenders (and fulltime transplants) from the big city down the river. The town of Hudson, directly across the Hudson River, has already turned into that kind of artsy preserve, and Athens may be next on the list. That's where the old Brooks Opera House fits in—a painstaking renovation should re-create a vintage entertainment venue on the second floor. "That space is really what sold the owners on the building," Kugeman said. "The beer is what's bringing people in now."

Crossroads Brewing Company

Opened: 2010.

Type: Brewpub.

Owners: Ken Landin and Janine Bennett.

Brewer: Hutch Kugeman.

System: 7-barrel system.

Annual production: 850 barrels in 2013.

Distribution: About 65 percent is sold at the bar and 35 percent to off-premises accounts. It's all draft, except for some bottles sold only at the bar.

Hours: 4 p.m. to 9 p.m. Monday, Wednesday, and Thursday; 4 p.m. to midnight Friday; 1 p.m. to midnight Saturday; 1 p.m. to 9 p.m. Sunday.

Food: Seasonal and farm-fresh pub menu.

Parking: On-street parking.

Defiant Brewing Company

6 East Dexter Plaza, Pearl River, NY 10965
(845) 920-8602 • www.defiantbrewing.com

You've heard of a man's man? Neill Acer is a brewer's brewer. "Being introduced to craft brewing for me was like being introduced to matches," he said. "You mean I can make fire? I can make beer? That's the greatest thing in the world." Perhaps that's why he named his brewery Defiant Brewing Company. It's not a sign of anger, he said, but a signal: He wanted to ensure that he could brew what he wanted and when he wanted.

Before launching Defiant, Acer had plenty of experience brewing in the Hudson Valley and New York City area. His résumé included the Mountain Valley (later Ramapo Valley) Brewpub and the short-lived West End Brewing Company on Manhattan's Upper West Side, among others. He also helped get Peekskill Brewery off the ground. Along the way, he helped train many of the brewers working in the New York region. "In some ways, it's the Golden Age of brewing, like the Golden Age of rail," he said. "The New York market is on fire right now."

Acer dove into his own brewery in 2008. Defiant is located in the commuter town of Pearl River, near the rail station. From the start, it has been a little different. It's a rough-edged place, looking more like the production brewery it is than a tasting room or pub. You've probably never seen so much copper in your life as you'll see on the tanks, kettle, and tuns lining the wall. "It is not a brewpub," Acer said. "It's a capital 'B' brewery." And yet Wednesdays through Sundays you can belly up to the very long bar opposite the row of copper-clad tanks and order beer and barbecue.

Credit the brewers: the same guys who fire up the brew kettle light up the smokers. "It's actually perfect for the sixteen-hour brew day," Acer said. "At the end of the day, when you're doing your second pitch, you can pull out the brisket . . . Both brewing and barbecue are best when they're not hurried." Acer's brewing philosophy? "We brew such a wide range—there's thirty different beers.

Beers brewed: Muddy Creek Lager, Medusa IPA, Little Thumper, O'Defiant Stout, Defiant Porter, many limited release or seasonals like Big Thumper, Christmas Ale, Orange Creamsicle, Four Horsemen series, Baron Von Weizen, Long Shadow Stout, Magnus Pongo (American strong ale), and others.

The Pick: Outside of Mexican restaurants, a toasty Vienna lager often seems to be an under-appreciated style. Defiant's Muddy Creek is a great example, crisp and malty. It's also a perfect accompaniment to barbecue.

We want to offer you a great glass of beer." While that means "no smoked watermelon double bocks," Acer does have some tricks in his fermenting tanks. Defiant has a Four Horsemen series, with each beer successively higher in alcohol. It also produces Orange Creamsicle Ale, with its hints of sweet orange and a big mouthfeel.

The core, "heavy lifter" beers include Medusa IPA and Muddy Creek Lager, a roasty example of the Vienna lager style, Acer said. (Muddy Creek reportedly was the town's former name, before someone found a pearl in the creek. More likely, the town realized Pearl River sounds more inviting.) Other regulars include the Prohibition Pilsner, Pale Ale, and O'Defiant Stout. To get a sense of Acer's "defiance," the chalkboard hanging from this beer's tank reads "Give us our counties back" and "England out of Ireland." An Irish flag hangs on the wall, too.

On my visit, Defiant's offerings on tap included Little Thumper, a 4 percent English ale, and Big Thumper, a 9.4 percent Imperial Pale Ale, each made with a single hop, the earthy English Fuggles. "Fuggles is a great hop, and it was fun to see what it could do," Acer said. There are eight tap lines at the brewery, and most of the beer there is sold in 10-ounce mugs. The next step up is a 25-ounce glass. "The smaller glasses work for people who want to try different things," said Defiant's Kyle Nicholson, who handles sales and sometimes works behind the bar. "The 25-ounce is for people who know what they like."

As a production brewery, Defiant sells most of its beer off-premises, with 80 percent going to accounts in the New York City metro area, including New Jersey. Defiant has been primarily draft-only, but Acer said he expected to launch a bottling line for 12-ounce beers by the end of 2013. "The market is so strong, especially the New York market," he said. He just wishes he had more time. "There's so much to beer. . . . I wish I had one hundred years of life to make more."

Defiant Brewing Company

Opened: 2008.

Type: Production brewery with a taproom that sells beer and barbecue.

Owner and Brewer: Neill Acer.

System: 15-barrel brewhouse with parts assembled from various sources.

Annual production: 2,000 barrels.

Distribution: Mostly off-premises in the New York metro area.

Hours: 2 p.m. to 10 p.m. Monday to Thursday; 2 p.m. to midnight Friday and Saturday; noon to 8 p.m. Sunday.

Food: In a word: barbecue.

Parking: Parking lot adjacent to nearby railroad tracks.

Gilded Otter Restaurant and Brewpub

3 Main St., New Paltz, NY 12561
(845) 256-1700 • www.gildedotter.com

Some people think of beer when they hear the word "Bohemian." Others think of a place like New Paltz. It's part college town (SUNY New Paltz) and part rock-climbing capital of the East, courtesy of the sheer rock faces on the nearby Shawangunk Mountains. It's filled with funky shops, and it seems tie-dye never went out of style here. Yet New Paltz also is steeped in history: Huguenot Street, named for the French Protestant settlers who came here in the late 1600s, is one of the oldest continuously inhabited streets in the country. There are half a dozen houses here that date to that era, plus a church and the remains of a fort. This combination of funkiness and stability suits the Gilded Otter Brewing Co. Restaurant and Brewpub, named for the ship that carried the Huguenot settlers to the New World (not for a species of critters inhabiting the nearby Wallkill River). The brewpub sits on a corner of Main Street, facing the 'Gunks, as local people call them, and Huguenot Street. The historic houses are just a short walk away.

Anyway, stability is the word. The pub opened in 1998, and brewer Darren Currier has been here since 2000. Rick Rauch remains the managing partner of the Catskill Mountain Brewing Co., Inc., the private corporation that owns the Gilded Otter. The building also lends itself to the air of stability, with the exterior's facade of fieldstones and the interior's half-timbered beams. The brewhouse winds its way around the joint. The mash vessels and brew kettle are behind the first-floor bar, and a set of tanks encircles the staircase to the second level, where more tanks and vessels wait. The mash and kettles "are pretty efficient, but after that we're moving beer around all over the place," Currier said.

If you check the Gilded Otter's website, you'll see an animated graphic that boasts of the brewpub's ability to do "true lager" in a "decoction brewhouse." Currier suggests that it's really an infusion system, although he can adjust mash temperatures as needed. If that seems a bit technical for you, know this: Currier is able to pull some

Beers brewed: Huguenot St. American Lager, Three Pines India Pale Ale, New Paltz Crimson Lager, Belgian Spring Wit, Stone House Irish Stout, Rail Trail Pale Ale, Back Porch Summer Lager, Hefeweizen, Mayday Maibock, Winter Wassail, seasonals, and limited releases.

The Pick: A sessionable lager for a hot summer day, the Huguenot St. (at a low 3.8 percent ABV) is an enticement to stick around New Paltz for a while.

great flavors out of his lagers—even the lighter ones—and that's not always easy to do. Check out the delicate notes of his Huguenot St. Lager, a low-alcohol (3.8 percent) pilsner, or the crisp maltiness of the Vienna-style New Paltz Crimson Lager.

The Rail Trail Pale Ale is a 5.2 percent California (West Coast) style, and is actually more boldly aroma-hopped than the Three Pines India Pale Ale. That's because the copper-colored Three Pines is brewed in the British style, with Fuggles and East Kent Goldings hops. Three Pines is the pub's bestseller, an indication of how things have changed since he started in 2000, Currier said. The bestseller back then was the light lager. "I've seen a lot more people come in who know more about beer," he said. "They're enjoying it more, with a more experimental palate. They're asking for different things. That's all good." The Back Porch Summer Lager, meanwhile, is built on the Huguenot St. Lager base and infused with blueberry. On my visit, the guest beer tap had Fort Collins Brewing's stout, and the last beer on my tasting flight was a blueberry lager blended with the stout. Colorado met the Hudson Valley, bringing a tart tang to roasty stout.

Aside from the six or seven beers on tap at any given time, you have a chance to see—if not taste—what you missed in Currier's brewing rotation. Behind the bar is a display of name plates under the heading: "Beers we've brewed in the past year and will again." On my visit, that included Grizzly Brown Porter, Dortmunder Gold, Kristall Weizen, Naked Under Me Kilt, and Winter Wassail. There's a fully stocked full-service bar. It's also a frequent venue for live music. The pub grub menu is bolstered by entrée choices such as pasta puttanesca, pasta Bolognese, Jambalaya, meatloaf, and seafood specialties. These dishes, and a mug or glass of Gilded Otter beer, are just what you'll want after a day of rock climbing or historic house hunting.

Gilded Otter Restaurant and Brewpub

Opened: November 1998.

Type: Brewpub.

Owners: Catskill Mountain Brewing Co., Inc. Rick Rauch is the general manager.

Brewer: Darren Currier.

System: 7-barrel Pub Brewing Systems brewhouse.

Annual production: 900 barrels.

Distribution: Primarily at the brewpub

Brewpub hours: 11:30 a.m. to 10 p.m. Monday to Thursday; 11:30 a.m. to 10:30 p.m. Friday and Saturday; noon to 9 p.m. Sunday.

Food: Full restaurant menu.

Hyde Park Brewing Company Restaurant and Brewery

4076 Albany Post Road (Route 9), Hyde Park, NY 12538
(845) 299-8277 • www.hydeparkbrewing.moonfruit.com

The patio out front of the Hyde Park Company offers a terrific view of Springbrook, the Hudson Valley estate of President Franklin D. Roosevelt (now a national historic site). It's a good place to sip one of brewer John Eccles's offerings and contemplate FDR's famous line marking the end of Prohibition in 1933: "I think this would be a good time for a beer."

Hyde Park Brewing has stood on this spot—in a building that once housed an original Howard Johnson motel—since 1996, making it one of New York's oldest continuously operating brewpubs. Eccles has been the brewer all that time, remarking in the first edition of this book that it would take an extraordinary offer of money to lure him away. He never left. Eccles would likely take no offense to this statement: He and the brewpub have lasted so long because Hyde Park is not fancy or blow-your-head-off experimental—but it is high quality. "Consistency is a key for us," said Angela LoBianco-Barone, who co-owns Hyde Park with her brother, Joey LoBianco. "And Johnny Eccles, he's been here eighteen years—he's a big reason for that."

Eccles makes both ales and lagers, but he favors lagers. Why? Here's his great observation from the first edition of this book: "Ales!" he snorted. "I could train a chimp to make ales. You have to know what you're doing to make lagers." So there. But don't be fooled. The Hyde Park beer menu includes an India Red Ale with lots of Cascade hops, a true descendant of those West Coast pale ales that started the whole craft beer thing. That beer replaced the Strong Old Bitter that was "the Pick" in the first edition. Sometimes a dry Irish stout and a porter are on tap, too. But there is only one dark beer on at a time, so the stout and the porter alternate with a third beer, Von Schtupp's Black Lager.

Beers brewed: Winkle Lager, Big Easy Blonde, Rough Rider Red Lager, India Red Ale, (rotating dark beers), Von Schtupp's Black Lager, Mary P's Porter, Chaos Dry Stout, and one tap for the brewer's choice.

The Pick: My pick is the Winkle Lager. Is it hoppy? The aroma says yes. Is it malty? The taste says yes. This is a remarkably balanced lager—malty, crisp, and refreshing. Say yes to it.

Here we start getting into Eccles's fascination not just with lagers, but also with German and other continental European techniques and ingredients. Big Easy Blonde is a light lager using Bavarian noble hops, and the brewpub's bestseller. Winkle Lager is a Bohemian-style pilsner with more malt character than you'd expect, and Rough Rider Red has Munich and Belgian malts for a taste reminiscent of a Vienna lager.

While Hyde Park isn't resistant to change, it is going to be sure of itself first. Just look at the décor. When I first visited it in the 1990s you could still sense the HoJoness of the original motel. The exterior has since been redone in stucco and stone, and the only reminder of its motor inn days is the circular logo in the bar floor.

Hyde Park Brewing's food menu has evolved, too. Many items are made with the house beers as a component, from the popular Cheddar Cheese Lager Soup to the Winkle Lager Cranberry Mayo on the Drunken Turkey Sandwich. The pub now sources many of its ingredients from local Hudson Valley farmers, crafts its own condiments using beer, and does its own charcuterie. The pizzas and burgers can be topped with almost anything—just check out the list of choices.

The pub is also known for live music, especially its Wednesday night open-mike blues jam. The crowd is a mix of tourists, primarily weekenders who come to the FDR sites, and locals who find it an enjoyable place to have a beer and take in sporting events.

And don't worry: Some things will change, just not at a breakneck pace. "We are going to be getting into some Belgian beers soon," LoBianco-Barone said. "But everyone has been so welcoming to what we do here. No one wants to change something that's not broken. Our success for eighteen years proves that."

Hyde Park Brewing Company Restaurant and Brewery

Opened: 1996.

Type: Brewpub.

Owners: Joey LoBianco and Angela LoBianco-Barone.

Brewer: John Eccles.

System: 7-barrel Pub Brewing Systems brewhouse.

Annual production: About 900 barrels.

Distribution: All beer served on-site or in growlers.

Hours: 4 p.m. to 10 p.m. Monday and Tuesday; 11 a.m. to 10 p.m. Wednesday and Thursday; 11 a.m. to midnight Friday and Saturday; 11 a.m. to 9 p.m. Sunday.

Food: Full restaurant menu, featuring burgers, pizzas, and more.

Parking: Yes.

Keegan Ales

20 Saint James St., Kingston, NY 12401
(845) 331-BREW • www.keeganales.com

Tommy Keegan started his career as a molecular biologist. He ended up running a brewery. His hometown is Patchogue, Long Island. He ended up in business in Kingston, in the Hudson Valley. He wanted to run a production brewery, not a brewpub. He now runs a tourist-friendly brewpub with plans to expand its kitchen service. So it's not surprising that he never intended for his bestselling beer to be a milk stout. And yet is. With all that, it's still clear that Keegan knows exactly what he's doing. "I enjoy brewing," he said. "That's what I do."

Since 2003, Keegan Ales has operated in downtown Kingston (the state's first capital) in a spot that has connections to New York's more recent craft-brewing history. In the 1990s, this was the site of the Woodstock Brewing Co., operated by Nat Collins. The old owners had taken out a loan with the city of Kingston, using the brewery equipment as collateral. When the business went belly-up, the city found itself with a brewhouse it didn't want, and the building owner had a space clogged with equipment he didn't want. Tommy Keegan ended up buying the old place and starting fresh.

Keegan had caught the brewing bug earlier while living and working in San Francisco. He bought his dad a homebrew kit and liked the idea so much he went back to the same shop a week later and got one for himself. His dad, by the way, took the hint and became a co-owner in the Brickhouse Brewery and Restaurant, a brewpub in Patchogue. Tommy Keegan returned east, found a university research job he didn't really like, and quit it for a post at Blue Point Brewing Company in his hometown of Patchogue. He eventually became head brewer there before his big move to the Hudson Valley.

Keegan Ales runs on a philosophy best described as keeping things simple. There are three core beers: a golden ale called Old Capital, a copper-red IPA called Hurricane Kitty, and a milk

Beers brewed: Old Capital (golden ale), Mother's Milk (milk stout); Hurricane Kitty (IPA), Joe Mama's Milk, and Super Kitty.

The Pick: Rich, smooth, and satisfying are common beer buzzwords, but they seriously undervalue the appeal of Mother's Milk. It's a winner.

stout called Mother's Milk. To those, Keegan has added a bigger version of the stout, called Joe Mama's Milk, with brown sugar and locally roasted coffee; and Super Kitty, a barleywine built off the IPA base. Mother's Milk, a 5 percent ABV stout brewed with lactose sugar, came as a surprise to Keegan. "I knew I wanted a black beer, but I didn't want a typical [dry Irish-style] stout," he said. "So I went with milk stout." He didn't know that much about it. He called his supplier to find out what size packaging the lactose sugar came in; it was a 50-pound bag. "So we threw in the 50 pounds, figuring we could add more or less later if it didn't work," he said. It worked. Mother's Milk won a gold medal at TAP New York and grew into the brewery's flagship. "We haven't touched the recipe since," he said.

In 2013, Keegan started his first series of one-off specials, including a Vanilla Honey Porter and Belgian tripel, to mark the brewery's tenth anniversary. He's not sure if he will continue the series. "I never intended to make a fourth beer after those first three," he said, echoing the recurring theme of Keegan Ales.

The food is simple, too. It's mostly barbecue. You order at the counter and find yourself a seat at one of the picnic tables scattered around the pub area. "We're not assigning you a seat, giving you a tablecloth, or having a maître d' assist you," Keegan said. "It keeps it simple and keeps it cheap." It also fits with the rustic feel of the place, with its exposed brick walls, high loft ceilings, and unfinished floors.

When Keegan Ales opened, the customers were "100 percent locals," Keegan said. "Then it was 90 percent, then 80 percent." Today, the Hudson Valley is hot and the tour buses stop at Keegan Ales. Even in winter, the Catskill ski resorts mean "half the people in here are wearing ski pants," he said. Which he probably intended all along.

Keegan Ales

Opened: 2003.

Type: Brewpub.

Owner and Brewer: Tommy Keegan.

System: 20-barrel DME brewhouse.

Annual production: 8,500 barrels.

Distribution: Brewpub, tasting room, and off-premises accounts from Saratoga Spring down to the New York City metro area; about 50 percent of sales are in bottles.

Hours: 4 p.m. to 10 p.m. Tuesday to Thursday; 11:30 a.m. to midnight Friday to Saturday; 1 p.m. to 10 p.m. Sunday.

Food: Barbecue served from a takeout counter.

Parking: Yes.

Newburgh Brewing Company

88 Colden St., Newburgh, NY 12550
(845) 569-2337 • www.newburghbrewing.com

George Washington slept here (or at least just a few hundred yards up the hill). He also probably had some beer, the dark, authentically cask-conditioned Colonial type. And he may have been amazed by the stunning view. You won't be the father of your country and you can't sleep at Newburgh Brewing Company, but you can appreciate the beer and the view.

Newburgh, launched in 2012 by Christopher Basso and Paul Halayko, is located in a ginormous four-story building, once home to a steam engine plant and later a paper box company. It overlooks perhaps the most gorgeous spot in the Hudson Valley—a bird's eye view of the Hudson Highlands, with West Point and Bear Mountain on the horizon. Look in the other direction, up the hill, and you'll see the Washington's Headquarters National Monument and the house where the founding father spent more time than at any other place during the Revolution.

Inside, you'll find the brewery on the ground floor. A spectacular Bavarian-style beer hall occupies the top floor, with large communal tables cut from old flooring and enough space (it seems) to host a full-court basketball game. The wood has been refinished, and the brick walls sandblasted. As for the long, curving bar with the beautiful inlaid detailing? It once stood in the Murphy's Brewery in Cork, Ireland. The irony is that despite this terrific pub space, the guys at Newburgh consider themselves to be running a production brewery first and foremost. "We're a brewery with a tap room, not a brewpub," Halayko said. Okay . . . but what a taproom.

Basso is the brewmaster, and worked for five years at Brooklyn Brewery under the guidance of Garrett Oliver. Halayko is a CPA who runs the business end of the company. Basso and Halayko were

Beers brewed: Year-round: Cream Ale, Brown Ale, New-Burton IPA, Paper Box Pale Ale; (seasonals and limited release) Aces Wild, The Newburgh Conspiracy, Chile Lime Stout, C.A.F.E. Sour, River-BREW Crown Maple Irish Red, and more.

The Pick: It's a toss-up between the NewBurton IPA, which really does have that northern English the-hops-are-there-but-not-overpowering character, and the Saison. Spicy and floral, the Saison is just 3.8 percent, so it's a real session beer.

high school buddies in the nearby town of Washingtonville, and even went to college together at Boston University. The dream to own their own brewery fell into place around 2011. They settled on Newburgh because, well, it's a town in need of a lift, which made property fairly inexpensive. "Breweries have often helped transform their neighborhoods," Basso said. "We think that can happen here." He operates a 20-barrel DME brewhouse, with seven fermenters, two bright tanks, and plenty of room to grow.

For every beer sold at the tap room, Newburgh sells three to off-premises accounts all along the Hudson Valley, the five boroughs of Manhattan, and Long Island. "We're right at the crossroads of [Interstates] 87 and 84, the Hudson River, and Stewart Airport," Halayko said. "It's a good place to be." It's even a short—albeit steep—walk to the ferry terminal, where you can catch a boat to the Beacon stop of the Metro North rail line to Manhattan.

As a brewer, Basso has a fondness for British-style ales. (Halayko attributes that to the years working with Oliver, a well-known fan of the British style.) But Belgian and German styles make their presence known, too. So do a handful of eclectic oddities. The year-rounders are Cream Ale, Brown Ale, NewBurton IPA, and Paper Box Pale Ale. The pale ale is probably hoppier than the IPA, which is made in the distinctly British style. "We're not huge hops guys," Halayko said. "We needed an IPA, but we made an IPA for ourselves."

There are big beers, like The Newburgh Conspiracy, an 11 percent ABV Imperial Stout, but the Newburgh guys aren't generally the type to blow your head off with hoppiness. "We like to drink beer because we like the taste of beer," Halayko said. "The buzz off a beer is great but it's not the goal." But don't think there's no creativity or innovation here. They make a hopped-up cream ale, called Aces High, with Sorachi Ace hops; a relatively light-bodied Chile Lime Stout; a Belgian strong ale called Sterk Aal van Hoodie (Hoodie is the brewhouse cat); and a beer called C.A.F.E. Sour. It's brewed with coffee—C.A.F.E. stands for "Coffee Acquired from Ethiopia."

Basso, who trained at New York City's French Culinary Institute, also offers a small but innovative menu, heavy on locally sourced meats, cheeses, and produce, with gastropub twists like house-made mayonnaise and mustards. There's also a Liège waffle, a Newburgh Brown Ale Float, and sorbets made with the house beers. The tap room is family friendly with board games, a ping-pong table, and high chairs so the kids can take a seat at those communal beer hall tables. There also is live music on occasion. "We do like the Bavarian beer hall feel,"

Halayko said. "We're glad that it seems to be a place where people feel comfortable trying our beers."

Newburgh Brewing Company

Opened: 2012.
Type: Production brewery.
Owners: Christopher Basso, Paul Halayko, and Charlie Benedetti.
Brewer: Christopher Basso.
System: 20-barrel DME brewhouse.
Annual production: 1,500 barrels; capacity around 4,800.
Distribution: Hudson Valley, New York City, and Long Island.
Hours: 4 p.m. to 9 p.m. Wednesday; 4 p.m. to 11 p.m. Thursday; 4 p.m. to midnight Friday; 1 p.m. to 11 p.m. Saturday; noon to 5 p.m. Sunday.
Food: Gastropub-style menu with locally sourced ingredients.
Parking: Limited off-street parking.

Peekskill Brewery

PEEKSKILL BREWERY

47–53 S. Water St., Peekskill, NY 10566
(914) 734-2337 • www.peekskillbrewery.com

There are two gadgets in the Peekskill Brewery that most brewpubs don't have. One device is visible to patrons and the other, extremely rare, is hidden away on the top floor. We'll get to those in a bit. Another distinction with Peekskill, certainly as a brewpub, is apparent when you step inside: You're in an entryway, with the glass wall and doorway ahead of you offering a direct view of the brewhouse. Do you want to eat in the upstairs pub or have a drink in the ground-floor taproom? You might have to ask a brewer for directions. "The brewers are the de facto greeters," said Jeff "Chief" O'Neill, the head brewer and designer of much of what you'll see (and drink) during your visit.

Peekskill opened in this commuter community on the Hudson River in 2007 and relocated a few blocks to the current location in 2012. It's still near the Hudson River waterfront, a short walk from the Metro North rail station. The move was a few small blocks for a pub but one giant leap for a brewing company. Peekskill traded in a 3.5-barrel brewhouse that was making about 300 barrels a year for a 15-barrel system that made 2,500 barrels in its first year and can do up to 3,000 barrels. "It's night and day," said O'Neill, who joined the brewery just as the transition was entering the planning stages. He previously worked as head brewer at Ithaca Beer Co. "We hired Chief to design the brewery," said Keith Berardi, a member of the family that owns and manages the place. "He put his stamp on everything here."

Everything about the place is sleek and industrial, from the logo design to the tanks and serving lines. The building was an Army storage center in the 1920s and has a fortified bunker feel to it. It is now divided. The upstairs pub offers a small but diverse, creative lunch and dinner menu featuring appetizers like Smoked Trout Cake and entrées ranging from bangers and mash to a pork confit sandwich. Local sourcing is a key element. And

Beers brewed: C.R.E.A.M. Ale, Skills Pils, Hop Common, AMAZEballs, Lower Standard, Eastern Standard, Higher Standard IPE, DRye Stout, Midnight Toker, Simple Sour, seasonals, and limited releases.

The Pick: On my visit, O'Neill had a beer called Flavor Savor, a 6 percent ABV saison wit fermented in the coolship. In a word: complex (that's a good word).

don't overlook the Brewer's Dinner, a four-course affair of chef's specials paired with the brewmaster's selections. The downstairs tap room is where you can belly up to a long, full-service bar with loads of spirits, ciders, and cocktails (and food, too).

Now let's get to that first gadget—the one you can see if you're in the first-level bar. It's a growler filler, built into a box fed by the lines from all the serving tanks. (In the brewery, the beers are fed into pumps, which split each line three ways: to the pub, to the taproom, and to the growler filler.) This is also a counter-pressure filler, which pushes the oxygen out of the bottle, replaces it with CO_2, and then fills it with beer from the bottom. It minimizes the oxygen contact with the beers, increasing the time it will take them to spoil. "It gives a nice, clean, not foamy pour and a complete fill," O'Neill said.

Other breweries have growler fillers of course, though perhaps not this high tech, but it's the other gadget that really sets Peekskill Brewery apart. It's not really high tech at all. It's called a coolship, and it's a shallow metal box where the just-brewed wort goes to cool in the open air. In a more typical brewery, the wort is chilled quickly and then sent to an air-locked fermenting vessel or, in some English-style breweries, to a deep open-topped fermenter. Some traditional Belgian breweries still use the coolships, but only a handful of breweries in the United States do, if even that many. O'Neill sends all his beers to the coolship for at least an hour. A couple of his beers ferment completely in the shallow box, located at the very top of the three-level brewhouse. O'Neill believes the coolships lead to "extra bright," or clear, wort that requires no filtering and no finings, which many brewers use to help clarify their beer. It can change the way the hops react, too, he said. "It creates a house character," he said. "We get a bright wort that leads to life as an unfiltered beer."

O'Neill is extremely proud of his coolship, his brewery, and his beers. Perhaps that's why he takes the further unusual step of having twelve to thirteen on tap at any time, a fairly high number. And there are typically a few guest beers, too, often from a local Hudson Valley or New York metro area brewery that Peekskill is happy to support.

While O'Neill clearly likes to experiment and innovate, he does have three year rounders: the Eastern Standard IPA, the brewery flagship; Simple Sour, brewed with wheat and dosed with the souring *Brettanomyces* yeast; and Hop Common, a citrus hop-infused steam lager. He also almost always offers AMAZEballs, made only with Galaxy hops from Australia. The Eastern Standard is the overall bestseller, but AMAZEballs is the most popular at the pub. In addition, O'Neill does variations on the IPA and always has a couple of Belgian styles going.

You can find dark beers, like a Black IPA or a stout made with flaked rye, but don't count on more than one or two at a time. "It's easy to have one too many dark beers," O'Neill said. "I tend to brew what I tend to drink."

For all his brewery design skills and attention to beer complexity, it may be surprising that O'Neill tends to shrug off precise questions about alcohol content and other numbers. "I don't worry too much about ABVs or IBUs," he said. "I go for the taste I want and then work backwards."

Peekskill Brewery

Opened: Original location in 2007; current location in 2012.

Type: Brewpub, with production for off-premises sales.

Owners: Keith, Morgan, and Kara Berardi.

Brewer: Jeff "Chief" O'Neill.

System: 15-barrel Metalcraft Fabricators.

Annual production: 2,500 barrels.

Distribution: Split roughly in half between on-premises sales and accounts in the Hudson Valley and the New York City area. It's mostly draft, with some limited 750-milliliter bottle releases.

Hours: Pub and tap room hours vary. Check the website before you visit.

Food: Gastropub menu with specials and the Brewer's Dinner option.

Parking: Limited off-street parking.

Rushing Duck Brewing Company

HAND CRAFTED IN ORANGE COUNTY, NY

1 Battiato Ln., Chester, NY 10918
(845) 610-5440 • www.rushingduck.com

Dan Hitchcock's Rushing Duck Brewing Company is a relative newcomer to the Hudson Valley brewing scene, but he's not worried about there being too much of a good thing. "There's nowhere near too many breweries," said Hitchcock, who founded his brewery in the Orange County village of Chester in 2012. "If we can get more consumers educated and drinking craft beer, then we could double the numbers and still be good." Besides, he added, having more breweries makes the Hudson Valley "a good beer destination." Chester, he said, qualifies "as a beautiful place, and there are educated beer people here already."

Hitchcock's confidence seems justified. A year into his venture he had built markets at seventy accounts from Westchester to Albany, and hadn't even attempted the gold mine of New York City yet. The brewery, which sits in an old building just off what used to be the railroad station depot square in Chester, can be a little hard to find. There is a tasting room, with Hitchcock's 7-barrel brewing system in the back. (The nearby Touch Base Sports Bar also offers Rushing Duck on tap.) Hitchcok owns the brewery with his parents, Les and Mary. It took a while to find the right place, and Hitchcock said he finally found it on Craigslist.

Now, about the name: Many beer enthusiasts know of growlers, the jugs that brewers fill with take-home beer. Growlers are descended from the old open pails that working men used to have filled at their local breweries. Getting beer that way used to be called "rushing the growler." In Bergen County, New Jersey, where the Hitchcock family is from, Dan's grandfather called his open beer pail the "duck." The combination of these two local colloquialisms—"rushing the growler" and "rushing the duck"—led to the brewery's name.

Hitchcock started homebrewing at the College of New Jersey, "when it was easier to make beer

Beers brewed: Year-round: Naysayer Pale Ale, Nimptopsical, and Beanhead Coffee Porter. Seasonals: War Elephant, Planet Funkatron, and more to come.

The Pick: A terrific toasted malt character makes the Nimptopsical a winner, and the 7.3 percent alcohol level makes it nearly impossible to pronounce after you've had a couple.

than to buy it." He found work after graduation at Weyerbacher Brewing Company in Easton, Pennsylvania. He started as a cellarman, then became a lead brewer after studying at the American Brewers Guild. After a few years, he "got the creative itch" and began exploring to find his own place. At Rushing Duck, after the first year about 75 percent of sales were to off-premises accounts and about 25 percent at the tasting room. "I'd like to do more here," he said. "I'm a control freak and I'd like to have more power over how the beer is poured and how you experience it. But if you want to grow, you need wholesale, so it's a balancing act." By mid-2013, Rushing Duck had three year-round beers and five seasonals, with plans to add brews. The flagship is Naysayer Pale Ale, the bestseller overall although it's outsold in the tasting room by a beer called Nimptopsical.

Another name check: Hitchcock took the word Nimptopsical from Benjamin Franklin, who used the term to refer to someone who drank too much. The Naysayer, at 5.2 percent ABV, is hopped with Columbus, Bravo, and Cascade. Hitchcock was going for a relatively high hop level, with a relatively low alcohol level. With Nimptopsical, a 7.3 percent Scotch Ale, Hitchcock went in the other direction, boosting the alcohol and increasing the malt for a toasted, malty character. But he doesn't want to get typecast as either a hop head or a malt advocate. "I appreciate balance," he said. "But I also think there are times when you want a good blow-your-face-off hoppy beer. They all have their place."

At Rushing Duck, that would include the year-round Beanhead Coffee Porter, infused with Guatemala Antigua beans from a local roaster, and the seasonal Planet Funkotron, made with the souring *Brettanomyces* yeast and spiced with coriander, orange peel, and grains of paradise. And the hop lover will want to try War Elephant, an 8.7 percent Double IPA, brewed with Simcoe, Galaxy, Summit, and Galena hops. For Hitchcock, it's all good. "I brew the beer I like to drink," he said.

Rushing Duck Brewing Company

Opened: 2012.
Type: Production brewery.
Owners: Dan Hitchcock, and Les and Mary Hitchcock.
Brewer: Dan Hitchcock.
System: 7-barrel brewhouse.
Annual production: 500 to 800 barrels.
Distribution: Hudson Valley, from Weschester County to Albany.
Hours: Noon to 5 p.m. Saturday.
Parking: In the square and around the brewery.

Brewing with New York Ingredients

Ask many of the brewers in this book if they use New York ingredients in their beers and the answer will likely be something along the lines of: "Yes . . . of course . . . we'd love to . . . *when we can*." Many will point proudly to a harvest ale made with fresh hops from a local grower, or to a fall pumpkin beer made with the produce of a nearby patch. Local honey, some local herbs like lavender, and local fruit are increasingly finding their ways into New York beers. The market incentive is clear: The decade-old demand for locally sourced ingredients in foods shows no signs of slowing down. Craft brewers, who pride themselves on the artisanal nature of their profession, are a logical fit for the "slow food," locavore movement. But there are difficulties, and New York's brewers, state government, and university researchers are trying to solve them.

The difficulties? The primary ingredients in beer—besides water, which New York has in abundance—are grain (barley malt) and hops. You'd think a big state like New York could supply all that, right? Not so fast. It's true that New York was once the nation's leading hop producer. That ended with a blight and then Prohibition, one hundred years ago. Today, the Pacific Northwest is the major hop region in the United States.

New York once had large producers of barley malt for the brewing industry, in places like Buffalo, but even then the grain was typically grown in the Midwest or farther west. The West, in the United States and Canada, is still the primary source of brewer's barley. It would take an enormous transformation of New York's farmlands to convert fields to hops and barley to supply the needs of the state's brewers. As you can see from this book, the number and size of New York breweries are rapidly expanding.

There are processing issues as well. Hops need to be dried and turned into pellets. Barley needs to be malted, and malt needs to be kilned to meet brewers' specifications. Until very recently, none of that happened in New York. Those are big hurdles.

In 2012, the New York State Brewers Association successfully persuaded Gov. Andrew Cuomo and state lawmakers to pass the New York Farm Brewery Law. It was based on the New York Farm Winery Act of 1976, which was widely credited with fostering the explosive growth of the state wine industry, which now tops three hundred wineries. Without going into ponderous detail, the new law offers economic and tax incentives, and loosens some of the operating rules and regulations, for brewers using New York ingredients. The law was written to take into account the limited supply of New York ingredients at the start, and builds in escalators, requiring the participating breweries to use more local ingredients as time goes on. The goal is to boost the amount of New York ingredients in New York beers and spur the development of New York farms and producers making beer ingredients.

Will it work? Already, in 2013, more than half a dozen breweries had obtained their farm licenses. Among the first visible signs were the breweries that opened satellite tasting rooms offering their beers, New York wines, and other local products. That's one of the side benefits of holding a farm brewery license.

The New York hop industry has been showing some signs of life for a few years, aided by the Northeast Hops Alliance, a growers group, and Cornell University. Cornell even hired a hops specialist a few years ago to foster the growth. Hops growers are now found around the state, especially in the Finger Lakes, Hudson Valley, and Long Island. The barley-growing and malting end of the business is moving a little slower, but already there are businesses popping up, pledging to grow and malt grain.

Still, many brewers interviewed for this book remain skeptical that the supply can meet demand, or that the specific hops and malts needed for the beers they want to make can be produced any time soon. But don't be afraid to ask brewers about using New York ingredients. You're certain to get an animated answer.

New York City

New York City is so big, in so many ways. Where do you start? It is richly historic; one of the oldest cities in America, it dates from the famed "purchase" of Manhattan Island for $24 in 1624. Washington's famous inaugural address was delivered here, architecture and invention thrived here, and the world's famous have lived and visited here.

It is strongly cosmopolitan, a melting pot since the earliest days of immigration, through the Ellis Island period and into today. It is still home to numerous strong ethnic neighborhoods. As one group arrives, establishes itself, becomes acclimated and successful, and moves to the suburbs, another replaces it. The city is also incredibly wealthy, with the financial clout of Wall Street, the New York Stock Exchange, the NASDAQ, the major banks, and the numerous corporate headquarters and wealthy individuals that call it their home. The world looks to New York as its financial center.

It is wonderfully creative, home to theater, art, dance, music, letters, and scholarship. It is a powerhouse of sports teams like the New York Yankees, baseball's winningest franchise, and the scrappy New York Mets, and some of the game's greatest have played here. Football, ice hockey, basketball—New York fans are rabid fans. They revel in their teams' glories and despair in their defeats.

New York is deeply symbolic. The Statue of Liberty stands in New York Harbor, a beacon to all of the world's oppressed and an icon of American freedom. New York is synonymous with freedom, hard work, and success to people the world over who have never been to America. It was this symbolism—this concentration of the American character and wealth—that led to New York's being targeted in the national tragedy of September 11, 2001. The horror of the World Trade Center disaster was numbing. Large parts of Manhattan were cut off, and it seemed everyone knew someone who died. The city mourned. But then it sprang back. It committed to clearing the debris—all of it. It carried on with business. Wall Street regained its bustle, companies took up temporary quarters, and the city, battered but defiant, went back to work. The skyline is different, to be sure. But in 2013, an antenna was installed at the top of the new One World Trade Center Tower, bringing its height to 1,776 feet. Yes, it's back.

The city is simply huge. New York encompasses 314 square miles, largely on a cluster of islands, and is home to over 7 million people in 5 boroughs: Manhattan, Queens, Brooklyn, the Bronx, and Staten Island. The breweries, by the way, are in Manhattan, Brooklyn, and Queens—for now anyway. (The Bronx Brewery was slated to open its own brewhouse by the end of 2013.) Whole libraries of guidebooks have been written on this city; get a good one. There's a lifetime's worth to see and do in New York.

Other breweries and brewing companies

The Bronx Brewery (www.thebronxbrewery.com), a successful contract-only brewer for a few years, was on the road toward opening its own 20-barrel brewhouse by the end of 2013. Big Alice Brewing (www.bigalicebrewing.com) of Long Island City and Bridge and Tunnel Brewery (www.bridgeandtunnelbrewery.com) of Maspeth are tiny nanobreweries operating out of small spaces without tasting rooms in Queens in 2013. Harlem Brewing Company (www.harlembrewing company.com), makers of Sugar Hill beer, and Jonas Bronck's Beer Company (www.broncksbeer.com) are contract-only brewing companies.

Other beer sites

There are way too many to list, but here's a sampling. Manhattan sites: d.b.a. (41 1st Ave.), Blind Tiger (281 Bleecker St.), The Ginger Man (11 E. 36th St.), The Pony Bar (637 10th Ave.), and Houston Hall (222 W. Houston St.). Brooklyn sites: The Spuyten Duyvil (359 Metropolitan Ave.), Tørst (615 Manhattan Ave.), Mugs Alehouse (125 Bedford Ave.), and Barcade (388 Union Ave.). Queens sites: Sunswick 3535 (35-02 35th St.) and Bohemian Hall & Beer Garden (29-19 24th Ave.).

Area Attractions

The *Statue of Liberty* (212-363-3200; www.nps.gov/stli) has been reopened to visitors (although Ellis Island had not been as of 2013). *Rockefeller Center* (45 Rockefeller Plaza, New York, NY 10111; 212-332-6868; www.rockefellercenter.com) includes the Christmas Tree, the ice rink, NBC studios, Radio City Music Hall, and more. ***Metropolitan Museum of Art*** (1000 Fifth Ave., New York, NY 10028; 212-535-7710; www.metmuseum.org) is the largest art museum in the United States, and one of the ten largest in the world. The ***World Trade Center Memorial*** (Visitors Center: 90 West St., New York, NY 10006; 212-225-1009; www.911memorial.org) is dedicated in remembrance of the events of Sept. 11, 2001.

This is just a small sampling of the city's attractions. Seriously, invest in a good guidebook.

Birreria (at Eataly)

200 Fifth Ave., Fifth Avenue at 23rd Street, New York, NY 10010
(212) 229-2560 • www.eataly.com/birreria

It's hard to get to Birreria. Not just because you might need a reservation. And not because it's on the top floor—the rooftop, actually—of a fourteen-story building in Manhattan's Flatiron district. It's hard because to get there you need to pass boatloads of cheeses, chocolates, olive oils, pastries, wines, sausages, pastas, herbs, truffles, and all the other assorted treasures of Italian cuisine. It's a wonder anyone makes it up to Birreria.

Birreria is the brewpub component, the crowning piece, of Manhattan's Eataly, a gourmet delight that includes seven eateries and dozens of food stalls in a giant New World Italian marketplace. Eataly is a creation of noted chefs Mario Batali, Lidia Bastianich, and other partners. Birreria is a collaboration between Eataly and three breweries: Dogfish Head Brewings & Eats of Rehoboth, Delaware; Birreria Le Baladin of Turin in northern Italy, and Birra del Borgo of Rome.

The on-site brewer is Peter Hepp Jr., who uses the 3.5-barrel system, double-batching everything in 7-barrel fermenters. (His predecessor, Brooks Carretta, moved on to Chicago in 2013 to set up the Birreria there.) Birreria has just three beers on tap at any time and all are served exclusively in real ale casks. Two beers are always available: Wanda, a dark English chestnut mild (4 percent ABV) and Gina, an American pale ale (5 percent) made with wild Roman thyme. The beers on the third tap get a little more daring—though they retain some English influence, courtesy of the real ale casking. This means many of the beers are low alcohol, although there have been brews in the 9 or 10 percent range on occasion. (Hepp is also producing the occasional barrel-aged version.)

The beers also often have some Italian influence, courtesy of the country's foods, flavors, and a fascination with ancient and modern brewing traditions. One of the limited releases that garnered Birreria the most attention came in December 2012. The beer was made with a yeast

Beers brewed: Birreria Wanda (dark English chestnut mild), Birreria Gina (pale ale with thyme), and a rotating limited release that sometimes features exotic or esoteric ingredients.

The Pick: Birreria Wanda combines the best of English brewing (cask-conditioning) and Italian flavor. Chestnut is a classic Italian beer ingredient, and dark mild is quintessentially English. The low-alcohol content makes this a perfect session beer to drink while contemplating the Manhattan skyline.

extracted from the abdomen of a hornet and cultured in a lab at Birra del Borgo. You're thinking: "What?!" It happened because the collaborators were trying to find the yeast used in ancient Italian brewing. Research indicates that yeast culture can be carried by wasps and hornets for centuries without mutating. So, they found a hornet in central Italy and . . . "Only one hornet really had to be put down to find its little secrets," Hepp said. "It kind of goes along with the old legend that hornets and wasps are good for the wine harvest. It just kind of leaked into beer."

If you're thinking this is the most difficult brewing Hepp has ever had to do, you should know this: He served in the Navy and brewed in the Middle East, where he had difficulty securing the proper equipment and ingredients for the not-really-authorized side activity. He thinks that's how he ended up landing the job at Birreria, where they prize the ability to invent as you go.

Aside from the three house beers, the list is extensive. Birreria has about a dozen draft lines, with beers from the three collaborators or other noted craft brewers, including New York state breweries like Captain Lawrence and Peekskill. There are a couple dozen bottled beers, too. Several times a year, Hepp is joined in New York by either Sam Calagione of Dogfish Head, Teo Musso of Baladin, or Leonardo Di Vincenzo of del Borgo. They turn out beers made with everything from pomegranate to myrrh. "The Italian beer scene is very innovative these days, and these brewers are right there at the forefront," Hepp said.

Birreria is also at the forefront when it comes to the view. The brewhouse is located on the top floor, along with the pub-dining area. Hepp's directions are priceless: "Come out of the elevator, look at the Empire State Building, and turn right." It really is a rooftop, open to the sky and the Manhattan skyline and able to be enclosed in glass when it turns rainy or cold.

And the food? Gourmet Italian pub fare, small-plate style (this is a part of Eataly, after all), with cheeses and sausages, mushrooms, salamis, and more. The food, meticulously sourced and prepared, is a complement to the beers. "Eataly is really tied into slow food, and so is Birreria," Hepp said. "Small batch and attention to detail. That sums up our food and our beers."

Birreria (at Eataly)

Opened: 2011.

Type: Brewpub.

Owners: Birreria is a part of the Eataly partnership and is a collaboration with Sam Calagione of Dogfish Head Brewings & Eats, Teo Musso of Birreria Le Baladin, and Leonardo Di Vincenzo of Birra del Borgo.

Brewer: Peter Hepp Jr.

System: 3.5-barrel JV Northwest brewhouse.

Annual production: 500 barrels.

Distribution: At the brewpub, exclusively cask-conditioned.

Hours: 11:30 a.m. to 10 p.m. Sunday to Wednesday; 11:30 a.m. to 11 p.m. Thursday to Saturday.

Food: This is Eataly, so expect top-quality, gourmet Italian specialties.

Parking: You're kidding, right?

The Brooklyn Brewery

79 N 11th St., Brooklyn, NY 11249
(718) 486-7422 • www.brooklynbrewery.com

Its probably the most recognizable name—and logo—in all of New York state brewing (excluding Anheuser-Busch, of course). The Brooklyn Brewery celebrated its twenty-fifth anniversary in 2013 with a firm grip on a segment of the American craft beer market and an eye toward international expansion.

You could write a book about Brooklyn Brewery, but your effort would have to share shelf space with the literary output from some of the brewery's principals. Founders Steve Hindy and Tom Potter wrote *Brew School: Bottling Success at the Brooklyn Brewery*, and brewmaster Garrett Oliver wrote *The Brewmaster's Table: Discovering the Pleasures of Real Beer with Real Food* and edited *The Oxford Companion to Beer*. Hindy is now at work on a history of American craft brewing.

That's appropriate, because Brooklyn Brewery is a big part of that history. It began as a celebrated practitioner of "contract brewing," building a renowned brand name with two beers, Brooklyn Lager and Brooklyn Brown Ale, before it had a brewery of its own. (Back then, Brooklyn made more money as a beer distributor than as a brewer.) In the mid-1990s, Hindy and Potter built a small brewhouse in Brooklyn, though most of its beer was still contract brewed elsewhere. Brooklyn also hired Oliver, who not only ramped up Brooklyn's recipes but also became a marquee name in craft-brewing circles worldwide. "We really started branching out when Garrett came on board and did the Black Chocolate Stout," Hindy said. Now its more than 210,000-barrel annual production includes cutting edge beers such as Black Ops, Sorachi Ace, Brooklyn BLAST! (a strong IPA that has become a regular), a line of bottle-conditioned beers, a line of Brewmaster's Reserve specials, and so on.

Beers brewed: Year-round: Lager, Brown Ale, Pilsner, East India Pale Ale, Pennant Pale Ale, and Blast! Seasonals: Black Chocolate Stout, Winter Ale, Monster Ale (barleywine), Dry Irish Stout, Oktoberfest, and Summer Ale, plus the Brewmaster's Reserve and Big Bottle series.

The Pick: I love a good American brown ale, and Brooklyn Brown is one of the prototypes. But I'll go with the first beer Garrett Oliver made for Brooklyn: the Black Chocolate Stout. It's rich, intense, and quintessentially American. But wait—my real favorite is the biscuity and spicy Pennant Pale Ale. Really . . .

In 2013, Brooklyn was making about 80,000 barrels at its own brewery (typically the smaller batch beers and seasonals) and about 130,000 at Matt Brewing Company (Saranac) in Utica, its longtime contract partner. Just a decade before, in 2003, the company's output had been 38,000 barrels. "We've had a good ten-year run," Hindy said. By the way, Hindy doesn't believe in being coy about the beer Brooklyn Brewery has produced under contract (perhaps it's the journalist in him). "There has been controversy [about contracting] in the industry, but my feeling is that it's best to be transparent about that," he said. "We have always said 'brewed in Utica' on the beers brewed in Utica." Besides, he notes, Anheuser-Busch started out as a contract brewer, too.

But let's not lose sight of the fact that there is a decent-sized brewery in Brooklyn. It has a 50-barrel brewhouse doing eight brews a day five days a week, and a 25-barrel system for smaller batches. The brewery has a line for 750-milliliter bottles and plans to install one for 12-ounce four packs of beers like the Brooklyn BLAST! Hindy believes they will eventually produce about 100,000 barrels in Brooklyn.

Along the way, the Brooklyn Brewery has become a groundbreaker in helping Brooklyn (and Williamsburg in particular), become the trendsetting hipster place it is today. (NYC Mayor Michael Bloomberg even said so in the introduction to *Brew School*.) That alone is a story, and one that Hindy, who worked as a journalist before he became a brewing magnate, can tell with some flair. He spent much of his career in the war zones of the Middle East. He enjoys telling the story of the day in 1995 when armed gunmen came into the brewery warehouse and put a gun to his head. Or the story of his run-ins with the mob guys who still wielded influence in the area. "Brooklyn was a very different scene then," he said. "But more and more young people were coming into the area, and I thought something was going to happen." The brewery put effort into rezoning its part of Williamsburg from industrial to residential (which is ironic since a brewery is a manufacturing facility and the move "put pressure on us," Hindy said).

Today, Brooklyn Brewery plays its part by hosting three thousand to four thousand visitors a week. There's often a two-week wait for tours. One effect of the rise in Brooklyn's fortunes is that even after several highly successful decades for the brewery, it still rents its buildings. "We never had the money [to buy] back then," Hindy said, "and today you can't have enough money to buy anything around here." In 2004, original partner Tom Potter sold his shares to Robin and Eric Ottaway, who Hindy expects will lead the company into the future. In the meantime, the brewery has its eyes overseas. It sells a lot of its beer in the Scandinavian countries, and even entered a partnership with Denmark's Carlsberg Brewing Company to build a joint brewery in Stockholm, Sweden. Brooklyn also has markets elsewhere in Europe, Asia, and other global outposts. "The main difference between us and everyone else is our export business," Hindy said. "We kind of cultivated that from the beginning, partly because we're here in New York and people from around the world come here and think they can sell our beer in their market."

In the United States, Brooklyn's markets are primarily east of the Mississippi, with outposts in Texas and Minnesota. Brooklyn Lager continues to be the brewery's bestseller (lagers in general are 50 percent of the total output here), but beer enthusiasts are known to wax poetic about the hard-to-find one-offs and reserves. Take Sorachi Ace, a single-hop varietal made with the Japanese-bred Sorachi Ace hop. Or the Black Ops, a winter-only Russian Imperial Stout. Fans have been known to stage missions worthy of the Navy Seals to secure some. Some of these beers have pushed the limit. One called Reinschweinsgebot was made with bacon. Once.

One of the big leaps forward in the proliferation of styles came in the mid-2000s, when the brewery began to produce the bottle-conditioned, Belgian-influenced beers called Local 1 and Local 2. "It was really, at first, for the beer geeks," Hindy said. "It's important to keep surprising and exciting those customers, to keep them coming back, which is what we want to do."

The Brooklyn Brewery

Opened: Company founded in 1988; brewery opened in 1996.

Type: Production brewery with much of its beer made under contract.

Owners: Steve Hindy and Robin and Eric Ottaway.

Brewer: Garrett Oliver (brewmaster).

System: 50-barrel primary brewhouse and 25-barrel small batch system in Brooklyn.

Annual production: 210,000 barrels in 2013—80,000 in Brooklyn; 130,000 at Matt Brewing Company (Saranac) in Utica.

Distribution: Throughout the eastern United States, with a large overseas market.

Hours: Limited; check the website to make reservations.

Parking: Limited

Chelsea Brewing Company

Pier 59, Chelsea Piers, New York, NY 10011
(212)-336-6440 • www.chelseabrewingco.com

Chelsea Brewing Company is the oldest continuously operating brewery in Manhattan, and the second
oldest in New York City (after The Brooklyn Brewery). This says something about Chelsea Brewing and about the
vagaries of operating a business—any business—in the largest and
most vibrant city in the United States. Chelsea head brewer Mark
Szmaida described the brewing philosophy: "We make regular beer,
really," he said. "For years, I've pretty much scoffed at making 'imperial' everything, and the whole wild yeast business. I enjoy those, but if
brewing is your business, then you want to make beer that sells, that
empties your tanks. You don't want beer sitting there forever."

In the dog-eat-dog world of New York City commerce, especially in
Manhattan, it's a wise man who makes something that sells. Many businesses, breweries among them, have failed to do that here. But make
no mistake: Chelsea's beers are interesting and inventive. You still need
that edge to succeed in New York. Take the beer Szmaida brewed for
Chelsea's one hundredth batch, the Hop Angel American-style IPA. It
was intended as a mild ale but came out at 11.5 percent ABV. "There
wasn't much mild about that," Szmaida said. He
originally planned to include the relatively familiar
West Coast Cascade hop, but when it was unavail-
able, he went with Columbus, Galena, and Chinook. The aroma is loaded with grapefruit and
pine. "A lot of people in the beer geek community
hate it because it's not Green Flash [an iconic San
Diego IPA], and some love it because it's not Green
Flash," Szmaida said.

Chelsea, for now, has something else to sell
besides its beer. The long, sleek brewpub sits amid
the Chelsea Piers, with a stunning view of the Hudson River. I say "for now" because owner Pat Green
is considering a move—perhaps out of Manhattan
and into a production brewery—within a few
years. Nothing stays the same in Manhattan for
long. In the meantime, you can see a lot of history

Beers brewed: Checker
Cab Blonde Ale, Sunset Red
Ale, Hop Angel IPA, Fruited
Wheat, Black Hole XXX Stout,
Frosty's Winter Wheat, sea-
sonals, and specials.

The Pick: I'll admit I was
blown away by the extra
dark and roasty Black Hole
XXX Stout (7.8 percent). But
the Checker Cab Blonde goes
down easy, dry, and smooth
—just the opposite of what
you'll feel in a typical Manhattan cab ride. It's made
for drinking by the river.

along this part of the Hudson. Pier 59, on which the brewpub sits, was the intended destination of the RMS *Titanic*, which sunk on her ill-fated maiden voyage after hitting an iceberg. The pier also was the area's major passenger line terminal for decades. More recently, Szmaida was in the brewpub on that cold day in January 2009 when an airplane that had just taken off from La Guardia Airport was successfully ditched in the Hudson by Capt. Chesley Sullenberger, with no loss of life. The plane came down around 48th Street and floated past Pier 59 (around 19th Street) some time later. "We saw the plane go by, and that night we were loaded with cops and fire and EMS," Szmaida said. Then, in 2012, Hurricane Sandy showed that a spot by the river has its disadvantages, too. The brewpub suffered flood damage and closed for several weeks.

Green's Chelsea Brewing Co. was among the first tenants in the Chelsea Piers development when it opened in the mid-1990s. Chelsea Piers now includes a sports complex, a bowling alley, a maritime complex for river excursions, and a photo and film production studio. It's also just a few blocks from another Manhattan reclamation project, the High Line, an elevated railroad track converted into an urban park.

The brewpub's beers also include the bestselling German Kolsch-style Checker Cab Blonde Ale and the Sunset Red Ale. Szmaida likes to liven things up with offerings such as a New York State of Mind Wet Hop IPA (with hops from the Finger Lakes) and a fall pumpkin beer (he mixes a "pumpkin elixir" that he can store to extend the seasons for this high-demand beer). Everything Szmaida makes is sold both at the pub and off-premises. Some 65 percent of the beer goes to off-premises accounts, though that changes in the summer when people flock to the waterfront. "New York City has been more of a Bud, Miller, [and] Coors town than, say, Philadelphia," Szmaida said. "But we're catching up. People are drinking better beer."

Chelsea Brewing Company

Opened: 1996.

Owners: Pat Green.

Brewer: Mark Szmaida.

System: 30-barrel DME system.

Annual production: 3,500 to 4,500 barrels.

Distribution: All draft beer; about 65 percent sold to off-premises accounts around the New York City area.

Hours: Noon to 10:30 p.m. Sunday to Friday; 11:30 a.m. to 10:30 p.m. Saturday.

Food: Gourmet pizzas, pastas, and pub cuisine.

Parking: An on-site parking garage.

508 Gastrobrewery

508 Greenwich St. (between Spring & Canal),
    New York City, NY 10013
(212) 219-2444 • www.508nyc.com

In the space halfway between the brew kettle and the fermentation tanks at Manhattan's 508 Gastro Pub & Brewery, you can watch the production of hand-crafted pasta. It doesn't go into the beer (although if you suggest that idea to brewer Chris Cuzme, he might take you up on it). The pub-brewery-restaurant is in the far west side of Manhattan (the western edge of SoHo), just a few blocks from the Hudson River. It's on Greenwich Street, between Canal and Spring streets, near the Holland Tunnel. This is New York City, where space is tight and logistical accommodations have to be made. And this is a gastropub brewery, where the food and the beer are both subject to the same high degrees of craftsmanship. "It's such a small brewery," Cuzme said. "I don't have to brew the same thing twice if I don't want to." And he has so many ideas he may never want to. That seems to be true for the rustic Mediterranean-American food, prepared by chef and owner Jennifer Lynn Hill, too.

Cuzme's energetic personality fits New York City and its brewing, food, and even music scenes. He's a professional musician who plays saxophone and bass, and a veteran of the craft beer scene. He's associated with the Wandering Star Craft Brewery in Pittsfield, Massachusetts, and still plays an active role in the New York City Homebrewers Guild. He even cohosts an online podcast on beer called "Fuhmentaboutit." He took over the brewhouse at 508 Gastrobrewery in December 2012, just weeks after it was flooded by Hurricane Sandy. He calls the brewing system a "franken-brewery." It's got a 2-barrel, electric-fired kettle, and tanks scattered throughout the basement level of the restaurant. "My first few weeks were just cleaning everything, taking everything apart, and putting it back together again," Cuzme

Beers brewed: On my visit, the lineup included Parting Glass Belgian Dubbel, Saxual Healing Imperial Stout, Hall Pass (an English tipple), a Blonde, and a Blonde with hibiscus and rose petals.

The Pick: Parting Glass may evoke something Irish, but the Dubbel showed strong signs of Belgian influence with more than a little hint of bubblegum, like some German wheats. It was a true gastropub mashup.

said. He dreams of upgrading and revamping the brew system, but in the meantime there are too many beers to brew.

In his first few months, Cuzme concocted such beers as Hall Pass, which he referred to as an "English tipple," a tribute to Dark Star Brewing Company's Sunburst. He made a blonde infused with hibiscus and rose hips, a Belgian dubbel called Parting Glass, a hoppy beer called Colonial Nugget, and an imperial stout called Saxual Healing. "I have carte blanche to brew what I want here," he said. That includes working with others in the NYC brewing community, or what Cuzme calls "brewlaborations." He made a brown ale with Tony Forder, editor of *Ale Street News*, and Hall Pass with his friend and Wandering Star colleague Alex Hall. He also wants to do frequent brewlaborations with local homebrewers. And he's playing around with some cask-conditioned real ales. He claims to have used his first paycheck to buy a small real-ale cask. Mention to Cuzme that all the beers show signs of good craftsmanship, despite the modest equipment and odd layout, and he smiles. "The fact that I can make clean beers in this setup is amazing," he said.

The 508 opened in 2008 as a restaurant and bar and added the brewery in 2011. Here's a bit of New York City trivia: The 508 is located in the building that was once home to Jonathan Larson, the playwright and composer most famous for *Rent*, a musical inspired by the time he lived in a second-floor flat. The place seats sixty and has a full bar. The menu features flatbread pizzas, burgers, shared small plates, and house-made pastas.

Hill said she initially encountered skepticism that a brewery could squeeze into the place. Now she's hoping to use it as a model for expansion. "Ideally, I'd like to cookie-cut this place and, with Chris overseeing the beer production, open a few more," Hill said. All of that is a little way in the future. "It's not necessarily the beer destination I'd like it to be, yet," Cuzme said. "But we're going to get there."

508 Gastrobrewery

Opened: The pub opened in 2008; the brewhouse opened in 2011.
Owner: Jennifer Lynn Hill.
Brewer: Chris Cuzme.
System: 2-barrel, electric-fired brewhouse.
Annual production: 250 to 300 barrels.
Distribution: Mostly on-premises.
Hours: 11 a.m. to midnight Monday to Friday; noon to midnight Saturday and Sunday.
Food: Eclectic gastropub menu.
Parking: No.

Greenpoint Beerworks/KelSo Beer Co.

·BEER CO

529 Waverly Ave., Brooklyn, NY 11238
(718) 398-2731 • www.kelsobeer.com

Heartland Brewery was never in the heartland. And Greenpoint Beerworks isn't in Greenpoint. Does it matter? In Brooklyn's Clinton Hill neighborhood stands a brewery called Greenpoint Beerworks, which makes beers for the Heartland pub chain in New York City, plus several other contractors. It's also the home of KelSo, a beer company owned by Kelly Taylor and his wife, Sonja Giacobbe (hence the name). A somewhat confusing setup to the casual observer, but easily sorted out when you understand that Taylor is at the center of it all. "Sonja and I started KelSo because we love beer, and we love the layers and the complexity and the nuance of fresh, handcrafted sessionable beers," Taylor said.

Taylor uses the word "layers" a lot when he talks about beer, so let's look at the layers of his story and how he got to this point. A native of Washington state, Taylor worked in international finance for several years before returning to his first love, beer. He had begun homebrewing while still an undergraduate in college. Later, he worked for some West Coast breweries, including the Karl Strauss Brewing Company in San Diego and Pyramid Breweries Cos. in Washington. Eventually, Taylor and Giacobbe came east to her hometown of New York.

That brings us to Heartland. Jon Bloostein, a stockbroker with a love of beer, started this string of pubs, all in Manhattan, in the mid-1990s. They began as brewpubs, each with its own on-premises brewhouse. Taylor was hired as an assistant at the original in Union Square in 2000 and worked his way up to running the brewhouse there. He also helped install the brewing systems at the Heartlands in Midtown and near Times Square.

By the time he became Heartland's overall director of brewing operations, he and Bloostein

Beers brewed: Heartland beers: Cornhusker Lager, Indian River Light, Red Rooster Ale, Indiana Pale Ale, Farmer Jon's Oatmeal Stout, and an array of seasonals. KelSo beers: Pilsner, Pale Ale, Nut Brown Lager, IPA, Industrial IPA, several seasonals, and specials.

The Pick: The KelSo Fuko is a special any flavor lover should try, but lagers are where KelSo stands out. The Nut Brown Lager is the type of full-flavored lager in which the yeast gets out of the way to let the malt and hops shine through.

had developed an idea. To save costs (and to open up space in the tight quarters of their Manhattan bars), they'd consolidate all of their brewing in one place. That place was supposed to be in Brooklyn's Greenpoint neighborhood, but a deal on a location fell through and things moved to Clinton Hill. "Once you have the licensing applied for and your tax ID number and all that, it's easier to change your address than your corporate name," Taylor said. So Greenpoint Beerworks opened in 2003 with a 30-barrel brewhouse in a two-story building, primarily cranking out Heartland's line of sessionable pub beers. Over the years, Taylor added more and more fermenters and storage tanks as the business grew, and also began brewing beer for other contractors. The major growth started in 2006 with the debut of the KelSo beer line. In effect, Taylor contracted with himself.

This is where Taylor really starts talking about beer and its layers. The initial plans he and Sonja had for KelSo did not include a lot of edgy, over-the-top extreme beers. They wanted beers you could drink in a session, but with a twist to keep you interested. "When we started in 2006, it seems everybody was doing aggressive stuff, double IPAs, sours," he said. "We just wanted to have a beer." So they started with beers that were 5 or 6 percent ABV and weren't hop monsters. And he tried to give them a distinctive twist.

His Pilsner uses Sterling, a hybrid hop based on the classic Czech Saaz, with what Taylor calls a more rounded character. The Nut Brown Lager is "like a German dunkel-y thing, but with American hops, so that's different." And the IPA uses a New Zealand hop called Nelson Sauvin. "We were the first to use that hop on a large scale," Taylor said. "It's clearly an IPA, but also clearly a different direction." Over time, however, some of the KelSo beers have become stronger and edgier. There's a Flemish sour red that is aged for three years, an 11 percent ABV Cabernet wine barrel-aged Imperial IPA, and a beer with hand-smoked malt called KelSo Rauchbier.

Perhaps the best example of KelSo's new extreme is a beer made for the Momofuko restaurant group in Manhattan. KelSo Fuku was launched after a taste test with the restaurant reps. "We determined it should be a little smoky, a little sour, and a little salty" to match Momofuko's Asian fusion cuisine, Taylor said. "They told us they appreciated the layers of complexity in our beer." There's that word "layers" again.

To taste all of these beers, there's no use going to Greenpoint Beerworks. Taylor stopped offering tours because the crowded brewery space isn't suited for them. But there's no shortage of outlets to find the beer. There are the Heartland pubs to start with, plus hundreds of KelSo accounts. Also, in early 2013, Heartland opened Houston Hall at

222 West Houston Street in Manhattan. It's a cavernous beer hall in an old parking garage, with beers made specially at Greenpoint.

In 2013, almost all of Geenpoint's production was draft (except for some limited barrel-aged beers in 750-milliliter bottles). But Taylor was considering contracting elsewhere to put some of his beers in cans. He expected the brewery will need to move in a few years, and at that point he'll install his own canning line, with the possibility of tours and food service, too.

Greenpoint Beerworks/KelSo Beer Co.

Opened: Brewery opened in 2003; KelSo beers launched in 2006.

Owners: Kelly Taylor and Sonja Giacobbe own KelSo; Heartland is an employee-owned business with Jon Bloostein as managing partner.

Brewer: Kelly Taylor.

System: 30-barrel Bavarian, with an annual capacity of about 24,000 barrels.

Annual production: 18,000 to 20,000 barrels total (about 6,000 are Heartland beer and 5,000 are KelSo, with the rest made for contract brewers).

Distribution: Mostly in the New York City metro area; all draft except for some 750-milliliter bottles of barrel-aged specials.

Hours: No public hours.

Parking: No.

Rockaway Brewing Company

46-01 Fifth St., Long Island City, Queens, NY 11101
www.rockawaybrewco.com

Call your company Rockaway Company and you're sure to evoke images of the beachfront, with crashing surf, gusting breezes, and cooling liquid refreshment. Rockaway Brewing is indeed by the water—but it's the East River, separating Long Island City in Queens from Manhattan.

Rockaway Brewing founders Ethan Long and Marcus Burnett opened their brewery in April 2012 in Queens. It was the first modern brewery in that borough. But they both have homes in Rockaway Beach and initially sold all their beer through the beachfront concession stands in Far Rockaway. "We started selling in Rockaway and people were really cool with the idea of local beer," Burnett said. Within a year, they had opened a tasting room and were selling growlers from the tiny brewery in Long Island City.

It's a story that began like so many others: A couple of homebrewers decided to go commercial. "We went on a cross-country trip with our families out West and we said, 'Wow there's a lot of breweries out here,'" Burnett said. "So we came back to here, where we live, and thought, 'There's not any breweries here.' That's stupid. This is a big place." So they spent $6,000 on a license and chose the spot, a former meatpacking operation, because Long has a second business nearby. (And it already had floor drains.) They have a 2-barrel system and four fermenters, and in 2013 were making 8 barrels every two weeks. "It's a classic nanobrewery," Bunett said. "We came from homebrewing and thought we'd get a big homebrew system and see what happens."

Initially, Burnett and Long did everything, but in their second year they hired a brewer. Both owners have other jobs; Burnett is a cinematographer and Long builds film sets. They opened the tasting room in the fall of 2012, "and that sort of covers the rent," said Burnett, who said making the business profitable is going to take some time and effort. "We've had a lot of goodwill and interest from the craft beer community, so that's

Beers brewed: Rockaway ESB, Black Gold, a dry Irish stout, Old School IPA, and High Plains Drifter Scotch Ale.

The Pick: The ESB has that classic buttery and malty English character.

helped. In the end, I'd like the brewery to support me, but right now I'm supporting the brewery." They have off-premises accounts in select bars in Queens, Brooklyn, and Manhattan. Burnett has dabbled in supplying the closest accounts in Queens by bicycle, and has his mind set on a large, souped-up tricycle to make that easier. "People think it's funny, but it's actually practical in New York City," he said.

Rockaway makes four beers, none of them extreme or over the top. The flagship is a malty English style ESB. There's also a dry Irish stout, an "old school" IPA, and a Scottish ale. "Our beers are kind of malt forward," Burnett said. "We never got into the hoppy things—we want beers that are drinkable, that you can have two or three of." Rockaway uses a counter-pressure filler for the growlers they sell out of the tasting room, a step many small breweries don't bother with but Burnett thinks is important. "For a brewery, if people don't enjoy your beer in the best possible circumstances, there's no reason to sell it," he said.

Burnett and Long dream of growing the brewery but know that will take time. "Our dream is to stay at 2 barrels until we get some traction," Burnett said. "This place can probably support 20 barrels." He pointed to the construction going on in 2013 around their end of Long Island City, with a promise of ten thousand new housing units. And while Long Island City may not have the Brooklyn hipsters, it does have a large and growing population of young urban professionals. "There's going to be a lot of people around here who want growlers," he said. "This is an auspicious time to be getting into craft brewing . . . In New York City, we're on an upswing. We're not one of those places that's oversaturated with breweries."

Rockaway Brewing Company

Opened: April 2012.
Owners and Brewers: Ethan Long and Marcus Burnett.
System: 2-barrel brewhouse.
Annual production: About 200 barrels.
Distribution: Rockaway Beach concession stands and select accounts in the NYC area.
Hours: Tasting room opens at 5 p.m. Wednesday through Saturday.
Parking: No.

SingleCut Beersmiths

19–33 37th St., Astoria, NY 11105
(718) 606-0788 • www.singlecutbeer.com

Just a few blocks away from SingleCut Beersmiths in Astoria, Queens, stands the Steinway piano factory. That's where they produce real, American-made Steinway pianos. "Those guys are the ultimate purveyors of craft," said SingleCut owner and brewer Rich Buceta. "They are my heroes. I'm so proud to be down the street from them." That pride shows in the care and attention to detail that Buceta puts into his brewery. He also carefully chooses his words when he calls SingleCut Beersmiths "the first microbrewery operating in Queens since the day Prohibition ended." That's "micro"—not nano—so the couple of tiny Queens breweries that got their start a little earlier are accounted for.

What's undisputed is the size and scope at SingleCut. Buceta launched with a 30-barrel brewhouse, a well-appointed tasting room (with a bandstand for live music), and 5,000 square feet of space. There's nothing nano about that, especially in New York City where a brewery with breathing room is hard to find. "I started out with a big commitment to brewing on the premises and not ever contracting out," Buceta said. "Our business plan was pretty explicit. We want to make sure we're big enough [and] comfortable in here so we never have to go outside our four walls." If they do, it'll just be to expand to adjacent space.

Buceta, like many modern craft brewers, got his start with the old 5-gallon homebrew kit. His "real" job was in advertising, in the fast-paced world of Manhattan. "I was homebrewing and doing well at it and really enjoying it, and at the same time my job was going proportionately in the other direction," he said. "So my supportive wife eventually said, 'if you're unhappy just quit.' So I quit." In 2007, he got a job at Greenpoint Beerworks, washing kegs to start. Eventually, he said, "I moved up to brewer and mastered the

Beers brewed: Year-round: Jan Olympic White Lagrrr, 19-33 Lagrrr, Billy 18-Watt IPA, Full-Stack IPA, and Dean Pacific Northwest Mahogany Ale. Seasonals: Half-Stack IPA Eric More Cowbell Milk Stout, Rüdy Double Umlaut Lager, and many others.

The Pick: Aside from its terrific back story, the Jan Olympic White Lagrrr is just an interesting beer, with a hint of orange in the aroma. The brewery's dry-house character is amplified by the use of Szechuan-style peppercorn.

mechanics of running a brewery. And I had developed some recipes of my own."

He began searching for his own place. "I knew our core market would be New York City, and I knew we needed to be visible to New York City," he said. "I didn't want to do Brooklyn because everyone was already in Brooklyn. At that time, there was nothing in Queens. It's the second-largest borough, so that was a pretty easy decision to make. He settled on the location because he needed a place that was zoned industrial and no more than ten minutes from the subway. Plus, "I knew we'd have a taproom, [so] it had to be place you'd want to go to," he said.

If you can read the signs around SingleCut Beersmiths, you can figure out that Buceta's second passion is the guitar. Take the name and the logo. The block-cut "S" in the name has a little notch in the top, resembling the cutaway in a solidbody electric guitar, which allows the player to have easier access to the upper frets. "I didn't want to do the clichés with the name, or just name it after our location," Buceta said. "I wanted something distinctive. SingleCut kind of makes you think of measure twice, cut once, so that evokes craftsmanship, too." That brings us to SingleCut's beers, most of which have names connected to the guitar, though some people may find them obscure. "Most people don't make the connection, and that's fine," Buceta said.

The story behind the recipe for the brewery's bestseller, Jan Olympic White Lagrrr, is one of those only-in-New York cultural tales. Buceta heard from one of his accounts, a Chinese restaurant called The Queens Kickshaw that wanted a beer for a special Christmas Eve dinner. "Jewish people are the only people who eat out on Christmas Eve, and the only restaurants that are open are Chinese, right?" Buceta said. "So they asked us to do a beer that combined Jewish and Chinese ingredients." As a homebrewer, Buceta had already made a beer flavored with Szechuan-style peppercorn. "Since it was primarily a wheat beer, it wasn't too far out to throw some matzo meal into the mash." The beer, Buceta said, was intended as seasonal, but became so popular it's now on year round.

SingleCut also has a series of IPAs, each higher in strength, that are called Billy 18 Watt, Half-Stack, and Full-Stack. (Music buffs will recognize the ascending series of amplifiers name-checked in this series.) Each is an IPA, but all are different, with varying hops and malts. Buceta is reluctant to go into much detail on the ingredients, though he does mention that one of the IPAs uses Nelson hops from New Zealand. "As a start-up brewer, my most valuable commodity is my recipes," he said. His beers run the full gamut, from lagers to stouts, but he seems genuinely interested in pushing the limits on lagers, which represent half his total production. He has a barrel-aged lager that he pushes through the line using nitrogen, a method typically associated with stouts or some English-style ales. "Lagers, and what you can do with them, is really kind of unmined territory," Buceta sad.

SingleCut generally has six beers on tap in the tasting room. Buceta also serves off-premises markets around the New York City metropolitan area and plans to package eventually. He said he's certain it will be a canning line, not a bottling line, when he moves in that direction. The tasting room in 2013 accounted for about 25 percent of his sales, a much higher number than he had planned for. It proved so popular he quickly decided to bring in food, and found a neighbor who makes savory meat pies to fill that niche.

The taproom also has a bandstand so Buceta can keep up with his love for music by showcasing local bands. And near the tap room bar is an upright piano, a housewarming gift from his neighbors at Steinway. Visitors to the tap room are encouraged to try it out "if they can play," Buceta said.

SingleCut Beersmiths

Opened: December 2012.

Owner and Brewer: Rich Buceta.

System: 30-barrel Specific Mechanical Brewhouse.

Annual production: 2,500 barrels in 2013; capacity is 3,500 barrels.

Distribution: Currently draft only, at the brewery taproom and selected New York City area accounts.

Hours: 4 p.m. to 11 p.m. Wednesday to Thursday; 4 p.m. to 1 a.m. Friday and Saturday; 1 p.m. to 8 p.m. Sunday.

Food: A neighboring business supplies savory meat pies to the tasting room.

Parking: No.

Sixpoint Brewery

40 Van Dyke St., Brooklyn, NY 11231
(917) 696-0438 • www.sixpoint.com

Stand at the corner of Van Dyke and Dwight streets in the Brooklyn neighborhood known as Red Hook and you'll see a corner bar called Rocky Sullivan's. It's hiding something: a brewery called Sixpoint, which opened in this neighborhood near the waterfront in 2004, before Brooklyn became the hip place to be.

Sixpoint occupies an L-shaped space around the bar, with frontage on both streets, and is easily identified by the big green barn doors marked with the six-pointed star, once a medieval symbol of brewing. It has many of the earmarks of a New York City brewery, most notably a lack of space (real estate is the most prized commodity in the NYC metro area).With a slogan of "Beer is Culture," Sixpoint is gaining traction by making an imaginative line of craft beers, from its core brews with interesting names like Sweet Action, The Crisp, and Resin, to smaller batches like its Mad Scientists collection and Spice of Life series. About 15 percent of its beers are made in the small brewery in Red Hook (in a 15-barrel brewhouse with 30-barrel fermenting and storage tanks), while the bulk is made at the Lion Brewery in Wilkes-Barre, Pennsylvania.

The brewery in Red Hook produces those beers made only on draft, typically the smaller batch brews. Under the supervision of Sixpoint head brewer Jan Matysiak, the Wilkes-Barre brewery makes the beers that are packaged—in this case, in cans. "It's the costs of New York City real estate," said Jeff Gorlechen, a Sixpoint company partner who handles marketing for Sixpoint. "Our costs for ingredients and materials [are] the same as everyone else's but it's cheaper to make the beer somewhere else and deliver it down here than it is to make it here." And yet there is brewing going on at Sixpoint Brewery in Red Hook, unlike some other New York City brewers who exclusively contract their production elsewhere.

Beers brewed: Year-round: Sweet Action, Resin, The Crisp, Bengali Tiger, Righteous Ale, and Brownstone. Seasonals: Harbinger (spring), Apollo (summer), Autumnation (fall), and Diesel (winter). Series: Mad Scientists, Spice of Life, and more.

The Pick: The winter seasonal, Diesel, is a perfect example of that hard-to-define Sixpoint quality. The pine-accented aroma screams IPA, while the rich roasty finish argues stout. The world's first Black India Pale Stout?

Sixpoint founder Shane Welch interned at Manhattan's Chelsea Brewing Company before starting on this venture. He was in the corner bar at Dwight and Van Dyke one day, musing about starting a brewery, when someone told him there was brewing equipment in the building out back. (It had belonged to a Brooklyn brewery that went out of business in 2001.) So Sixpoint began brewing and developed loyal followers, including Gorlechen, who rode his bicycle to the brewery to check it out and ended up handling its marketing and becoming a partner. "At that time, nobody was coming to Red Hook," he said. "Now, Brooklyn is the greatest thing since America was invented. . . . We were here before all that."

For a brewery with a decent amount of production—38,000 barrels in 2012—Sixpoint has a portfolio of products that are hard to define. That's the way they roll in Red Hook, it seems. The six core beers include Sweet Action, the brewery's first and the bestseller in the New York metro area, according to Gorlechen. What style is it, exactly? Sixpoint literature describes it as part pale ale, part wheat, and part cream ale. The label bears no hint of style. "You have to drink it to get it," Gorlechen said. In many places outside New York, the big seller is Crisp, a noble-hopped European-style lager. "It tends to do well where there is not local craft lager," Gorlechen said. Crisp was one of the first Sixpoint beers made at Lion Brewery when production began in Wilkes-Barre in 2011. The Red Hook brewery was clearly too small for a lager.

Sixpoint also has four rotating seasonals, but stays true to its experimental origins with the Mad Scientists series (a new beer every two months), and the Spice of Life series, for which the base beer stays the same but the hops change each time (and only a single hop variety is used for each batch).

Each year, Sixpoint and BeerAdvocate join to create dozens of special beers to be sold at Beer for Beasts, an annual festival in Brooklyn. All proceeds benefit the Humane Society of New York. Sound like a great place to visit? The Sixpoint Brewery in Red Hook was open for tours until 2010, and the sometimes-crowded weekend events became "legendary," Gorlechen said, with people staying for hours. But the needs of the brewing process—and the unpredictability of crowds—led the brewery to stop having visitors. "We're in New York City but we're tucked into a corner," Gorlechen said. "We have six hundred accounts in New York City. So that's where people find us and learn about the beer."

Sixpoint Brewery

Opened: 2004.

Type: Production brewery.

Owners: Shane Welch and Jeff Gorlechen.

Brewer: Jan Matysiak.

System: 15-barrel brewhouse on-site in Brooklyn.

Annual production: 38,000 barrels; about 15 percent is made on-premises in Brooklyn, while the rest is made at Lion Brewery in Wilkes-Barre, Pennsylvania.

Distribution: East Coast, with some Midwest and Austin, Texas, accounts.

Hours: No tours or tasting room.

Parking: No off-street parking.

Wine Regions
(Spirits and Ciders, Too)

Love beer? Like wine? How do you feel about distilled spirits or hard cider?
If you're the type of person who likes to play the field when it comes to drinking, New York is for you. Here's a look.

Wine

As the number of New York breweries operating or soon-to-be operating climbs toward 100, the number of wineries has soared past 300—with expectations that it would reach 350 by early 2014.

The state has five official wine regions, or American Viticultural Areas (AVAs), recognized by the federal Alcohol and Tobacco Tax and Trade Bureau for labeling purposes. Some of these are broken up into smaller, member-driven wine trails. Wines produced in other areas of the state can be labeled with the words "New York." The five official wine regions are:

Long Island: Primarily centered on the North Fork, in eastern Suffolk County, this is the state's newest AVA, dating back forty years. It's best known for Chardonnay and for reds like the classic Bordeaux blends (called "Meritage" wines in the United States), Cabernet Sauvignon, and Merlot.

Hudson River: The oldest wine region in New York, and one of the oldest in America, these wineries are located primarily in and around the Shawangunk Mountains on the west side of the river, and in Columbia, Dutchess, and Westchester counties on the east side. Specialties include Seyval (a French-American hybrid), Chardonnay, blended reds, and fruit wines.

The Finger Lakes: Most of these wineries stand along Canandaigua, Keuka, Seneca, and Cayuga lakes, although some are popping up along the smaller lakes to the east and west. Cayuga and Seneca also have their own AVA designations, meaning some wines can be labeled as coming from a particular lake region. The overall specialties in the Finger Lakes are Riesling, Pinot Noir, sparkling wines, and ice wines, along with some native grape wines and hybrids.

Lake Erie: This is the state's largest grape-growing region and largest producer of juice from native grapes like Concord. Many of the vineyards are along the state Thruway corridor south of Buffalo. The region is becoming known for wines like the French-American hybrid Seyval and the European vinifera Riesling.

Niagara Escarpment: Located along Lake Ontario, this region is warmed by the lake and has been known primarily for its native American and French-American hybrid grapes. Many wineries also produce ice wine.

Take note: You'll find wineries in other areas, such as the Thousand Islands, southern Adirondacks, and around Cooperstown. Many of the wines made in these areas come from cold-hardy grapes, or from other fruit. For more information, visit www.newyorkwines.org

Spirits

Distilleries making spirits are popping up all over the state, with a recent burst in New York City boroughs like Brooklyn and Queens. You'll also find them in the Hudson Valley, the Finger Lakes, the Thousand Islands, and even in cities like Utica. More than thirty were licensed as of the middle of 2013, and produced liquors ranging from vodka and gin to whiskey, brandies, and liqueurs. Keep an eye out for them—a New York distillers promotional organization had yet to get under way. Some of the better-known New York distillers include Tuthilltown Spirits in Gardiner in the Hudson Valley, Finger Lakes Distilling near Watkins Glen, and Breukelen Distilling in Brooklyn.

Hard Cider

One of the oldest alcoholic beverages produced in the state, hard cider is now also the only one that can be sold legally in both grocery stores and liquor stores. More than a dozen cideries were open in the state as of 2013. Noted cideries include Bellwether Cider of Trumansburg in the Finger Lakes, Warwick Valley Wineries of Warwick in the Hudson Valley, and BlackBird Cider Works in Niagara County.

Long Island

If you think of Long Island as one long expanse of suburban sprawl, you're only half right. If you think of it as the rich playground of the Hamptons, the crowded beaches for city dwellers seeking summer relief, and the charming seaside, you're closer to filling in the whole picture.

Nassau County is the congested half; Suffolk the more bucolic. Drive out to the eastern end and you'll pass farms, wineries, and open fields, almost as if you were in, say, the Finger Lakes. Oddly enough, all but one of the Long Island breweries profiled in this section are in Suffolk County. Space considerations and real estate prices must have something to do with it. (Only one is actually in the Hamptons.)

If you're out on Long Island, especially in the summer, you're going to be lured to the many beaches by the sound of the crashing surf. They are well worth it. Some of the little seaside villages are charming, like Port Jefferson and Greenport (both home to breweries). And the Hamptons are, well, the Hamptons. If celebrity sighting and gawking at huge mansions are your thing, that is where you want to be.

Long Island is physically separated from the rest of the state by water on all sides, linked only by eight bridges, two tunnels, and regular ferry lines. And it is a long island, 110 miles from Montauk Point to the eastern approaches of the Verrazano Narrows Bridge. The Verrazano? That's right. Take a look at the map: Brooklyn and Queens are both on Long Island. Many New York natives don't know that.

Long Island also represents almost all of New York's saltwater coastline. Here's where you'll find the surviving fishing fleets, Fire Island National Seashore and Jones Beach State Park, and ferries to Block Island and Martha's Vineyard. On Long Island, you're never more than ten miles from the water, whether it's the relatively sheltered waters of Long Island Sound, the safe harbors of the Great and Little Peconic Bays, or the long reaches of the Atlantic Ocean.

Three highways run the length of the island: the Long Island Expressway down the middle; the combination of the Belt Parkway, Southern State Parkway, and the Sunrise Expressway along the southern side; and the Northern State Parkway along the Sound. With a combination of service roads and connector roads, you can quickly get to any spot on the island . . . except, of course, when there's traffic. And usually there's traffic, which gets extra heavy in the summer as people crowd onto the island to hit the beaches. But don't sweat it. You're near the ocean. And there's beer.

Other breweries and brewing companies

Spider Bite Beer Company (www.spiderbitebeer.com) is an award-winning, contract-only brewer based in Holbrook. Fire Island Brewing Company (www.fireislandbeer.com) is also contract-only. The Blind Bat Brewery (www.blindbatbrewery.com) is a nanobrewery operated part-time by owner Paul Dlugokencky; he hoped to move to a larger operation in Farmingdale by the end of 2013. Crooked Ladder Brewing Company (www.crookedladderbrewing.com) in Riverhead, Rocky Point Artisan Brewers (beer.donavanhall.net) on the north shore, Montauk Brewing Company (www.montaukbrewingco.com) on the eastern tip of Long Island, Moustache Brewing Company (www.moustachebrewing .com) in Riverhead, and Oyster Bay Brewing Company (www.oyster baybrewing.com) in the north shore town of the same name, were just getting under way as this guide went to press.

Other beer sites

Long Island is a big place, but a few beer sites worth mentioning are the several locations for the Croxley's Ale House chain of multi-tap beer bars, including Farmingdale (190 Main St.), Smithtown (155 W. Main St.), and Franklin Square (129 New Hyde Park Rd.); Mr. Beery's (4019 Hempstead Turnpike, Bethpage); and Fadely's Deli & Pub (422 W. Main St., Patchogue).

Area Attractions

Long Island has a number of *beaches*. Jones Beach, designed by Robert Moses and opened in 1929, is still quite the attraction, packed cheek to cheek in the high season, with bathhouses, pools, baseball fields, a boardwalk, picnic areas, and a restaurant. Fire Island National Seashore is a long (32 miles), skinny barrier island with only minimal highway access. There is a park at either end—Smith Point County

Park at the east end and Robert Moses State Park at the west end—which have parking lots, but otherwise the resort communities on Fire Island are reached by a number of ferries. The beaches in the Hamptons are public but beware of limited parking (or high parking fees). *Montauk Point*, the easternmost tip of New York state, is a flat, windswept, wild area. The Point is home to Montauk Point State Park and the Montauk Point Lighthouse (2000 New York 27, Montauk, NY 11954; 631-668-2544; www.montauklighthouse.com).

New York's biggest collection of *wineries* is on the North Fork, along Routes 25 and 25A. (www.nofowine.com). The *Cradle of Aviation Museum* (Charles Lindbergh Blvd., Garden City, NY 11530; 516-572-4111; www.cradleofaviation.org), located in Garden City, is dedicated to Long Island's historic role in the development of the aircraft industry. *Sagamore Hill and the Roosevelt Museum at Old Orchard* (20 Sagamore Hill Rd., Oyster Bay, NY 11771; 516-922-4788; www.nps.gov/sahi) served as Theodore Roosevelt's "summer White House" from 1885 until his death in 1919. (Note: At the time this book went to press, the house itself was closed for a rehabilitation project but the Theodore Roosevelt Museum, visitors center, and park grounds were open.)

Barrier Brewing Co.

3001 New St., Unit A2, Oceanside, NY 11572
(516) 594-1028 • www.barrierbrewing.com

"What doesn't kill you," an old saying goes, "makes you stronger." By that score, Barrier Brewing Co. should be the Superman of Long Island beer. Blame Sandy, whether you call it a hurricane or a "superstorm," which hit Barrier Brewing hard in 2012 just a few months after it opened its current location in Oceanside, on the south side of Long Island. "We had a difficult second year, that's for sure," said Craig Frymark, who co-owns the brewery with partner Evan Klein. "For half the year, we made no beer and generated no revenue."

By early 2013, Barrier was back up and running, but its timeline shows the difficulty. The company started in January 2009 but didn't make its first brew until June 2010. That was on a 1-barrel system, which Klein, then working alone, had to brew on twelve times a week to keep up. Soon, Frymark joined, and they moved to the current location with a new 5-barrel brewhouse. Production shut down for the first three months of 2012 during installation.

They brewed from March until the end of October that year. Then the storm hit. They lost everything electrical, plus items like the keg washer and the glycol chillers, and half the beer inventory. They were able to clean up the remaining equipment and start again. They got help from fellow Long Island brewers—none of whom suffered such extensive damage—and from Brewery Ommegang (page 90) in Cooperstown through some collaboration brews. "It was tough," Klein said, "but this is what we've always wanted to do, so we're making it happen. It's a good thing we like it, because this is really our third start-up in three years." Their motto, by the way, is "We brew it. We bring it."

The dream for Frymark and Klein began several years ago, when they were both working at Sixpoint Brewery in Brooklyn. "We had the Saturday shift, and at the end of the brew day, we'd each

Beers brewed: On my visit, beers included Green Room American Pale Ale, Money West Coast IPA, Antagonist ESB, Bulkhead India Red Ale, Saisoff (a hoppy saison), Medulla English IPA, and Icculus German Kolsch.

The Pick: Green Room, one of Klein and Frymark's earliest beers, combines the best of a West Coast IPA hop character with a European-style toasted and biscuity malt base.

bring out some homebrew," Frymark said. "And we talked about our own brewery." They knew what they wanted, too. They wouldn't contract any beers out to other breweries, for one thing. Frymark said that never appealed to them. "The kind of people we are, we knew that we wanted to make our own beers," Klein said. "I can see the benefits of contract, but not for us."

They also shared a vision for how they would operate, and what beers they would make: a lot of them, across every imaginable style. That explains why there is no flagship Barrier beer. They made forty-seven different beers in their first year, despite all the hardships. "We try to steer clear of a flagship beer," Klein said. "We have flagship styles like IPAs or Belgians or Germans. But we don't want to be limited." That was a necessity, he added, back when he was brewing lots of small batch beers on the 1-barrel system, but it carried over to the new brewhouse. Their 5-barrel DME system has four vessels—mash tank, lauter tank, boil kettle, and whirlpool—which is unusual for its small size. But that does make it efficient. "We'd rather make four different 5-barrel beers than one 20-barrel beer," Frymark said.

Barrier's accounts, almost all draft-only for now, seem okay with that. They have 120 accounts throughout Long Island, New York City, and the lower Hudson Valley. "It's great—if they have a Barrier tap handle, then we can fill that space with what we want," Klein said. And it doesn't mean the beers are strictly one-offs, never to be seen again, either. "Every beer, or almost every beer, will come back again and again during the year," Klein said. The sheer number of brews they make, which include 8 or 9 IPAs and a bunch of saisons, is reflected in the tap setup in their tasting room. The beers are identified by numbered billiard balls, not by specific tap handles.

In 2013, Barrier began taking advantage of space in their former warehouse home vacated by another tenant after Sandy, and began building a new tasting area. The older tasting room was limited by its location in the working brewhouse area and by the slow traffic during the post-Sandy recovery. Klein and Frymark look forward to bringing more people to the brewery, and to building their identity and generating more retail sales. "It's a better margin, of course," Klein said.

Assuming no other disaster, natural or otherwise, occurs, Frymark and Klein plan to grow. Their 5-barrel system is smaller than that in many craft brewhouses, but they resist the "nano" label. "We don't use nano or micro or even craft," Frymark said. "We're a brewery that makes beer. That's it."

Barrier Brewing Co.

Opened: 2010.

Type: Production brewery.

Owners and Brewers: Evan Klein and Craig Frymark.

System: 5-barrel DME brewhouse.

Annual production: About 1,500 barrels.

Distribution: Long Island, New York City, and Westchester County. Almost all draft in 2013; limited 22-ounce and 750-milliliter beers.

Hours: New tasting room under construction in 2013. Check website for details.

Parking: Yes.

Black Forest Brew Haus

Black Forest Brew Haus

2015 New Highway, Farmingdale, NY 11735
(631) 391-9500 • www.blackforestbrewhaus.com

Tucked away in a corner of Long Island dominated by light industrial buildings and offices, you'll find a little piece of Germany: a solid dark wood interior, Wiener schnitzel and sauerbraten on the menu, and some classic "bier." The Black Forest Brew Haus in Farmingdale even has a German-built brewing system with two copper vessels, which measures its output in hectoliters, not barrels. Yet the place is not exclusively German. The menu features good old American pub fare, and brewer Joe Hayes does produce the occasional IPA or other brew, like the Oatmeal Blueberry Brown that was on tap during my summer visit.

Black Forest opened in 1998. Todd Waite is the managing partner, but there is an affiliation with a two-hundred-year-old German brewer called Privatbrauerei Hoepfner, in Karlsruhe, in the northern part of the Black Forest region. There were originally supposed to be several of these brewpubs in the United States, but only one other, in Detroit, ever started up. (It's no longer associated with the Black Forest on Long Island.) In its early days, everything from the grain to the recipes came straight from Germany, with some limits on what the on-site brewer could do. The malt was going to be shipped in containers (like the ones you see on ships) to reflect the size of the American operation.

Hayes took over the brewhouse in 2003 and has much more freedom to operate. "Most of the beers are still true to the German style, the lagers and the wheats," Hayes said. "But I get to tweak them a bit." He increased the hop level on the Pilsner, for example, to better reflect American tastes. "And when I do ales, like the IPA, I get to play around," Hayes said, describing an IPA that came in at 110 IBUs with Chinook and Centennial hops—unheard of in Germany. "That keeps it interesting, both for me and for the customers." Hayes has no assistant, and he works hard. His

Beers brewed: Amber, Pilsner, Hefe-Weizen, Rye Steam, Helles, IPA, and both German and non-German seasonals.

The Pick: Anyone who thinks a light-colored lager only means pilsner can go straight to Helles. (I always wanted to say that.) Black Forest's Helles lager (*helles* is German for "light") is the real deal, a malt-forward but refreshing sip of German beer tradition.

grain is stored in a room near the entrance, and he has to manually carry the bags over to the brewhouse on the other side of the dining room and pour the malt into the mash tun. On my visit, Hayes, who trained at the University of California, Davis, was somewhat appropriately wearing a T-shirt that read "Haulin' Oats."

Black Forest produces three year-round beers: a malty sweet Amber, a light and crisp Pilsner, and a wheat of some kind or another, depending on the season. "In the summer, it's going to a Hefe[weizen]," Hayes said, but at other times it could be a Dunkel Weizen or a Weizenbock. For the lagers, Hayes is able to do a real decoction mash—the slow, intense method favored by German traditionalists, which is said to boost the malt character, especially of lighter-colored lagers. It's certainly true that Black Forest's lagers are intensely malty. Hayes is able to do the less time-consuming single infusion mash for his ales. In all, he makes about twenty-five beers during the course of a year. The beers are naturally carbonated in the conditioning tanks and unfiltered.

Not long after he was hired, Hayes was sent to Germany to check out an affiliated brewery near Heidelberg. He noticed something odd. "On their sign, in Germany, they called it a brew house—h-o-u-s-e," he said. "Here on Long Island, we spell it h-a-u-s. It's kind of funny."

Black Forest Brew Haus

Opened: 1998.

Type: Brewpub.

Owners: Todd Waite (managing partner) and Friedrich Hoepfner (partner).

Brewer: Joe Hayes.

System: 10-barrel Beering-Fooding system.

Annual production: 900 barrels.

Distribution: Only at the brewpub, or growlers.

Hours: 11:30 a.m. to 11 p.m. Monday to Thursday; 11:30 a.m. to 1 a.m. Friday and Saturday; 11 a.m. to 10 p.m. Sunday.

Food: Lots of German influence, but otherwise American pub fare

Parking: Yes.

Blue Point Brewing Company

161 River Ave., Patchogue, NY 11772
(631) 475-6944 • www.bluepointbrewing.com

You don't get to be the biggest brewery on Long Island—and in the top forty nationally—by standing still. Blue Point Brewing Company has been successful from the get-go. It's not only the biggest Long Island brewery, it's also the oldest production brewery on the island.

Here's an example of not standing still. For a decade, part of the brewery's signature was its direct-fired, brick-lined brew kettle. That's what put the "toasted" in the brewery's flagship, Toasted Lager. In 2009, the brewery installed a new stainless steel brewhouse and it didn't skip a beat. Toasted Lager still rules. And yet they don't rest on that, either.

In 2003, the brewery launched a beer called Hoptical Illusion, a citrus-resiny American IPA that has won lots of fans and became its second-leading seller. In 2013, Blue Point also seemed poised for yet another big winner, Mosaic, a grapefruit bomb of an IPA. Of course, Blue Point has brewed many other beers along the way. "We're always experimenting, always looking for something," said Curt Potter, Blue Point's director of branding and communication, who served as my guide to the brewery. "It's one of those things you know when you see it. That's their [owners Mark Burford and Peter Cotter] philosophy of creating beers."

Blue Point Brewing opened in 1998 in Patchogue, centrally located on the southern side of the island, facing the Great South Bay, and beyond that, Fire Island. The nearby town of Blue Point is home to the legendary (and authentic) Blue Point oysters. The species nearly disappeared, and it has taken some extraordinary effort to restore them. No such efforts have been needed with Blue Point beers. The story began with friends Burford and Cotter, who used to drink in a joint—yes, that is the right word—called Fadeley's

Beers brewed: Year-round: Toasted Lager, Blueberry Ale, RastafaRye Ale, Oatmeal Stout, Hoptical Illusion, Pale Ale, Toxic Sludge Black IPA, and White IPA. Seasonals and limited releases: Double Blonde, ESB, No Apologies (Double PA), Old Howling Bastard, and Sour Cherry Imperial Stout.

The Pick: I've had beers, especially West Coast-style IPAs, with some intense citrusy grapefruit aromas. But I don't think I'd ever had the grapefruit explosion I found in the Mosaic IPA, a limited release in 2013. It seems destined to make it back in the rotation. If it's not around, the Hoptical Illusion is a more than adequate IPA.

Deli that actually served what passed for decent beer in the 1970s. (Remember when German imports were the pinnacle of good beer drinking?) Burford and Cotter had both traveled, and so developed an appreciation for good beer. Burford eventually ran a homebrew shop, then became brewmaster at the short-lived Cobblestone Winery and Brewery in Huntington. Cotter handled sales. By 1998, Cobblestone failed and the duo combined to open Blue Point. They bought the Peter Austin-designed direct-fire brewhouse from Wild Goose Brewery in Cambridge, Maryland, which had gone out of business, and set up shop in an old Penguin Ice factory. They found some talented people to help with graphics—their slightly askew buoy logo, designed by Jim McCune, may be one of the most recognizable in craft beer—and got brewing.

Burford and Cotter managed a lot of diversity within the relative constraints of the original Peter Austin system, which generally has been used by brewers to specialize in British-style ales. Blue Point's eight year-round beers, five seasonals, and assorted limited-release beers still show some British influence, from a selection of core pale ales and IPAs to an ESB, Oatmeal Stout, barleywine called Old Howling Bastard, and an Imperial Stout (a sour cherry version). Yet its flagship and one of its earliest beers is a lager, the coppery, malt-accented Toasted Lager. "Toasted has been really popular from the start," Potter said, adding that it accounts for up to 30 percent of Blue Point's total sales. The Hoptical Illusion is the second bestseller, a 6.8 percent ABV American-style IPA. Also popular is the Blueberry Ale, which may have been mistakenly thought of as a beer intended to appeal strictly to women. "We're always amazed by the feedback we get from guys on that one," Potter said.

Some of Blue Point's beers demonstrate the brewery's commitment to various causes. It sends a portion of proceeds from RastafaRye Ale to a charity for underprivileged children, and its Toxic Sludge Black IPA debuted in 2010 in response to the BP oil rig disaster in the Gulf of Mexico. "That was supposed to be a one-time thing, but it took off and now we do it year round," Potter said. More recently in 2012, Blue Point hosted a collaboration beermaking effort to support its Long Island neighbor, Barrier Brewing Co. in Oceanside (page 237), which suffered severe damage in Hurricane Sandy.

Blue Point sells its beers all along the East Coast, from New Hampshire to Florida, in all sorts of packaging, from kegs to 12- and 22-ounce bottles to 12- and 16-ounce cans. (Not all the beers are available in every package.) It contracts its packaged beers at various places; the largest contract provider has been Genesee Brewing Company in

Rochester. "We'd brew more here, but there is definitely a space issue," Potter said.

Many smaller breweries are jammed into one building that's not always very large. Blue Point is more of a compound, a complex of buildings and spaces that's on the small side. Everyone's favorite space in good weather is the "beer garden," set up amid the buildings and outfitted with picnic tables. It hosts several events each year, including a major cask ale festival. The indoor tasting room is pretty cool, too, especially its tiled mosaic bar. The room has a sort of cluttered, home-bar feel, and it's a popular spot. And there's another benefit for Long Islanders who get tired of bumper-to-bumper traffic: It's just a ten-minute walk from the Long Island Railroad stop. "We give discounts for people with railroad tickets," Potter said.

Blue Point's role in the development of Long Island's craft beer scene can't be overlooked. In the first edition of this book, the last word in the Blue Point entry went to Burford, who said the brewery was "brewing beers for exploration." I'll give the new last word to a Long Island brewing colleague, Greg Martin of Long Ireland Beer Company in Riverhead (page 254). "You have to give credit to Mark and Pete and Blue Point," Martin said. "In 1998 when they started, there was no craft beer on Long Island. But they started brewing and selling and paving the way for guys like us today."

Blue Point Brewing Company

Opened: 1998.

Type: Production brewery, with some beer made off-premises under contract.

Owners: Mark Burford and Peter Cotter.

Brewer: Mark Burford and Christian Ryan.

System: 30-barrel brewhouse.

Annual production: 63,000 barrels (including contracted beers).

Distribution: Throughout the East Coast in kegs, bottles, and cans.

Hours: 3 p.m. to 7 p.m. Thursday and Friday; noon to 7 p.m. Saturday.

Parking: Limited.

The BrickHouse Brewery & Restaurant

67 W. Main St., Patchogue, New York 11772
(631) 447-BEER • www.brickhousebrewery.com

Brewer Charles Noll has a trick up his sleeve when it comes to keeping the rotation varied at The BrickHouse Brewery & Restaurant in Patchogue, Long Island. His signature brew is called Anarchy Ale. The trick is that, while it's always a hop-heavy beer, it's almost never brewed the exact same way twice. He might change the type of hops or the alcohol level or even the color. "The most common question I get from customers here is 'What's new?' or 'What's next?'" Noll said. "So I can always say, 'Well the Anarchy Ale is new.'" Of course, BrickHouse offers more beers than that, and Noll juggles a core of bestselling brews with a rotation of seasonals and specials.

The BrickHouse opened in 1996, pre-dating the better known Blue Point Brewing Company production brewery (page 242) a few blocks away. Blue Point owner Mark Burford once served as the BrickHouse brewer, and today BrickHouse uses Blue Point for keg washing and storage. But there's a stronger connection to another New York brewery. BrickHouse majority owner Tom Keegan is the father of Tommy Keegan, who runs Keegan Ales in Kingston (page 196) on the Hudson River.

The BrickHouse building has a lot of history and is billed as the oldest commercial building in Patchogue, a seaside town between the rampant suburbia of Nassau County and the Hamptons. Its foundation was built from ship's ballast back in 1850. The building was once a stop on the Underground Railroad, and then was a general store called Shands. Today, BrickHouse is a comfortable and friendly pub with a main bar area, upstairs room, and beer garden. It also hosts live music, and the crowds for these events serve as a representation of BrickHouse's clientele and the kind of beers they drink. "If it's a Grateful Dead cover band," Noll said, "I'll sell lots of IPA. If it's a head-banging, fist-bumping group, I'll sell a lot of Street Light."

Street Light is the lightest beer in the Brickhouse rotation, and Noll uses it "to woo the Budweiser drinkers." But, he notes, "craft beer is huge, and so a lot of people are coming in looking for the interesting stuff we have." That lineup

Beers brewed: Street Light, Beowulf IPA, Boy's Red, Nitro Boom Stout, Mother Chugga, Keller Bier, Smokin Betty, Main Street Coffee Porter, and limited releases.

The Pick: Mother Chugga is Noll's beer but he swears he didn't pick the name. In any case, it's a full-bodied, satisfying brew at 6 percent ABV.

includes several that are almost always on tap, from the Hurricane Kitty, a Sierra Nevada-style American pale ale, to Brickhouse Red, which Noll said he uses "to woo people away from Kilians [MillerCoors' Irish red]." Also usually on tap are Nitro Boom Stout, Mother Chugga (an English-style amber ale), and Beowulf IPA, a British-style India pale ale hopped with Fuggles.

In honor of its brewery connections, BrickHouse also generally carries Keegan Ales' Old Capital (or another Keegan brew) and Blue Point's flagship, Toasted Lager. But it doesn't put any other guest beers on tap. Oddly, both Keegan Ales and BrickHouse have an IPA called Hurricane Kitty, but they aren't the same. They don't even use the same yeast, Noll said.

The food menu includes a raw bar—oysters, clams, and shrimp—like you'd expect to find in a place just a short distance from the crashing surf. The kitchen also serves burgers and sandwiches, steaks and seafood, entrees like Jambalaya and sauerbraten, and a "famous" marinated flank steak.

Noll brews on a 10-barrel Bohemian system—the kind with the beautiful copper cladding—that sits in the front of the main bar area. Almost all of BrickHouse's beer production is sold on-premises, although as the brewery adds kegs it might expand a little to more off-premises accounts. One recent such venture came when New York City's famed 21 Club came looking for a house beer. Noll brewed them what he called a "toned-down," slightly less hoppy version of his Beowulf IPA. "That was a great thing," he said. "It kind of elevated our status."

The BrickHouse Brewery & Restaurant

Opened: 1996.
Type: Brewpub.
Owners: Tom Keegan (majority partner).
Brewer: Charles Noll.
System: 10-barrel Bohemian brewhouse.
Annual production: 900 to 1,000 barrels.
Distribution: Mostly on-premises; a few off-premises accounts, all draft.
Food: Pizza, pasta, burgers, and a raw seafood bar.
Hours: 11 a.m. to 2 a.m. Monday to Saturday; 11 a.m. to 1 a.m. Sunday.
Parking: No off-street parking but municipal lots nearby.

Great South Bay Brewery

25 Drexel Drive, Bay Shore, NY 11706
(631) EZ-AT-GSB
www.greatsouthbaybrewery.com

Rick Sobotka's Great South Bay Brewery beers may knock you out, but they won't put you to sleep. Sobotka is an anesthesiologist by trade and a brewery owner on the side. His Great South Bay Brewery occupies a large space in Bay Shore, Long Island. The space looks big enough to be an airplane hangar, but the brewery and tasting room currently take up just a small portion. "We definitely built this with room to grow," said head brewer Greg Maisch.

Great South Bay had beers on the market for a few years before opening on its own in 2013. The beers had previously been made under contract at Greenpoint Beerworks/KelSo (page 221) in Brooklyn before then. As of 2013, Great South's brews were all ales, but Maisch said they expect to do lagers down the road. It's the same with packaging: The brewery debuted draft-only beers but its brewers hope to install a bottling line within the year.

Sobotka is an Upstater. He grew up in the Southern Tier town of Apalachin, most famous for being the site of a big Mafioso summit and raid back in 1957. He learned to brew from his dad, a well-known and respected homebrewer. The men in the family had learned like that for generations, dating back to Rick Sobotka's great-grandfather, who had brewed and distilled back in Poland. Sobotka studied at SUNY Binghamton, then did some beer travels, eventually apprenticing at the San Diego Brewing Company in California and Breckenridge Brewery in Colorado. Then he went to medical school. But the brewing itch never subsided.

Sobotka designs the beers, and Maisch tweaks them for production in the 30-barrel brewhouse made by Allied Beverage Tanks, Inc. of Chicago.

Beers Brewed: Blonde Ambition, Massive IPA, Robert Moses Pale Ale, Blood Orange Pale Ale, Snaggletooth Stout, Pumpkin Ale, Kismet Saison, Sleigh Ryed (a winter red rye), Hoppocratic Oath Imperial IPA, Bayliner Weisse, Conscious Sedaison (saison), Marauder Scotch Ale, and Lager.

The Pick: How could something like Blood Orange Pale Ale put anyone to sleep? It comes in a clear glass growler to better accentuate that sunset hue. But the taste is what sells it—an orange flavor, both tart and sweet, and a lingering bitterness that keeps you coming back for more.

"They start with Rick—it's his concept," Maisch said. The beers start with Robert Moses Pale Ale (named for the guy who masterminded many of the beaches, parks, and roadways on Long Island and beyond). This is a classic American West Coast pale with Cascade and Amarillo hops and a "sessionable" alcohol content of 5 percent. That beer is also the base for the Blood Orange Pale, in which blood oranges are added to the tank during fermentation. The orange flavor definitely comes through, and the pith adds another layer of bitterness on top of the hops. If you're looking for hops, however, check out the Massive India Pale Ale, made with Simcoe, Centennial, Cascade, and Chinook hops. The brewery bills this 6.8 percent ABV beer as an "East Coast" IPA.

The rest of the lineup has the occasional "straight" beer like lager but often veers into a creative range of flavors and additives. The Snaggletooth Stout, for example, is brewed with flaked oats, cinnamon, licorice root, and Long Island apples. The Sleigh Ryed Red Ale has rye and juniper berries. And Great South Bay is not afraid to go big, either. Marauder, a bourbon barrel-aged Scotch Ale, weighs a hefty 10 percent ABV. And there's the beer Sobotka called Hoppocratic Oath, a 9 percent Imperial IPA brewed with Simcoe, Summit, Cascade, Centennial Chinook, and Citra hops.

The doctor even offers cards at the brewery, with the "Hoppocratic Oath" written on the back: "It has been granted to me to brew a beer; this awesome responsibility must follow the true standard of craft brewing and not deviate to lesser forms of liquid fabrication," it reads in part, later adding: "I enjoy the endless adventure that craft beer offers."

Great South Bay Brewery

Opened: Previously brewed under contract; opened its own brewery in 2013.

Type: Production brewery.

Owner: Rick Sobotka.

Brewers: Rick Sobotka and Greg Maisch.

System: 30-barrel Allied Beverage Tanks brewhouse.

Annual production: 1,900 barrels in 2013; expected to double in 2014.

Distribution: Nassau and Suffolk counties, with plans to move into New York City by 2014.

Hours: 3 p.m. to 8 p.m. Thursday to Friday; noon to 5 p.m. Saturday and Sunday.

Parking: Yes.

Greenport Harbor Brewing Company

234 Carpenter St., Greenport, NY 11944
(631) 477-6681 • harborbrewing.com

You pass so many farms and wineries on the way to Greenport Harbor Brewing Company that you might think you're in the Finger Lakes, or at least not on densely populated Long Island. But this is the North Fork, on the island's eastern end—a land of vineyards and berry farms next to the sea—and this is where you'll find Greenport, a place with an intense focus on beer.

As of 2013, Greenport Harbor Brewing has two locations. The first (farther east) is the original brewhouse and tasting room in the little coastal village of Greenport, where seafood restaurants abound and the ferry runs across to nearby Shelter Island. It's located in an old firehouse. (Check out the century-old red brick "Greenport Jail" next door, too.) Meanwhile, Greenport was building a larger production brewery a little farther west along Route 25 in Peconic, with wineries on every side. They're keeping the existing 15-barrel system in the old Greenport firehouse and installing a new 30-barrel system in Peconic, for a 45-barrel total that should make the brewery one of Long Island's largest.

The story of Greenport Harbor begins with John Liegey, a New Yorker, and Rich Vandenburgh, a Bostonian. As they relate on their website, they bonded over the bad beer they drank in college. Soon they were homebrewing and learning everything they could about beer and the beer business. They began thinking of opening a brewery, and in the spring of 2008 Rich bought an old firehouse in the Village of Greenport. Renovations were carried out with the help of friends and family. They also got help from DJ Swanson, who showed up one winter day looking for a brewing job. Swanson had previously worked as a brewer at the John Harvard's Brewery & Ale House in Lake Grove, farther west on Long Island, then had several other jobs, including a stint as a distillery manager.

Beers brewed: Year-round: Harbor Pale Ale, Black Duck Porter, and Other Side IPA. Seasonals: Summer Ale, Anti Freeze, Rye Saison, and Leaf Pile (pumpkin ale), plus the Project Hoppiness IPA series and other specials.

The Pick: Even on a summer day, the Black Duck Porter was a winner (perhaps the stiff ocean breezes helped). The beer is full and round, with a crisp, clean finish that leaves you wanting more.

On July 4, 2009, Greenport Harbor Brewing opened with Swanson at the helm of the 15-barrel DME brewhouse. He was later joined by assistant brewer Greg Doroski. Since the beginning, Greenport has brewed all its beers on its own equipment, never contracting out to another brewery. That was true even after the brewery found New York City accounts less than a year after opening. "We were doing single [15-barrel] batches at first, but since we got into the city, it's been double batching all the way," Swanson said.

Until the new brewery is running, all the beers are draft. And they're all clean-finishing, since Swanson and Doroski both have a deep-seated dislike of the buttery aromas that come with the compound known as diacetyl. That makes the beers, whatever the style, quenching. Swanson said he hates the term "drinkable," but that is a great way to describe them.

The brewery has three fulltime beers and four seasonals, plus enough specialties and one-offs to total forty different beers in the first four years of operation. The flagship beer is Harbor Pale, an American pale ale made with 30 percent wheat malt and hopped with Warrior, Glacier, and Cascade (although the brewers do tweak elements of each beer from time to time). The next most popular beer, Black Duck Porter, may not sell as much in volume as the Harbor Pale, but Swanson said it does have the highest number of steady accounts. It's his baby, and one they don't tweak so often. "Nobody messes with the porter," he said. Its characteristic creaminess is due in part, the brewers say, to the use of Thomas Fawcett & Sons dark crystal malt. (There is, by the way, a version called Canard Noir, which uses the same base but substitutes a Belgian saison yeast.)

In the specialty category, Swanson and Doroski have embarked on what they call "Project Hoppiness," a series of different India pale ales. "There's black IPA, English-style IPA, and so on," Doroski said. "I guess you could say the IPA category is unlimited." Take, for example, the brewery's Citrus IPA. It has real mashed-up whole fruits like orange, lemon, lime, and tangelo—pith and all—mixed in. It's also got an extraordinarily low level of hops, considering it's an IPA. "The pith from the fruit actually adds some bitterness that was lost with the reduction in hops," Doroski said. The brewers did add some Citra hops to later batches, because the name led people to assume there was Citra in it.

The Citrus IPA is one of several Greenport Harbor beers that have food products in them. The Blonde Summer Ale has orange blossom honey, and the Devil's Plaything, brewed for a New York City restaurant called Salvation Taco, has both Latin American and Thai peppers. And yet Swanson contends that "Keep it simple" is his brewing philosophy.

"You can get a lot of flavor out of a simple set of ingredients," he said, "so that's how most of our beers are formulated."

Greenport Harbor gets my vote for the most creative logo in New York. The design features the image of a sperm whale shaped to resemble Long Island, right down to the North and South Forks at the tail. The brewery cranks out more beer—and operates its tasting room longer—in the busy summer months. "It can get pretty dead around here in the middle of winter," Swanson said. Production will certainly increase, perhaps along with distribution, once the new brewhouse is up and running.

Greenport Harbor Brewing Company

Opened: 2009.

Type: Production brewery (two locations after 2013).

Owners: John Liegey and Richard Vandenburgh.

Brewers: DJ Swanson and Greg Doroski.

System: 15-barrel DME (original brewhouse); 30-barrel system planned for the second location.

Annual production: 3,000 barrels in the original brewhouse.

Distribution: Long Island, New York City, and Westchester County (draft only until the new brewhouse opens).

Hours: Seasonal; call ahead.

Parking: Limited.

John Harvard's Brewery & Ale House

2093 Smithaven Plaza, Lake Grove, NY 11755
(631) 979-2739 • www.johnharvards.com

The Long Island branch of a small national brewpub chain is located just about where you'd expect it—on the edge of a strip mall parking lot, along a busy road crowded with Target, Old Navy, Carrabba's, and other signposts of suburbia. Since the chain is John Harvard's Brewery & Ale House, which began in Cambridge, Massachusetts, near Harvard University, you'd expect Lake Grove's branch to be near a college campus. In this case, the nearby college is the State University of New York at Stony Brook, one of the largest university centers in the state college system.

The village center of Stony Brook is full of authentic Long Island charm, from cedar shake and fieldstone homes to specialty shops to an idyllic little coastal harbor. And although it's part of a chain, John Harvard's offers some claims to Long Island individuality, too. The brewers are allowed to make their own choices in beer, within some limits. The brewhouse at Lake Grove is run by David DeTurris. Like other John Harvard's brewers, he has the ability to play around—seemingly more so than brewers at, say, the Gordon Biersch chain. And so the Long Island John Harvard's has a rich, somewhat sweet dark beer called Pinstripe Porter. That's not something you'd expect to go over well in the greater Boston area.

The first John Harvard's opened in Cambridge's Harvard Square with Grenville Byford and Gary Gut at the helm. Other current locations include Framingham, Massachusetts; Providence, Rhode Island; and two seasonal ski center locales: Jiminy Peak in Hancock, Massachusetts; and Holiday Valley, in Ellicottville, New York. Long Island clearly has one of the success stories. It even won the 2002 F.X Matt Memorial Cup at the TAP New York festival for the best brewery in New York state.

The company slogan is "Real Beer, Honest Food." Corporate history tells the tale of the young John Harvard, the English clergyman for whom Harvard University is named, watching William Shakespeare brew beer in Southwark, England. We

Beers brewed: Long Island Light Lager, Penguin Pils, Amarillo Anonymous, John Harvard's Pale Ale, Vacation? IPA, Dunkel Weisse, and Pinstripe Porter.

The Pick: The namesake Pale Ale is one of those classic, retro-1990s American pale ales, hoppy but not overloaded. But I was impressed with the Dunkel Weisse, a bubblegum-infused dark wheat that seems perfect for a breezy day at the shore.

are told that Shakespeare wrote, in addition to his plays and sonnets, a book of brewing recipes that John Harvard brought with him to America in 1637. According to the story, the book was found in 1992 and inspired the brewpub's beers. You can decide for yourself how "real and honest" the story is, but don't doubt the sincerity of the slogan. The menu is innovative and eclectic with a number of regional influences. The desserts are excessive, just the way you want them. A few local specialties may show up, but the food varies little from pub to pub. The pubs also have very similar brewing equipment with which they brew the same core beers. Each location has a handpump for serving cask-conditioned versions of some of the beers.

The brewhouses exchange recipes and information, a practice the brewers find very helpful. If a brewer runs into a problem, chances are someone else has had the same trouble and can offer a solution, or at least some ideas. Brewers also formulate some of their own beers and are encouraged to tweak the core beers toward local tastes. All in all, John Harvard's is a brewpub chain that seems more at home in parts of Long Island than almost anywhere else.

John Harvard's Brewery & Ale House

Opened: 1997.

Owners: Part of the John Harvard's Brewery & Ale House chain.

Brewer: David DeTurris.

System: 14-barrel Pub Systems brewhouse.

Annual production: 2,400 barrels capacity.

Distribution: On-premises and growlers.

Hours: 11:30 a.m. to midnight Sunday to Thursday; 11:30 a.m. to 1 a.m. Friday and Saturday.

Food: Pub menu.

Parking: Yes.

Long Ireland Beer Company

817 Pulaski St., Riverhead, NY 11901
(631) 403-4303 • www.longirelandbrewing.com

For a couple of years, Greg Martin and Dan Burke made their first commercial beers in Connecticut and then brought them over to their home territory in New York. The trouble is, their home is on the eastern end of Long Island. "There were some long trips by water or by road," Martin said. Now, Long Ireland Beer Company is established in its own brewery in Riverhead and sells its beers across the island and into New York City and the lower Hudson Valley.

Martin and Burke do it by trying to "fill in the blanks" in their customers' craft beer lineup. "That's been our philosophy," Martin said. "Let's say a bar has a bunch of IPA taps. That's fine, but we can fill in the gaps. Give us a hole, a tap handle, and we'll fill it, perhaps with something malty as an alternative." That explains two of the brewery's leading beers: Celtic Ale and Breakfast Stout.

Even within the Irish theme—both Martin and Burke have Irish ancestry—these beers are different. Celtic Ale is certainly malty, but it's not really a traditional Irish red ale, even though it contains honey and oats, two traditional Irish ingredients. And the Breakfast Stout, which contains both lactose sugar and roasted coffee, is not going to be confused with an Irish style like Guinness. "We basically said, if everyone is going hop heavy, we'll go malt," Martin said. "We want to stand out." That's not to say they don't count some hoppy beers among the dozen or so they produce yearly—they have an IPA hopped with Columbus, Centennial, Citra, and Summit, and they've added locally grown North Fork Long Island wet hops to a fall seasonal version. They also have a seasonal Pumpkin Ale, which, like those produced by other New York metro area breweries, is a hot commodity in the fall. "It pays the bills," Martin said.

Martin and Burke started on this path as coworkers and homebrewers back around 2003. When they finally decided to embark on a brewery,

Beers brewed: Celtic Ale, Breakfast Stout, IPA, and Pale Ale. Seasonals: Raspberry Wheat, Summer Ale, Winter Ale, Pumpkin Ale, and others.

The Pick: The Celtic Ale is a smooth, malty beer that is an antidote to a world of over-hopped brews, but the unusual Breakfast Stout, with its ultra-low 3.5 percent ABV level, is a welcome session beer that is true to that term.

they didn't have a brewhouse of their own. A friend, Rob Leonard of New England Brewing Company in Woodbridge, Connecticut, offered them space in his brewhouse. That's how they ended up on those long journeys, usually by ferry, when they launched in 2009. "We'd take a 50-foot box truck, load up with used kegs, and go over there on the 6 a.m. ferry, then start our brews, clean the old kegs, do some filtering, keg off from the tanks, and pray we could make the 10 p.m. ferry back." When they didn't, Martin said, the drive only added twenty minutes, "but on the boat, you can just sit and think, so that was nice."

Eventually, Celtic Ale got too big to be accommodated in New England Brewing's schedule, so its production was transferred to Olde Saratoga/Mendocino Brewing Company (page 161) in Saratoga Springs while the Breakfast Stout and Pale Ale stayed in Woodbridge. But Martin and Burke wanted their own brewhouse, and they found it in a 15-barrel system that began life with New Haven Brewing Co. in Connecticut, and later served a brewery in New Hampshire. "The funny thing is, Rob Leonard started brewing on that system in New Haven, so he was familiar with it," Martin said.

In March 2011, Long Ireland had shifted all its production to Riverhead, the town that sits at the base of the two forks of eastern Long Island along the Peconic River, just before it turns in the estuary leading to Peconic Bay. The brewhouse, though officially listed at 15 barrels, is "weird," Martin said. They can boil up to 22 barrels in it, so their batches are oversized. Martin handles most of the recipe development and marketing, while Burke is the day-to-day brewer. Most of the beer is draft, for now, although they have small bottling systems for both 12-ounce and 22-ounce sizes. Like many brewers, they find bottling to be a pain. "I told people that in the first two weeks that [12-ounce] bottling line saw more cursing than any naval ship," Martin said.

The tasting room is spacious and handles a few hundred people on weekends. The brewery is located close enough to the eastern Long Island wine trails to pick up some side business that way. "I like being the first stop on their day," Martin said, and echoing reports I'd heard from brewers in the Finger Lakes wine region, he added. "I hate being the last stop in their day." But you don't have to be part of a tour. The guys at Long Ireland will fill a growler for you as long as someone is in the brewery. "If they ring the bell and we're here, we'll accommodate them," Martin said. "I feel bad for people without beer."

Long Ireland Beer Company

Opened: Company launched in 2009; on-premises brewing started in 2011.

Type: Production brewery.

Owners and Brewers: Greg Martin and Dan Burke.

System: 15-barrel JV Northwest (modified to boil 22 barrels).

Annual production: 2,885 barrels in 2012; 4,000 barrels projected for 2013.

Distribution: Long Island, New York City, and the lower Hudson Valley.

Hours: 3 p.m. to 7 p.m. Thursday and Friday; 1 p.m. to 6 p.m. Saturday and Sunday.

Parking: Yes.

Port Jeff Brewing Company

22 Mill Creek Rd., Port Jefferson, NY 11777
(877) 4PJ-BREW • www.portjeffbrewing.com

"We make beer. Adjacent to boats." Now that's a cool slogan for a brewery in a pretty cool place. Port Jeff Brewing Company is in the heart of the seaside community of Port Jefferson on Long Island's north shore. The tasting room even features a curved wooden bar, shaped like a boat. The tasting room, by the way, is open seven days a week, 364 days a year, including Thanksgiving morning for growler fills. It's closed only on Christmas. That is fairly unusual for a small brewery, but for Port Jeff, it makes sense. "Because of where we are, a lot of people stumble in," owner and brewer Mike Philbrick said.

The brewery and tasting room is in a small plaza called Chandler Square, near the main ferry port connecting central Long Island with Connecticut. It has a bustling little waterfront commercial district with an active marina and seafood restaurants. Philbrick discovered it was a good place to open a craft brewery, even if his brewhouse is a little cramped. It has a 7-barrel system, though he would "really love to have a 15 or a 30, but that can't be done in this space." Philbrick does double-batch his brews in 14-barrel fermenters, and he has a separate warehouse nearby. About 85 percent of his production is draft, and he has small bottling systems for 22-ouncers and 750-milliliter "cork and cage" bottles. Like some other Long Island brewers, he's looking into the concept of contracting with a mobile canning operator that would come to the brewhouse to package the beers.

Philbrick opened Port Jeff in the fall of 2011. Like many start-up craft brewers, he started as a homebrewer and launched his commercial operation by maxing out his credit cards. He grew up mostly in Connecticut and attended Temple

Beers brewed: Year-round: Schooner Pale Ale, Port Jeff Porter, and Party Boat IPA. Seasonals and limited releases: Centennial Sunset Lager, Boo Brew, White's Beach Wit, Dead Ryes Ryes-N-Bock, Runaway Ferry Imperial IPA, and several other limited beers.

The Pick: A refreshing coriander- and orange-influenced wit is ideal for a seaside retreat, and White's Beach Wit, a Celis White knockoff, meets that expectation. Pierre Celis would be proud.

University in Philadelphia. The thriving beer scene in Philly and surrounding areas of Pennsylvania jump-started his interest in beer. For a while, he volunteered at Victory Brewing Company in Downingtown, Pennsylvania, and later interned at Iron Hill Brewery in Lancaster. He came to Port Jefferson because his wife is from nearby Stony Brook, home to a large SUNY campus. The couple was walking on the beach on Christmas Day 2009 when he decided to open a brewery.

But Philbrick traces his serious beer chops back to the day in Philly when he decided to switch from extract to all-gain home brewing. The motivation: Celis White, a well-known Belgian witbier. "You can't duplicate that beer with extract," Philbrick said. "It just can't be done." The Celis knockoff he brewed then evolved into a beer that is still in the Port Jeff lineup as the summer seasonal White's Beach Wit. "Because of where we are, the summer seasonal is something we make a lot of," he said.

The bestseller and flagship is the Schooner Pale Ale, which accounts for more than 30 percent of his sales. It's a 6.5 percent ABV "loose pale ale," Philbrick said. Its popularity, by the way, is accounted for mostly in an area that is within five to ten miles of Port Jefferson, including Stony Brook. "It sells here really well, so it is like the local beer for this area," Philbrick said. "That's great." The second most popular beer in the Port Jeff lineup is its Porter, "and it's not really a close second." A higher percentage of its sales goes to Port Jeff's accounts across Long Island, New York City, and parts of the Hudson Valley.

In 2013, Philbrick launched Party Boat IPA. He predicted that it would instantly join the year-round lineup and possibly move up the line in sales, certainly passing the Porter and perhaps rivaling the Schooner Pale Ale. If it does, it's going to put more pressure on the brewhouse. "We're in a position where we need to figure out how to make more beer," Philbrick said, "and that's where we've been since day one."

Port Jeff Brewing Company

Opened: 2011.
Type: Production brewery.
Owner and Brewer: Mike Philbrick.
System: 7-barrel brewhouse.
Annual production: 1,600 barrels.
Distribution: Long Island, New York City, and Hudson Valley; mostly draft.
Hours: Noon to 8 p.m. daily.
Parking: Limited.

Southampton Publick House

40 Bowden Square, Southampton, NY 11968
(631) 283-2800 • www.publick.com

In choosing to call his brewpub the Southampton Publick House, owner Donald Sullivan chose the word "publick" or "public" deliberately. "In the Hamptons, there's an awful lot that's private," he said, "but we called this a public house in the literal sense of what that means. It's a public place, centrally located in the village, where anyone can come in and meet and greet and enjoy themselves. . . . We want to be an open door kind of place," he said. Adding the "k" just reinforced that old English pub vibe. It's a beer place for the same reason. "After all, beer is the common man's beverage," he said. "Beer is our mission."

Southampton Publick House opened in 1996, making it the oldest brewery on Long Island and one of the oldest continuously operating in the New York City metro area. The location has been a tavern of some sort since about 1900. For a long time, in the 1940s to the 1970s, it was a joint called Herb McCarthy's. Now it's a full-service restaurant, a spacious place with a couple of large dining rooms, a bar area, and outdoor seating areas. But beer is the focal point, with food there playing a supporting role, Sullivan said.

For fifteen years, the beer was made under the direction of Phil Markowski, a somewhat legendary brewer in the New York–Long Island area. (He's now at Two Roads Brewing Co. in Stratford, Connecticut.) Southampton beers are now in the capable hands of brewer Evan Addario, who operates the 15-barrel DME system from Canada that was installed when the place opened. In a nod to the challenges of operating in a one-hundred-year-old building, the brewhouse is a little scattered. The mash vessels and brew kettle are in a visible space off the main dining room, but the fermenters are behind the bar and the serving tanks and keg storage are below that. "There's a lot of physically moving beer around the place," Sullivan said.

Southampton brews another 10,000 barrels under contract at other breweries and has moved that business around a bit. In 2013, it was using

Beers brewed: Big Brown Ale, Sully's Irish Ale, Scotch Ale, Biere De Mars, Burton India Pale Ale, Keller Pils, Southampton Double White, Southampton Altbier, Montauk Light, and some limited releases.

The Pick: Close your eyes and take a sip of Southampton's Burton India Pale Ale. You might think you're in the north of England. It's a mineral-accented, dry-finishing classic of an authentic English IPA.

Olde Saratoga/Mendocino Brewing Company (page 161) in Saratoga Springs, and Susquehanna Brewing Company in Pittston, Pennsylvania. The flagship beer has changed, too. In Southampton's first few years, a German-style *altbier* (brewed with ale yeast) called Secret Ale was the bestseller. It has since been eclipsed by Double White, a "double-gravity" version of a Belgian wit beer. That makes it a relatively high-alcohol wit (6.6 percent ABV) with hints of coriander and curacao orange. Other beers hit many of the marks established by long traditions of European brewing, be they German, Belgian, or English.

Sullivan calls it a "Eurocentric" brewing philosophy. "I think a beer should be true to the style you're setting out to brew," he said. "If you tell me it's an IPA, then I'm expecting an IPA." He has even had Europeans who visit the Hamptons stop in and tell him the beers remind them of what they drink back home. Sullivan is quick to point out he's not criticizing other brewers that play faster and looser with styles. It's just not his thing at Southampton.

The building is not flashy from the exterior; in fact, it's partly hidden by hedgerows and resembles the clubhouse of a high-class golf club or even one of the nearby fancy homes. Sports are a focus here, from the TVs offering the NFL Sunday ticket to the in-house, off-track betting setup. "It's sort of an upscale sports bar," Sullivan said.

And just because Sullivan says the focus is on beer, don't forget the food. The menu is pub fare for the most part, with sandwiches and salads complemented by some hearty entrées of steak and seafood. You can even get the famed Long Island Duck. The place serves lunch, dinner, and weekend brunch, and provides catering and rooms for private functions. That all goes back to Sullivan's notion of having a place where the public is welcome, even in the Hamptons. "We want to be part of the community, not cut off from it," he said.

Southampton Publick House

Opened: 1996.

Type: Brewpub, with some packaged beers brewed under contract.

Owner: Donald Sullivan.

Brewer: Evan Addario.

System: 15-barrel DME in the pub.

Annual production: 2,400 barrels on-premises; another 10,000 through contracts.

Distribution: On-premises, plus local accounts on Long Island.

Hours: Call for hours.

Food: Full restaurant menu.

Parking: Yes.

Beerwebs

We live in the age of the Internet, which means constantly updated (we hope) information on New York's beer scene is available at your fingertips. Here are some helpful sites:

New York

New York State Brewers Association

www.thinknydrinkny.com

The official site of the state brewers association, with listings of breweries, newsletters, lobbying efforts, and more.

The Barley Corner

www.thebarleycorner.tumblr.com

Don Cazentre's blog on all things beer, particularly in New York state. Look here for updates on New York breweries.

The Foaming Head

www.foaminghead.com

Kevin Burns and his team offer brewery profiles, tasting notes, beer events, a guide to beer shops and bars, and more, covering all of New York state.

In the Name of Beer

www.inthenameofbeer.com

Greg Back blogs about his journeys across New York state in search of good beer.

Finger Lakes Beer Trail

www.fingerlakesbeertrail.com

Offers maps, brewery information, and a calendar of beer-related events in the Finger Lakes region (Rochester and Syracuse, too).

Brew Central New York

www.brewcentralny.com

A site that aggregates news and features about beer, spirits, and cider in the Central New York area, including Syracuse, Binghamton, and Cooperstown.

Hudson Valley Beer Trail

www.hudsonvalleybeertrail.com

Coverage of breweries, distilleries, restaurants, and more in the Hudson Valley.

National

Brewers Association

www.brewersassociation.org

This Boulder, Colorado-based association represents more than one thousand breweries. The site offers news, statistics, business information, guides to commercial brewing and homebrewing, a brewery finder, and more.

Ale Street News

www.alestreetnews.com

The website for the largest circulation beer newspaper in the country offers features, columns, news stories, and regional guides to breweries. *New York Breweries* authors Lew Bryson and Don Cazentre are regular contributors.

BeerAdvocate

www.beeradvocate.com

This top-rated site offers reviews, beer finders, events, features, and more, and covers the whole world of beer.

Glossary

ABV, ABW. Alcohol by volume, alcohol by weight. These are two slightly different ways of measuring the alcohol content of beverages, as a percentage of either the beverage's total volume or of its weight. For example, if you have 1 liter of 4 percent ABV beer, 4 percent of that liter (40 milliliters) is alcohol. However, because alcohol weighs only 79.6 percent as much as water, that same beer is only 3.18 percent ABW. This may seem like a dry exercise in mathematics, but it is at the heart of the common misconception that Canadian beer is stronger than American beer. Canadian brewers generally use ABV figures, whereas American brewers have historically used the lower ABW figures. Mainstream Canadian and American lagers are approximately equal in strength. Just to confuse the issue further, most American microbreweries use ABV figures. This is very important if you're trying to keep a handle on how much alcohol you're consuming. If you know how much Bud (at roughly 5 percent ABV) you can safely consume, you can extrapolate from there. Learn your limits.

Adjunct. Any non-barley malt source of sugars for fermentation. This can be candy sugar, corn grits, molasses or other nonstandard sugar, corn or rice syrup, or one of any number of specialty grains. Wheat, rye, and specialty sugars are considered by beer geeks to be "politically correct" adjuncts; corn and rice are generally taken as signs of swill. However, small amounts of corn used as a brewing ingredient for certain styles of beer is slowly gaining acceptance in craft-brewing circles, and I had a "pre–Prohibition double bock" made with 25 percent rice that was fantastic. So keep an open mind.

Ale. The generic term for warm-fermented beers. (See "A Word About . . . Ales and Lagers" on page 170.)

Alefruit. A term invented by Lew Bryson to signify the juicy esters produced by some yeasts, aromas, and flavors of a variety of fruits: pear, melon, plum, peach, lemon drop, and pineapple. Bryson uses "alefruit" when he can't tease out the exact fruits (or when he can but doesn't want to sound pretentious).

Barley. A wonderfully apt grain for brewing beer. Barley grows well in relatively marginal soil and climate. It has no significant gluten content, which makes it largely unsuitable for baking bread and thereby limits market competition for brewers buying the grain. Its husk serves as a very efficient filter at the end of the mashing process. And it makes beer that tastes really, really good. Barley comes in two types: two-row and six-row, named for the rows of kernels on the heads of the grain. In days past, two-row barley was plumper and considered finer. Six-row barley was easier to grow, had a better yield per acre, and higher enzymatic power, but a somewhat astringent character. These differences have been lessened by crossbreeding. Most barley grown in North America is six-row, for reasons of soil and climate. (Incidentally, the grain's kernels, or corns, are the source of the name "John Barleycorn," a traditional personification of barley or beer.)

Barrel. A traditional measure of beer volume equal to 31 United States gallons. The most common containers of draft beer in the United States are half- and quarter-barrels, or kegs, at 15.5 gallons and 7.75 gallons respectively, though the one-sixth-barrel kegs (about 5.2 gallons), known as sixtels, are becoming popular with microbrewers. (See *hectoliter*.)

Beer. A fermented beverage brewed from grain, generally malted barley. "Beer" covers a variety of beverages, including ales and lagers, stouts and bocks, porters and pilsners, lambics and *altbiers*, cream ale, Kolsch, wheat beer, and a whole lot more.

Beer geek. A person who takes beer a little more seriously than the average person does. Often homebrewers, beer geeks love to argue with other beer geeks about what makes exceptional beers exceptional. That is, if they've been able to agree on which beers are exceptional in the first place. A beer geek is the kind of person who would buy a book about traveling to breweries . . . the kind of person who would read the glossary of a beer book. Hey, hi there!

Bottle-conditioned beer. A beer that has been bottled with an added dose of live yeast. This living yeast causes the beer to mature and change as it ages over periods of one to thirty years or more. It will also "eat" any oxygen that may have been sealed in at bottling and keep the beer from oxidizing, a staling process that leads to sherryish and "wet cardboard" aromas in beer. Bottle-conditioned beer qualifies as "real ale."

Brewer. One who brews beer for commercial sale.

Breweriana. Brewery and beer memorabilia, such as trays, coasters, neon signs, steins, mirrors, and so on, including the objects of desire of the beer can and bottle collectors. Most collectors do this for fun, and a few do it for money (breweriana is starting to command some big prices; just check eBay), but the weird thing about this for me is the number of breweriana collectors—about a third, from my experience—who don't drink beer.

Brewhouse. The vessels used to mash the malt and grains and boil the wort. The malt and grains are mashed in a vessel called a mash tun. Brewhouse size is generally given in terms of the capacity of the brewkettle in which the wort is boiled. A brewery's annual capacity is a function of brewhouse size, fermentation and aging tank capacity, and length of the fermentation and aging cycle for the brewery's beers.

Brewpub. A brewery that sells the majority of its output on draft or on the premises, or a tavern that brews its own beer. Either of these may sell other brewers' beers, and often do. These days, many larger brewpubs are branching out by launching adjacent or free-standing production breweries.

CAMRA. The CAMpaign for Real Ale. A British beer drinkers' consumer group formed in the early 1970s by beer drinkers irate over the disappearance of cask-conditioned ale. They have been very vocal and successful in bringing this traditional drink back to a place of importance in the United Kingdom. CAMRA sets high standards for cask-conditioned ale, which only a few brewers in the United States match.

Carbonation. The fizzy effects of carbon dioxide (CO_2) in solution in a liquid (e.g., beer). Carbonation can be accomplished artificially by injecting the beer with the gas or naturally by trapping the CO_2, which is a by-product of fermentation. There is no intrinsic qualitative difference between beers carbonated by these two methods. It's brewer's choice, essentially. Low carbonation will allow a broader array of flavors to come through, whereas high carbonation can result in a perceived bitterness. Most American drinkers prefer a higher carbonation.

Cask. A keg designed to serve cask-conditioned beer by gravity feed or by handpump, not by gas pressure. These casks may be made of wood, but most are steel with special plumbing.

Cask-conditioned beer. An unfiltered beer that is put in a cask before it is completely ready to serve. The yeast still in the beer continues to work and ideally brings the beer to perfection at the point of sale, resulting in a beautifully fresh beer that has a "soft," natural carbonation and beautiful array of aromas. This is a classic British-style "real ale." The flip side to achieving this supreme freshness is that as the beer is poured, air replaces the beer in the cask, and the beer will become sour within five days. Bars should sell the cask out before then or remove it from sale. If you are served sour cask-conditioned beer, send it back. Better yet, ask politely for a taste before ordering. Cask-conditioned beer is generally served at cellar temperature (55–60 degrees F) and is lightly carbonated. Cask-conditioned beers are almost always ales, but some American brewers are experimenting with cask-conditioned lagers.

Cold-filtering. The practice of passing finished beer through progressively finer filters (usually cellulose or ceramic) to strip out microorganisms that can spoil the beer when it is stored. Brewers like Coors and Miller, and also some smaller brewers, use cold-filtering as an alternative to pasteurization (see *pasteurization*). Some beer geeks complain that this "strip-filtering" robs beers of their more subtle complexities and of some of their body.

Contract brewer. A brewer who hires an existing brewery to brew beer on contract. Contract brewers range from those who simply have a different label put on one of the brewery's existing brands, to those who maintain a separate on-site staff to actually brew the beer at the brewery. Some brewers and beer geeks feel contract-brewed beer is inherently inferior. This is strictly a moral and business issue; some of the better beers on the market are contract-brewed.

Craft brewer. The new term for microbrewer. Craft brewer, like microbrewer before it, is really a code word for any brewer producing beers other than mainstream American lagers like Budweiser and Miller Lite. (See "A Word

About . . . Brewpubs, Microbreweries, Nanobreweries, and Craft Breweries" on page 129.)

Decoction. The type of mashing often used by lager brewers to wring the full character from the malt. In a decoction mash, a portion of the hot mash is taken to another vessel, brought to boiling, and returned to the mash, thus raising the temperature. (See *infusion*.)

Dry hopping. Adding hops to the beer in postfermentation stages, often in porous bags to allow easy removal. This results in a greater hop aroma in the finished beer. A few brewers put a small bag of hop cones in each cask of their cask-conditioned beers, resulting in a particularly intense hop aroma in a glass of the draft beer.

ESB. Extra special bitter, an ale style with a rich malt character and full body, perhaps some butter or butterscotch aromas, and an understated hop bitterness. An ESB is noticeably bitter only in comparison to a mild ale, a style not often found in America.

Esters. Aroma compounds produced by fermentation give some ales lightly fruity aromas such as banana, pear, and grapefruit, among others. The aromas produced are tightly linked to the yeast strain used. Ester-based aromas should not be confused with the less-subtle fruit aromas of a beer to which fruit or fruit essences have been added.

Extract. More specifically, malt extract. Malt extract is kind of like concentrated wort (see *wort*). The malt is mashed and the resulting sweet, unhopped wort is reduced to a syrup, which is then packaged and sold to brewers. In extract brewing, the extract is mixed with water and boiled. Specialty grains (such as black patent or chocolate malts, wheat, or roasted barley) and hops can be added for flavor notes and nuances. It is actually more expensive to brew with extract, but you need less equipment—which can be crucial in cramped brewing areas—and less training, which makes it a lot easier. But the quality of the beer may suffer. Some people claim to be able to pick out an extract brew blindfolded. I've had extract brews that had a common taste—a kind of thin, vegetal sharpness—but I used to have excellent extract brews at the Samuel Adams Brew House when it was open in Philadelphia. My advice is to try it yourself.

Fermentation. The miracle of yeast; the heart of making beer. Fermentation is the process in which yeast turns sugar and water into alcohol, heat, carbon dioxide, esters, and traces of other compounds.

Final gravity. See *gravity*.

Firkin. A cask or keg holding 9 gallons of beer, specially plumbed for gravity or handpump dispense.

Geekerie. The collective of beer geeks, particularly the beer-oriented, beer-fascinated, beer-above-all geeks. They sometime can fall victim to group thinking and a herd mentality, but they are generally good people, if a bit hopheaded and malt-maniacal. If you're not a member of the geekerie, you might want to consider getting to know them: They usually know where all the best bars and beer stores are in their town, and they're more than happy to share the knowledge and even go along with you to share the fun. All you have to do is ask. See the Beerwebs listing (page 261) for links to the better beer pages, a good way to hook up with them.

Gravity. The specific gravity of wort (original gravity) or finished beer (terminal gravity). The ratio of dissolved sugars to water determines the gravity of the wort. If there are more dissolved sugars, the original gravity and the potential alcohol are higher. The sugar that is converted to alcohol by the yeast lowers the terminal gravity and makes the beer drier, just like wine. A brewer can determine the alcohol content of a beer by mathematical comparison of its original gravity and terminal gravity.

Great American Beer Festival (GABF). Since 1982, America's breweries have been invited each year to bring their best beer to the GABF in Denver to showcase what America can brew. Since 1987, the GABF has awarded medals for various styles of beer, with three medals for each style. To ensure impartiality, the beers are tasted blind and their identities hidden from the judges. GABF medals are the most prestigious awards in American brewing because of the festival's longevity and reputation for fairness.

Growler. A jug or bottle used to take home draft beer. These are usually either simple half-gallon glass jugs with screwtops, or more elaborate molded glass containers with swingtop seals. I have traced the origin of the term growler back to a cheap, four-wheeled horse cab in use in Victorian London. These cabs would travel a circuit of pubs in the evenings, and riding from pub to pub was known as "working the growler." To bring a pail of beer home to have with dinner was to anticipate the night's work of drinking, and became known as "rushing the growler." When the growler cabs disappeared from the scene, we were left with only the phrase, and "rushing the growler" was assumed to mean hurrying home with the bucket. When Ed Otto revived the practice by selling jugs of Otto Brothers beer at his Jackson Hole, Wyoming, brewery in the mid-1980s, he called them growlers. Now you know where the term really came from.

Guest taps/guest beers. Beers made by other brewers that are offered at brewpubs.

Handpump. A hand-powered pump for dispensing beer from a keg. Either a handpump or a gravity tap is always used for dispensing cask-conditioned beer; however, the presence of a handpump does not guarantee that the beer being dispensed is cask conditioned.

Homebrewing. Making honest-to-goodness beer at home for personal consumption. Homebrewing is where many American craft brewers get their start.

Hops. The spice of beer. Hop plants (*Humulus lupulus*) are vines whose flowers have a remarkable effect on beer. The flowers' resins and oils add bitterness and a variety of aromas (spicy, piney, citrus, and others) to the finished beer. Beer without hops would be more like a fizzy, sweet, "alco-soda."

IBU. International bittering unit, a measure of a beer's bitterness. Humans can first perceive bitterness at levels between 8 and 12 IBU. Budweiser has 11.5 IBU, Heineken 18, Sierra Nevada Pale Ale 32, and Pilsner Urquell

43. A monster like Sierra Nevada Bigfoot clocks in at 98 IBU. Equivalent amounts of bitterness will seem greater in a lighter-bodied beer, whereas a heavier, maltier beer like Bigfoot needs lots of bitterness to be perceived as balanced.

Infusion. The mashing method generally used by ale brewers. Infusion entails heating the mash in a single vessel until the starches have been converted to sugar. There is single infusion, in which the crushed malt (grist) is mixed with hot water and steeped without further heating, and step infusion, in which the mash is held for short periods at rising temperature points. Infusion mashing is simpler than decoction mashing and works well with the right types of malt. (See *decoction*.)

IPA. India pale ale, a British ale style that has been almost completely co-opted by American brewers, characterized in this country by intense hop bitterness, accompanied (in better examples of the style) by a full-malt body. The name derives from the style's origin as a beer brewed for export to British beer drinkers in India. The beer was strong and heavily laced with hops—a natural preservative—to better endure the long sea voyage. Some British brewers claim that the beer was brewed that way in order to be diluted upon arrival in India, a kind of "beer concentrate" that saved on shipping costs.

Kräusening. The practice of carbonating beer by a second fermentation. After the main fermentation has taken place and its vigorous blowoff of carbon dioxide has been allowed to escape, a small amount of fresh wort is added to the tank. A second fermentation takes place, and the carbon dioxide is captured in solution. General opinion is that there is little sensory difference between kräusened beer and beer carbonated by injection, but some brewers hold that this more traditional method produces a "softer" beer.

Lager. The generic term for all cold-fermented beers. Lager has also been appropriated as a name for the lightly hopped pilsners that have become the world's most popular beers, such as Budweiser, Castle, Brahma, Heineken, and Asahi. Many people speak of pilsners and lagers as if they are two different styles of beer, which is incorrect. All pilsners are lagers, but not all lagers are pilsners. Some are bocks, hellesbiers, and Maerzens.

Malt. Generally this refers to malted barley, although other grains can be malted and used in brewing. Barley is wetted and allowed to sprout, which causes the hard, stable starches in the grain to convert to soluble starches (and small amounts of sugars). The grains, now called malt, are kiln-dried to kill the sprouts and conserve the starches. Malt is responsible for the color of beer. The kilned malt can be roasted, which will darken its color and intensify its flavors like a French roast coffee.

Mash. A mixture of cracked grains of malt and water that has been heated. Heating causes starches in the malt to convert to sugars, which will be consumed by the yeast in fermentation. The length of time the mash is heated, temperatures, and techniques used are crucial to the character of the finished beer. Two mashing techniques are infusion and decoction.

Megabrewer. A mainstream brewer, generally producing 5 million or more barrels of American-style pilsner beer annually. Anheuser-Busch InBev and SAB/MillerCoors are the best-known megabrewers.

Microbrewer. A somewhat dated term, originally defined as a brewer producing less than 15,000 barrels of beer in a year. Microbrewer, like craft brewer, is generally applied to any brewer producing beers other than mainstream American lagers. (See "A Word About . . . Brewpubs, Microbreweries, Nanobreweries, and Craft Breweries" on page 129.)

Nanobrewery. One of the fastest-growing segments of craft brewing, these generally use equipment capable of producing batches of 3 barrels or less. You might think of them as glorified homebrewers, but make no mistake: They have commercial licenses and distribute beer to bars and other outlets. Some are housed in residential areas and do not have tasting rooms. But keep in mind, some nanos are making pretty good beer.

Original gravity. (See *gravity*.)

Pasteurization. A process named for its inventor, Louis Pasteur, the famed French microbiologist. Pasteurization involves heating beer to kill the microorganisms in it. This keeps beer fresh longer, but unfortunately also changes the flavor, because the beer is essentially cooked. "Flash pasteurization" sends fresh beer through a heated pipe where most of the microorganisms are killed; in this method, the beer is only hot for a few seconds, as opposed to the twenty to thirty minutes of regular "tunnel" pasteurization. (See *cold-filtering*.)

Pilsner. The Beer That Conquered the World. Developed in 1842 in Pilsen (now Plzen, in the Czech Republic), it is a hoppy pale lager that quickly became known as pilsner or pilsener, a German word meaning simply "from Pilsen." Pilsner rapidly became the most popular beer in the world and now accounts for more than 80 percent of all beer consumed worldwide. A less hoppy, more delicate version of pilsner, called budweiser, was developed in the Czech town of Budejovice, formerly known as Budweis. Anheuser-Busch's Budweiser, the world's best-selling beer, is quite a different animal.

Pitching. The technical term for adding yeast to wort.

Production brewery. Essentially, the opposite of a brewpub. Production breweries make most of their beer to be packaged and then sold at other sites, usually through a distributor network. But some production breweries now have tasting rooms that serve food, or adjoining pubs, further blurring the lines.

Prohibition. The period from 1920 to 1933, when the sale, manufacture, or transportation of alcoholic beverages was illegal in the United States, thanks to the Eighteenth Amendment and the Volstead Act. Prohibition had a disastrous effect on American brewing and brought about a huge growth in organized crime and government corruption. Repeal of Prohibition came with the ratification of the Twenty-first Amendment in December 1933. Beer drinkers, however, had gotten an eight-month head start when the Volstead Act, the enforcement legislation of Prohibition, was amended to allow sales of 3.2 percent ABW beer. The amendment took effect at midnight on April 7. According to Will Anderson's *From Beer to*

Eternity: Everything You Always Wanted to Know About Beer, more than 1 million barrels of beer were consumed on April 7—the equivalent of 2,323,000 six-packs each hour.

Quaffability. Quaff means to drink large quantities. With craft brews, this usually means a pint or more. A pale ale generally is quaffable; a double-bock generally is not. A good, truly quaffable doublebock would be dangerous, given the style's typical alcohol levels!

Real ale. See *bottle-conditioned beer* and *cask-conditioned beer*.

Regional brewery. Somewhere between a micro- and a megabrewer. Annual production by regional breweries ranges from 35,000 to 2 million barrels. They generally brew mainstream American lagers. However, some micro-brewers—The Boston Beer Company, New Belgium Brewing Company, and Sierra Nevada Brewing Co., for instance—have climbed to this production level, and some regional brewers, like Anchor Brewing Company in California, Matt Brewing Company (page 111), and August Schell Brewing Company in Minnesota, have reinvented themselves and now produce craft-brewed beer. (See "A Word About . . . Brewpubs, Micro-breweries, Nanobreweries, and Craft Breweries" on page 129.)

Reinheitsgebot. The German beer purity law, which has its roots in a 1516 Bavarian statute limiting the ingredients in beer to barley malt, hops, and water. The law evolved into an inch-thick book and was the cornerstone of high-quality German brewing. It was deemed anticompetitive by the European Community courts and overturned in 1988. Most German brewers, however, continue to brew by its standards; tradition and the demands of their customers ensure it.

Ringwood. The house yeast of Peter Austin and Pugsley System breweries. A very particular yeast that requires an open fermenter, it is mostly found in the northeastern United States. Some well-known examples of Ring-wood-brewed beers are Geary's, Shipyard, and Magic Hat. Ringwood beers are often easily identifiable by a certain nuttiness to their flavor. A brewer who isn't careful will find that Ringwood has created an undesirably high level of diacetyl, a compound that gives a beer a buttery or butterscotch aroma. Note that smaller amounts of diacetyl are perfectly normal and desirable in some types of beer.

Swill. A derogatory term used by beer geeks for American mainstream beers. The beers do not really deserve the name, since they are made with pure ingredients under conditions of quality control and sanitation that some micros only wish they could achieve.

TAP New York Craft Beer and Food Festival (TAP NY). This annual festival, held every spring, seems to have settled in at the Hunter Mountain ski resort. Originally a Hudson Valley festival, it has grown to encompass the whole state. Eight prizes are awarded in two categories: Hudson Valley beers and statewide beers. The F. X. Matt's Memorial Cup is awarded to the brewery judged best in the state; the Matthew Vassar Brewers' Cup goes to the best brewery in the Hudson Valley. Gold, silver, and bronze medals are awarded to the three top beers in each category. All judging is blind, and the cups are based on average point totals across the range of beers a brewery brings to the festival. It's a great time, and I intend to make it an annual event on my schedule.

Terminal gravity. See *gravity*.

Three-tier system. A holdover from before Prohibition, the three-tier system requires brewers, wholesalers, and retailers to be separate entities. The system was put in place to curtail financial abuses that were common when the three were mingled. Owning both wholesale and retail outlets gave unscrupulous brewers the power to rake in huge amounts of money, which all too often was used to finance political graft and police corruption. The three-tier system keeps the wholesaler insulated from pressure from the brewer, and puts a layer of separation between brewer and retailer. Recent court rulings have put the future of the regulated three-tier system in serious doubt, however, which could spell paradise or disaster for beer drinkers.

TTB (formerly ATF, or BATF). The federal Alcohol and Tobacco Tax and Trade Bureau, formerly the Bureau of Alcohol, Tobacco and Firearms, a branch of the Treasury Department. The TTB is the federal regulatory arm for the brewing industry. It has to inspect every brewery before it opens, approve every label before it is used, and approve all packaging.

Wort. The prebeer grain broth of sugars, proteins, hops, oils, alpha acids, and whatever else was added or developed during the mashing process. Once the yeast has been pitched and starts its jolly work, wort becomes beer.

Yeast. A miraculous fungus that, among other things, converts sugar into alcohol and carbon dioxide. The particular yeast strain used in brewing beer greatly influences the aroma and flavor of the beer. Yeast is the sole source of the clovey, banana-rama aroma and the taste of Bavarian-style wheat beers. The original Reinheitsgebot of 1516 made no mention of yeast. It hadn't been discovered yet. Early brewing depended on a variety of sources for yeast. These included adding a starter from the previous batch of beer; exposing the wort to the wild yeasts carried on the open air (a method still used for Belgian lambic beers); always using the same vats for fermentation (yeast would cling to cracks and pores in the wood); or using a "magic stick" (which had the dormant yeast from the previous batch dried on its surface) to stir the beer. British brewers called the turbulent, billowing foam on fermenting beer *goddesgood*— "God is good"—because the foam meant that the predictable magic of the yeast was making beer. And beer, as Ben Franklin said, is proof that God loves us and wants us to be happy. Amen.

Index

Page numbers in italics indicates illustrations.